Florida
Archaeology

NEW WORLD ARCHAEOLOGICAL RECORD

Under the Editorship of

James Bennett Griffin

Museum of Anthropology
University of Michigan
Ann Arbor, Michigan

In preparation:

Dean R. Snow, The Archaeology of New England
Ronald J. Mason, Great Lakes Archaeology

Published:

Jerald T. Milanich and Charles H. Fairbanks, Florida Archaeology
George C. Frison, Prehistoric Hunters of the High Plains

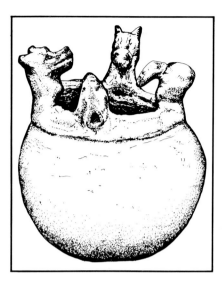

Florida Archaeology

JERALD T. MILANICH
CHARLES H. FAIRBANKS
The University of Florida
Gainesville, Florida

ACADEMIC PRESS
A Subsidiary of Harcourt Brace Jovanovich, Publishers
New York   London   Toronto   Sydney   San Francisco

ACADEMIC PRESS, INC.
111 Fifth Avenue, New York, New York 10003

United Kingdom Edition published by
ACADEMIC PRESS, INC. (LONDON) LTD.
24/28 Oval Road, London NW1 7DX

Library of Congress Cataloging in Publication Data

Milanich, Jerald T
    Florida archaeology.

    (New World archaeological record series)
    Bibliography: p.
    Includes index.
    1. Indians of North America––Florida––Antiquities.
2. Florida––Antiquities. I. Fairbanks, Charles
Herron, Date   joint author. II. Title.
III. Series: New World archaeological record.
E78.F6M54   975.9'01   80–524
ISBN 0–12–495960–1

PRINTED IN THE UNITED STATES OF AMERICA

80 81 82 83   9 8 7 6 5 4 3 2 1

Passing through a great extent of ancient Indian fields, now grown over with forests of stately trees, Orange groves and luxuriant herbage. The old trader, my associate, informed me it was the ancient Alachua, the capital of that famous and powerful tribe, who peopled the hills surrounding the savanna, when, in days of old, they could assemble by thousands at ball play and other juvenile diversions and athletic exercises, over those, then, happy fields and green plains; and there is no reason to doubt of his account being true, as almost every step we take over those fertile heights, discovers remains and traces of human habitations and cultivation.

WILLIAM BARTRAM IN 1774
(Harper 1958:126)

Contents

vii

8

Fort Walton, Pensacola, and Safety Harbor: The Mississippian Peoples

9

Peoples of the Historic Period

10

Archaeology of the Seminole Peoples

Preface

In the fall of 1972 James Bennett Griffin approached Charles Fairbanks, his former student, about the possibility of writing a book on Florida archaeology. Fairbanks, in turn, approached Jerald T. Milanich, his former student, about serving as coauthor, and this project was conceived. As many other archaeologists have discovered, conception can be all too easy; in that brief moment of creativity, little thought is given to the project's more serious long-term ramifications. We immediately drew up a few chapter outlines and wrote Chapters 1, 2, and 4. In the next two years, while we were jointly involved in a research project on the Georgia Coast, we completed Chapters 6, 7, and 10, and prepared a draft of Chapter 5. At that point, Griffin inquired about his grandchild, examined the manuscript, and determined that the overdue project was too far along to abort. Would we finish it, please? After nearly six more years, it was finished.

The final accounting shows that Fairbanks was primarily responsible for Chapters 1, 2, and 10, and Milanich for Chapters 3—9. After such a long and arduous gestation period, both of us are very glad to reach the birthing, no matter the number of toes.

Preparing the manuscript has been a learning experience; our own knowledge of Florida archaeology has increased considerably (although some of our colleagues may disagree), and we have become aware of those areas of Florida archaeology that are in need of urgent investigation, such as nineteenth-century Seminole archaeology or the entire southwestern coastal region. We have also increased our awareness of the contributions that other archaeologists have made to Florida, most notably John M. Goggin, Ripley P. Bullen, and William H. Sears. A glance at the bibliographic sources clearly shows the importance of their work to our understanding of Florida archaeology. Nor should Gordon R. Willey's contributions be overlooked.

Today, many archaeologists are involved in research in Florida, and some of the best work is being carried out by graduate students trained in the state. Their theses and dissertations have provided us with detailed, problem-oriented interpretations; we are confident that similar sources will greatly benefit future work. Another group that has provided important data used in this study is the Florida Anthropological Society and its local chapters in the state. These avocational archaeologists have worked long and hard to help uncover the past; and they have always supported the work of others. Much of our data regarding distribution of sites and complexes come from their work.

We encountered several problems in preparing this introduction to Florida archaeology. Some have been taxonomic, such as: What should we call cultures formerly included within the rubric "Weeden Island" that are apparently not Weeden Island—in the sense that that term applies to archaeological complexes in northern Florida? We have referred to them as Weeden Island *period* cultures—not a very satisfactory solution but one that points out the need for a better resolution of the problem. Other problems have revolved around when to lump and when to split. When it came to Weeden Island we split; but we lumped the St. Johns region and Central Florida. (In general we have been lumpers.) Still other problems resulted from a simple lack of data concerning some periods and areas. For instance, we have very little quantified data on the Paleo-Indian or Archaic periods beyond projectile point categories, and we have divided the late Paleo-Indian and early Archaic periods somewhat differently than others have done. Recent research in Sarasota County by Carl J. Clausen and by Wilburn Cockrell is rectifying that situation, however, and we were able to include some of their findings in Chapter 3.

We have not included a separate chapter on South Florida, although the Lake Okeechobee Basin, for which we have excellent information, was treated separately. Although we know a great deal about the general culture sequence for southeastern Florida (and little about southwestern Florida), we found that much of the interpretive data on culture process were presented as analogous with the historic Calusa and Tequesta Indians. Consequently, the archaeology of those South Florida areas is included with the discussions of the Tequesta and the Calusa in Chapter 9. Analysis of data from the Granada site in Miami (excavated by the Division of Archives, History and Records Management of Florida) and research planned for the southwestern coast by the University of Florida should help remedy the lack of interpretive data on prehistoric sites in those areas.

Another problem was the level on which to prepare the book and the amount of primary data that would be presented. We decided to write the book as an introduction to the archaeology of Florida—an overview that would appeal not only to students but also to the many people who are not professional archaeologists yet are interested in the state's archaeology. We have only mentioned briefly, or relegated to figures and tables, detailed information on such things as potsherds, which, although certainly important as a tool to the archaeologist, actually played only a small part in behavioral systems. We have tried instead to focus on the behavioral patterns that can be derived from quantifying archaeological artifact complexes and their contexts. The resulting coverage is uneven; we know more about, and therefore can infer more information from, some archaeological complexes than others.

This study represents Florida archaeology according to our interpretations, which are certainly subject to change as more data become available. We hope that you enjoy the book and that in reading it you will experience some of the same pleasures in uncovering new knowledge that we experienced in our own archaeological investigations.

Acknowledgments

Many people have contributed to the preparation of this manuscript. We are indebted to our colleagues in Florida archaeology, both professional and avocational, who have provided most of the data on which our synthesis is based. William H. Sears was kind enough to read and critique the Lake Okeechobee Basin portion of Chapter 7, and Carl J. Clausen read and commented on Chapter 3. Kathleen A. Deagan and John W. Griffin allowed us to cite their unpublished data, Kathy's on the Apalachee Indians and John's on the archaeology of South Florida. James Bennett Griffin and Christopher Peebles both reviewed the manuscript and made worthwhile suggestions. In every case, however, we remain responsible for our interpretations and use of our colleagues' data and suggestions.

Lydia Deakin, Sharon Parr, and Annette Fanus typed portions of drafts of the manuscript, and Phyllis Durrell typed the final version. D. Gerald Evans and Deborah Harding of the Florida State Museum aided the project in many ways, including reading early drafts and aiding in the selection of artifacts for the illustrations. Malinda Stafford and Joan Metzger of the museum expertly drew all of the figures, and Kay Purington, Joan Metzger, and Jimmy Franco, also of that institution, helped with photographing and preparing the final illustrations. Ann S. Cordell assisted in checking bibliographic references.

The staff of the University of Florida's P.K. Yonge Library of Florida History, which is directed by Elizabeth Alexander, greatly facilitated our use of that excellent collection. We are also very greatful to Vernon J.

Knight of the University of Florida for compiling the index and to the staff of Academic Press for its advice and cooperation. And we would be remiss in not acknowledging the gentle but firm prodding by James Bennett Griffin, scientific editor of this series, which eventually led to our completion of the project.

Florida
Archaeology

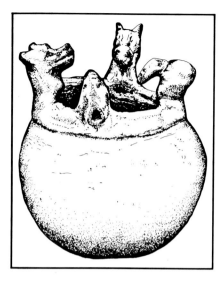

1

Archaeology in Florida

Indians have lived in Florida for thousands of years and have left abundant evidence of their presence. However, as long as there were large numbers of Indians still living in Florida, they, rather than their past remains, were the object of interest. Only when the living Indians were reduced to relatively insignificant numbers did their past become of general interest.

Today, as a result of work by a dozen or so professional archaeologists employed in the state and several hundred avocational archaeologists interested in Florida's past, we know a great deal about the aboriginal peoples and the ways in which they lived. Certainly much more could have been learned during the colonial period had anyone queried the Indians who were then still living in their traditional ways (and had the proper questions been asked). But few early visitors to Florida were interested in the aboriginal past.

The early explorers and first colonists indeed saw Indians and their villages and mounds, but they usually took little interest in investigating or recording how or why the mounds were constructed. The French Huguenots under Ribault seem to have observed the Timucua interring their dead in burial mounds similar to those that are now known to date back for more than 1500 years. Pedro Menéndez de Avilés saw temples and houses of chieftains on top of large shell mounds at the Calusa capitol on Mound Key, but he and other Spaniards did not provide us with very informative descriptions of the town. Other early travelers, however, did mention Indian sites of several types. John and William

Bartram noted many Indian remains, some of which can be closely identified and have even been investigated in the twentieth century. None of these early observers, however, were either archaeologists or diggers.

The first actual digging, probably not really archaeology but rather antiquarianism, seems to have been undertaken by a New Hampshire physician, John Durkee, who had come to Jacksonville for his health. In 1834 he excavated in a burial mound on the St. Johns River below Jacksonville and wrote his brother of his observations (Hoole 1974). As with so much of the early digging in Florida and elsewhere, it was nearly a century and a half before these observations were to be published. In the course of the Second Seminole War, another physician, Dr. Samuel Forry, excavated part of a mound during a lull in his duties as a military surgeon.

None of the scattered observations on mounds or middens during the early and middle years of the nineteenth century contributed much to our knowledge of Florida's past except to further demonstrate that humans are interested in the past, whether it is one's own or someone else's. Until the middle of the nineteenth century, archaeology, at least in the United States, was in what Willey and Sabloff (1974:21 – 41) have called the Speculative Period. The then emerging students of both archaeology and the American Indian were content to build speculative fabrics on a minimum of actual data in order to further their own investigations of the age, racial group, or interests of ancient man. Some excavations were conducted, generally without much coherent purpose except to find things. In 1859, Daniel G. Brinton published a book about the Florida peninsula in which he summarized his own travels and the little coherent information available at that time (Brinton 1859). Henry R. Schoolcraft in a monumental work on the American Indian devoted a brief summary to the elaborate Gulf Coast pottery that we now classify as Weeden Island (Schoolcraft 1854:75 – 82). However, these scattered excavations and descriptions probably did little to spread any reliable information about the Indians in Florida's past.

Somewhat better work was stimulated in 1861 by the publication of an English translation of A. von Morlot's work on kitchen middens, more commonly known in Florida as shell mounds (Morlot 1861:284 – 343). This Danish archaeologist demonstrated that in Scandinavia highly significant information could be recovered from these trash piles of early peoples. Previously, speculation had alternated between considering them intentionally constructed platforms and viewing them as the natural result of hurricanes. Morlot set a fashion in archaeology that has continued intermittently down to the present, and his contribution cannot be ignored. One of the men who chose to dig in Florida middens was Jeffries Wyman, the first director of the Peabody Museum then just established at Harvard University. He first dug in the shell middens along the St. Johns in 1867, and continued with more excavations in 1869, 1871, and 1874 (Wyman 1868, 1875). Wyman, a scientifically trained observer in the natural sciences, concluded that the shell mounds were indeed made by Indians, thus offering a final answer to the debate that had continued for several decades. He was able to demonstrate that the mounds were prehistoric and that there was some stratigraphy in them with older artifacts below younger types.

Wyman's pioneering work was shortly followed by a series of excavations by S. T. Walker, perhaps the most important of which was at Cedar Key on the Gulf Coast. There he observed stratigraphy rather crudely and applied an evolutionary framework to his data (Walker 1880, 1883, 1885). At that time the Smithsonian Institution and the associated Bureau of American Ethnology were engaged in a widespread survey of aboriginal sites in the United States. Their interest, in contrast to that of Wyman and Walker, was largely in the "monuments," that is, in the burial mounds. The bureau's field agent, J. P. Rogan, dug two mounds in Alachua County and located a number of others that were listed and briefly described in a catalogue published by Cyrus Thomas (1894). Rogan's excavation evidently left much to be desired by modern standards, and Thomas's summary does little but list the mounds. They are so vague that it is often impossible to determine the exact location or content of the sites. The work of Rogan and Thomas, however, did focus the attention of this classificatory — descriptive period on the very numerous and interesting sites and artifacts present in the state.

The closing decade of the nineteenth century is marked by the very extensive work of Clarence B. Moore, a wealthy Philadelphian who had already traveled widely and had made his first visit to Florida in 1875. Moore equipped himself with a coal-fired steam-powered house boat, the *Gopher*, in which he traveled to aboriginal sites during the winter season. His first Florida excavations took place along the St. Johns River in 1892. During subsequent winters he worked his way around the entire peninsula before moving on to more western sites. Moore excavated the readily accessible burial mounds and many middens within reach of waters navigable by the *Gopher* during the next 11 years.

In the light of modern archaeological technique and method, it is easy to criticize the work of this energetic man, but he did, however, dig carefully, keep respectable notes, and observe astutely. Noting changes in typology of both artifacts and mounds, he showed a preference for burial mounds that contained elaborate grave goods, which in this region usually were pottery. Perhaps his greatest contribution was that he published his reports with an abundance of illustrations and a highly commendable promptness. Recent comparison of his field notes with his publications shows that he did little further analysis; in effect, he published illustrated field notes. Generous with the artifacts, Moore deposited them widely in museums in the Northeast. The fact that Florida had no such institutions at that time is probably all that prevented Moore from distributing the artifacts within the state. Today, as Willey (1949a) has amply demonstrated, it is possible to fit much of Moore's work into modern classifications, and the reading of his reports is the starting point for research in much of the southeastern United States. Although C. B. Moore showed a preference for sites with more eye-catching objects of material culture (which is, of course, one of the more important foundations of all archaeology), his excavations salvaged materials that would in all likelihood have been widely dispersed and unreported by other diggers.

The rising tide of winter visitors to Florida brought some with an avocational interest in the past and in archaeology. These visitors occasionally did a little superficial digging, but the great strides of the 1890s were not repeated except for Frank H. Cushing's discovery at Key Marco on the lower Gulf Coast of elaborate and varied wooden objects submerged in muck. This discovery brought to light a range of both ritual and subsistence artifacts not usually recoverable in the eastern United States. Cushing felt that the muck deposits represented refuse collected under pile dwellings, such as those certainly suggested by mid-nineteenth-century reports of such houses in the Upper Rhineland and Switzerland (Cushing 1897). Cushing's discoveries created a stir at the time, although his imaginative reconstructions of the culture of Key Marco are now largely revised (Gilliland 1975). Cushing, like Moore, did much to call to the attention of the public the range and abundance of archaeological materials in the peninsula.

As C. B. Moore turned to other areas in the Southeast, and as World War I occupied the attention of many, there was a hiatus in the serious study of archaeology in Florida. During the war years, a drainage development near Vero on the east coast uncovered a human skeleton in presumed association with the remains of mammoth and other Pleistocene animals. The opinions of contemporary experts differed as to whether this and the similar find at Melbourne a few years later could be taken as valid evidence of the presence of man in the New World during glacial times. Hrdlička at the United States National Museum (Smithsonian Institution) argued that the Vero and Melbourne finds were intrusive into the Melbourne geological formation, and few were prepared to counter his opinion. More recent examination of the skulls has suggested that they may indeed belong to the Paleo-Indian period (Stewart 1946). Certainly the peninsula was the home of many species of big game during the closing years of the glacial period, and recent evidence suggests that humans as well as mammoths found Florida a pleasant place. This material will be further discussed in a later chapter, although no final answers are possible at this date.

All these varied activities meant that by 1920 the archaeology of Florida was at least started, but very little coherent work had been done. It was recognized, however, that the state had many differing cultures and varied geographic areas. In Florida, some work had been done in both classification of artifacts and cultural units, and in the development of at least a beginning chronological framework. No continued program was underway and no institution within the state was engaged in archaeological research or teaching. Both field and analytical techniques were either in their infancy or were ignored by the few people working sporadically in the area. The land boom of the early 1920s brought many new residents, quite a few of whom were informed and interested in archaeology. The stage should have been set for continuing, intensive work in the state.

During 1923–1924 a major excavation was undertaken at the large complex site of Weeden Island on the western shore of Tampa Bay. Under the auspices of the Smithsonian Institution, field work was directed by Matthew W. Stirling under the general direction of Jesse W. Fewkes (Fewkes 1924). As both Fewkes and Stirling were professionally trained, this can be considered the first truly scientific archaeological program in the state. Nearly 90 years after the digging of Dr. Durkee, archaeology in Florida reached adulthood. The excavations established the type site for the Weeden Island culture. For the first time there was an accurate description by trained persons of the complex burial-mound pattern and the spectacular pottery that had been described by Holmes 20 years earlier. More importantly, the Weeden Island excavations established an interest in the area by the Bureau of American Ethnology and the Smithsonian Institution.

When the Civil Works Administration was organized in 1933 as part of Franklin Roosevelt's schemes to combat the Depression, Matthew W. Stirling realized that Florida and archaeology were admirably suited for each other. Archaeology was almost solely a matter for hand tools, and thus would employ large numbers of workers; it did not compete with any private business; and Florida's climate meant that work could be carried out during the winter months. As a result, nine projects were carried out in Florida, with a few in Georgia, North Carolina, Tennessee, and California. Stirling also realized that the large numbers of people assigned to the projects could undertake excavation at sites that would not usually be attempted. For the next 7 years the various relief agencies were to contribute a great fund of information on the archaeology of the United States and to develop chronologies and classifications in nearly every section. Much of what was learned in Florida would be put to use elsewhere in the years to come.

The Civil Works Administration began projects on nine sites at six different locations: Perico Island and three sites on the Little Manatee River in Manatee County, the Englewood Mound in Sarasota County, the large Belle Glade group near Lake Okeechobee in Palm Beach County, the Ormond Beach Mound in Volusia County, and two sites on Canaveral Peninsula in Brevard County. Trained supervisors were the directors, but unfortunately no provision was made in the Civil Works Administration or the succeeding Works Project Administration for post-excavation analysis. Gordon R. Willey (1949a) was able later to analyze the data from sites on the Gulf Coast and to use the material in his pioneering Gulf Coast study. Willey, Jennings, and Newman reported on the Ormond Beach Mound somewhat later, leaving only the Canaveral sites largely unreported. The notes from the sites as well as the collections themselves were catalogued in the National Museum of the Smithsonian Institution and were thus made available to students of Florida archaeology. As the directors of the six projects for the most part remained active in archaeology, the outlines of the archaeological information were generally available. While the primary goal of the emergency relief archaeological projects was to provide employment and thus purchasing power, they did set the pattern for large-scale publicly supported excavations.

During the Depression, an additional, and more prolonged, effort in archaeology was the work conducted by the Civilian Conservation Corps in the Ocala National Forest. Some of the project leaders conducted site surveys and limited excavations in this area during their free time. Reports of their findings, which were solely descriptive and published in a very limited mimeographed format, did, however, provide a base of site locations and typological information on which later work could build.

The result of all this early work, perhaps most importantly that undertaken through the participation of the various federal agencies, was to make the Florida public more aware of the state's archaeological resources and of what should be done about them. The Florida Historical Society formed a committee on archaeology that published an inventory of the then known sites. For a brief period, Florida had a state archaeologist, although his work was seemingly confined to one excavation at Marineland. The Florida Geological Survey began an archaeological survey conducted by Clarence Simpson, who located a large number of sites and freely shared his information with later workers. The Simpson Collection, made by Clarence and other members of his family, is presently curated at the Florida State Museum.

Although C. B. Moore and others had discovered historic objects in some sites and had demonstrated that the Florida Indians continued to build burial mounds after Spanish settlement, it was not until 1939 that specifically historical archaeology was undertaken in the state. In that year, W. J. Winter began a series of excavations in St. Augustine under the sponsorship of the National Park Service and the St. Augustine Restoration Society. This work was to serve as a valuable foundation for future work in the city and eventually to develop into a full-scale problem-oriented program of historical archaeology.

The formation of the Southeastern Archaeological Conference in 1938 (in which persons working in Florida were not directly involved— probably because of lack of institutional affiliation) served as a means of developing regional chronologies for the entire area. When institutional archaeology did begin, it could find a ready placement for Florida chronologies in the framework of the whole southeastern region.

When archaeological work was halted by World War II, there was a generally understood chronology for the Southeast, some valuable excavations at sites that were to become type stations (Weeden Island and Safety Harbor), recognition of the St. Johns area and the Gulf Coast as specific culture areas, and a beginning of a local chronology. Gordon R. Willey and Richard B. Woodbury had begun a survey of the western Gulf Coast and published a chronology (Willey and Woodbury 1942). Immediately after the war, archaeology seemed suddenly to spring to life with a number of developments that have persisted to the present.

In 1946 the Florida Park Service established a program of archaeology conducted by John W. Griffin and Hale G. Smith. Two years later John M. Goggin was appointed as archaeologist within the Department of Sociology at the University of Florida, Gainesville. Although the Florida Park Service's interest in this program was short-lived, it did result in considerable survey and some excavations. A conference on Florida archaeology was held by interested individuals and institutions at Daytona Beach in 1948, and a broader conference was held at Rollins College in 1949. Proceedings of the latter conference were edited by John Griffin (Griffin, ed. 1949). These formal and informal conferences involved people from neighboring states and served to define the immediate goals of the discipline in the state. Upon the withdrawal of the park service from the field, the Florida State Museum, a part of the University of Florida, became active in archaeology by continuing the development of the park service's extensive collections and by preparing archaeological exhibits. Working in conjunction with the academic department at the University of Florida, the museum began a fairly broad program of excavation, perhaps more concentrated in the northern half of the state. Largely descriptive, the reports appeared regularly and included a museum series of publications. Ripley P. Bullen, William H. Sears, James A. Ford, William Bullard, E. Thomas Hemmings, and Jerald T. Milanich have held the position of archaeologist at the Florida State Museum and have greatly expanded the program of research and publication. Elizabeth Wing, working in zooarchaeology, has contributed a major auxiliary in the identification and interpretation of animal remains excavated from both prehistoric and historic sites. In addition, she has trained a number of students in this useful discipline.

When John M. Goggin joined the Department of Sociology at the University of Florida in 1948, he began programs of survey, excavation, and the training of students. The demand for courses in anthropology and archaeology steadily increased until a separate department of anthropology was established in 1962 with Goggin as its first chairman. Following Goggin's death in 1963, Charles H. Fairbanks became chairman and continued the program of survey and research. The department received permission to grant master's degrees in 1963, and a doctoral program was begun soon thereafter. Both master's degrees and doctorates are now being granted on a regular basis; 33 master's degrees and 13 doctoral degrees have been granted to specialists in various areas of archaeology as of May 1980. Several specific programs were initiated under Goggin that did much to advance the discipline throughout the state. In 1948 the Florida Anthropological Society (F.A.S.) was established, and its journal, *The Florida Anthropologist*, continues to be published. This society is one of the oldest state societies in the country. While the bulk of its publications have been on archaeological subjects, it still remains a society dedicated to the whole discipline of anthropology, and it receives support from persons with a broad range of backgrounds and interests.

Goggin also established a statewide archaeological site file which has grown over the years until it now contains more than 12,000 cards, each detailing the location and characteristics of a specific archaeological site. In recent years copies of the site file have been requested by other institutions, and the master file is now located in the office of the state archaeologist in Tallahassee. Whereas university initiative led to the founding of this statewide survey, it is estimated that about two-thirds of the sites have been first reported by avocational archaeologists. In no other area of archaeology has the help of the nonprofessional or avocational archaeologist been so valuable.

In addition to locating and describing the archaeological sites in Florida, Goggin had a number of other research goals. Among these were the definition of the cultural subareas of the state and the definition of the chronological stages found there. He also developed the concept of cultural tradition beyond what was then in current usage. His approach focuses attention on the persistence through time of those distinctive ways of behavior that characterize a specific human group (Goggin 1949). With the publication of Willey's *Archeology of the Florida Gulf Coast* in 1949, a major landmark was reached for the Weeden Island and related complexes along the Gulf Coast. Goggin concentrated on the northern and eastern parts of the state and published a definitive study (1952) of the northern St. Johns River area.

Until the 1950s, most of the archaeology done in Florida had been concerned with prehistoric sites, and Goggin had been active in that phase. Boyd, Griffin, and Smith (1951) had done some excavation in Spanish—Indian mission sites in the Tallahassee area, and the Florida Park Service had carried out some limited additional work. Goggin embarked on a complex study of the historic era with special reference to the Spanish colonial period. This resulted in highly valuable studies of Spanish olive jars (Goggin 1960) and, posthumously, of a definitive study of Spanish majolica (Goggin 1968). His investigations of Spanish sites took him to the Caribbean, Mexico, and Panama, but his major interest remained the Spanish—Indian mission system.

At about the same time that Goggin was achieving breakthroughs in the identification and dating of Spanish artifacts, more work was beginning in sites of the colonial period. In 1951 Florida State University in Tallahassee had established the first department of anthropology in Florida and was actively engaged in studying the Apalachee missions. With the approaching quadricentennial of Florida's founding, the Historic St. Augustine Preservation Board was established. Along with the St. Augustine Historical Society, it undertook a series of excavations in the historic city designed to collect data on specific buildings that were either being or could be developed as preserved historic houses. In the decade following the quadricentennial, a continuing program of colonial archaeology was developed in St. Augustine through the cooperative action of the Historic St. Augustine Preservation Board, the University of Florida, Florida State University, and the Society of Colonial Dames (Deagan 1974). This approached the problems from the newly emphasized processual archaeology in which specific explanations of cultural process were sought rather than simply digging because the sites were there. It already shows great promise of contributing to both history and archaeology substantial new or revised explanations of the colonial era. During the same time investigation began at sites pertaining to black history, initially at the slave cabins of the Kingsley Plantation on Ft. George Island north of Jacksonville. The development of historical, particularly colonial and plantation-periods, archaeology in Florida somewhat preceded similar developments in other nearby states.

To some extent these concerns with the European and African traditions were concurrent with the development of underwater archaeology in the state. The first known underwater work occurred in 1952 during the attempt by the National Park Service to find some evidence of the French Huguenot fort at Fort Caroline on the St. Johns River east of Jacksonville. Later, Goggin did much to develop a strong program for the instruction of students and research in underwater sites. His work at Oven Hill, a Seminole site on the Suwannee River, provided a strong foundation for the definition of the cultural remains of that tribal group. Of course, underwater archaeology was not confined to historic sites. Especially in the underwater caves in the northern karst (limestone-underlain) region of the state, Goggin did much pioneering work. In that region at Devil's Den, he found human skeletal material with the same fluoride content as extinct mammals. Gradually, a series of finds, largely in the Ichetucknee, Santa Fe, Withlacoochee, and other rivers of North Florida, showed a thick scatter of Clovis points, the related Suwannee point, and simple bone points. These were frequently in the same localities as bones of extinct mammals, often at shallow spots that had once been river fords. Reexamination of the mammal bones disclosed that a small percentage showed cut marks, evidently the result of butchering. However, as such an underwater program was expensive to maintain in terms of equipment, it was gradually abandoned at the University of Florida.

Another aspect of underwater archaeology was that concerned with submerged shipwrecks off Florida's coasts, largely the east coast where Spanish ships laden with treasure had been lost to the summer and fall hurricanes. After 1964 the program of state-supervised salvage of these wrecks substantially increased. Until 1967 the recovered materials comprising the state's share of salvaged material was preserved in the laboratory at the Department of Anthropology at the University of Florida. The proper cleaning and preservation of materials recovered from marine sites is even more important than that for land remains, since sea salts cause severe deterioration even after artifacts are removed from the ocean. Florida has probably the oldest program of conservation and preservation of underwater artifacts of any state. Since 1967 the conservation program has been located in Tallahassee at the Division of Archives, History and Records Management.

The emergence of this state agency was the result of a long series of legislative and administrative developments beginning in the middle 1960s. For some time archaeologists in the state had felt the need for the revival of the position of state archaeologist. Legislation was secured to this end by statutes protecting historic or prehistoric sites on state lands. This was followed by the establishment of the Division of Archives, History and Records Management, within the Office of the Secretary of State. L. Ross Morrell was the first state archaeologist, and he soon assembled a staff which made that office the largest single employer of trained archaeologists within the state. As much of the program has been, of necessity, concerned with salvage archaeology due to the rapidly expanding interstate highway program, they have done little problem-oriented archaeology. They have, however, been able to publish a significant number of reports regarding the vast assortment of sites investigated. In addition, they are charged with acting as liaison with the state park system and with reviewing Environmental Impact Statements for the entire state. These reports, required under the National Environmental Protection Act and the Moss — Bennett Bill, have resulted in a great number of specific surveys. Although these are often piecemeal because they deal with specific developments, the Division has begun and encouraged others to begin programs of systematic survey of individual Florida counties or areas.

In addition, the director of the Division is the liaison officer for nominations to the National Register of Historic Places and is charged with nominating historic or archaeological sites to the National Register. Florida has, as have most other states, placed mostly historic houses on this protective list, although a number of archaeological sites are present. As the coordinator of historic preservation for the entire state, the Division of Archives, History and Records Management fills an important need in the state. The Division also manages the new Museum of Florida History in Tallahassee that supplements the Florida State Museum in Gainesville.

The 1960s saw both a proliferation of state universities, with six new ones added to the already existing three, and a dramatic increase in the number of departments of anthropology. The University of South Florida at Tampa was the first of the new universities to be established, having an anthropology department and archaeologist as chairman. Florida Atlantic University was next with another archaeologist as chairman of anthropology. By 1970 the four anthropology departments in state universities (UF, FSU, USF, and FAU) were all chaired by archaeologists. Of these the University of Florida, Florida State University, and Florida Atlantic University had active programs of archaeology with field schools doing work in the state. Florida State University was largely occupied with the panhandle area, whereas Florida Atlantic University had a long-range program at the large Fort Center site just west of Lake Okeechobee. This was a cooperative program, in which the University of Florida and Colgate University were also involved, under the overall direction of William H. Sears of Florida Atlantic University. Somewhat later Florida Technological University at Orlando added a program in anthropology as did Florida International University at Miami. Neither of these institutions, however, developed a program of active research and training in Florida archaeology. Several community colleges developed programs in anthropology during the same period, such as St. Johns River Junior College, Santa Fe Community College, and Miami—Dade Community College. While some were engaged in sporadic field research, their contribution was mainly to provide students for the 4-year colleges, and enrollments in anthropology courses and especially in field schools increased steadily.

Among the private institutions in the state, only Eckerd College, the University of Miami, and Rollins College developed programs in anthropology, and only Miami and Rollins have any research programs in archaeology. Certainly anthropology was becoming widespread in the state, and archaeology was usually an important element in this spread.

The Florida Anthropological Society gradually developed a series of regional chapters that were often active in site survey and sometimes in excavation. Most of the members of the society were avocational archaeologists and few had great interest in the other fields of anthropology. The annual meetings and the society's quarterly publication were mainly concerned with papers on archaeological subjects. The society, in addition, served as a sort of spokesman for archaeology in the state. Its membership was sufficiently large to provide a fairly stable base for the publication program in spite of continuously rising printing costs.

It is difficult to assess the accomplishments in Florida archaeology by the beginning of the last quarter of the twentieth century. Certainly much has been learned about the prehistoric and colonial inhabitants of the state during the 140 years since John Durkee first dug in a burial mound on the St. Johns River bank. The explorations of Clarence B. Moore did more than any other early work to bring to public attention the varied archaeological resources of the state. Most later work must start with Moore's excavations as a baseline for research. Probably no archaeological work in the state has been so wide ranging geographically or been published so promptly as that of Moore. The relief agency excavations of the early 1930s were probably the next major step. While they did large-scale work for virtually the first time, publication was delayed and they contributed less to our contemporary knowledge than much other work. The work of Gordon R. Willey and his milestone publication *Archeology of the Florida Gulf Coast* (1949a) made 1949 the real beginning of scientific reporting in the state. It has not been equalled in value by any publication of Florida archaeology. The program in anthropology and archaeology at the University of Florida, begun under the late John M. Goggin in 1948, is perhaps the greatest continuing contribution to knowledge of Florida's past. His work in establishing chronological frameworks by systematic excavation of stratigraphic cuts did much to firmly establish the chronology of Florida. Goggin, along with Hale G. Smith, began an extensive program in historic archaeology that has tremendously increased our knowledge of the early Spanish occupation of the state.

At the other end of the scale, the early speculations raised by the discovery of Vero and Melbourne Man have gradually been extended by survey and excavation. We now have in several places good evidence of early humans in association with glacial animals (Devil's Den, Warm Mineral Springs, Little Salt Spring), and we can expect this early occupation to yield additional information in the near future. For most of the state, we have clear understandings of the relationships and chronological ordering of the occupations. What remains to be done is to define more clearly the growth and development of human adaptations to the natural environments of the state and the ways in which people have adapted the varied resources to their own use.

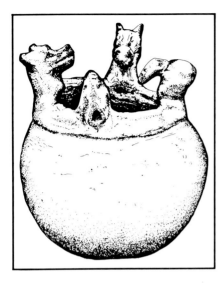

Geographical and Temporal Boundaries

The ancient wisdom expressed in the statement that "no man is an island, complete in himself" expresses the reality that all people are part of the world around them. They must interact with their fellow humans, with the plants and animals, and with the inorganic environment in which they live. Thus a discussion of Florida archaeology must take into account the environment in which the cultures of the past have existed. Culture is never a passive occupant of the environment. As humans must exploit the resources of their milieu in order to survive, they must continually adjust or adapt to a more proficient use of those resources. In a very real sense those cultures, and the human beings who carry them, will be successful and survive only if they can develop cultural, technological means to derive more from their environment than they must expend in work to procure the things that they want and need. As their technology improves, it does so largely by discarding those procedures that are uneconomic and by emphasizing those ways of life that return more for their effort. It is thus on a geographic, or rather ecological, stage that the panorama of human history in Florida has been displayed.

Natural Environment

Florida is largely a peninsula extending from the southeastern corner of North America into the Caribbean. It could have been a major cross-roads of trade where ideas were exchanged only if trade or communication with the Antilles had been frequent. Such appears not to have been the case as there is little evidence for direct human contact between Florida and the Caribbean lands. Most influences and relationships seem always to have come from the north or northwest. The major causes of change in Florida cultures, then, have been the processes of adjusting to Florida's environmental conditions; often techniques adapted to other environments were changed to suit local or new conditions. These ways have been varied, producing a number of distinctive cultural areas in Florida prehistory, just as contemporary Florida shows a number of regional specializations.

Matthew W. Stirling first defined several distinctive archaeological areas of the state in 1936. These were later expanded by Goggin (1947) as knowledge of the state increased. Since that time archaeologists have somewhat modified the areas Goggin defined, although the basic alignment remains much the same. In this chapter we will briefly describe the geographic extent of the major areas, their ecological situation, and the cultural adaptations characteristic of each area. A further expansion of this brief overview will be made in subsequent chapters. It must be remembered that the boundaries of these cultural areas are somewhat arbitrary, fluctuating with time, and are only approximations of the real distributions they attempt to represent.

Some habitats are common to much of Florida and will be briefly discussed before the introduction of the archaeological areas. Because of its peninsular shape, perhaps the most visible part of Florida is the coastal zone, one of the longest in the country. This coastal strip actually consists of two major elements: the coastal strand and the lagoon system. The coastal strip itself is made up of the ocean (or the Gulf of Mexico on the west), the beach, and the dunes. None of these is especially favorable for any human inhabitants except recent sun-seeking tourists who have housing and air-conditioning for protection against the elements. The strand was also exposed to frequent storms, especially the summer and fall hurricanes, and had few resources that could be used by the Indians. Especially on the Atlantic Coast, the sandy beaches offer little purchase for vegetation in the turbulent surf. As a result, fish and shellfish (except for the tiny coquina) are scarce.

The beach and foreshore are generally just as inhospitable. The difficulty met by Jonathan Dickinson, shipwrecked on these shores in the late seventeenth century, indicates the difficulty of finding anything to eat along open coasts. The Gulf Coast of Florida is less open, has more sheltered lagoons, and seems to have been more intensively occupied. The coastal strand, however, when it does occur, is generally not a favorable spot for Indian habitations.

In back of the dunes and beyond a strip of more stable, older dunes is a lower elevation, often a coastal lagoon, or perhaps a marsh area. These coastal lagoons, fed by drainage from the interior and sheltered from the coastal winds, offer a rich and broad range of resources. If cord grass marshes are present, it is there that many of the food chains start. Decaying marsh grass, microorganisms, and various algae supply food for a host of more complex life forms. The lagoons are frequently brackish and thus offer a home for many shellfish, principally oyster. As they frequently open to the sea, the lagoons serve as a zone of interchange between inland species and marine species. It is along these coastal lagoons that much of the aboriginal population lived as long as hunting, fishing, and gathering were the major sources of the food supply. Aside from shellfish and fish, plants and animals from the more inland areas were usually available along the lagoons or could be procured by short trips farther inland. The major land animals were deer, raccoon, and turkey, with bear, rabbits, and varieties of turtles also available. Especially along the west coast where land and sea finger into each other in myriad bays and estuaries, these coastal lagoons then and now offer many resources. Along them the Indians could exploit the bounties of both land and sea.

Large areas of inland Florida, especially the flat woods of the northern half of the state, bear extensive stands of longleaf or slash pine. Locally these are often called pine barrens because they offer so little in the way of subsistence. The pines are highly resistant to the forest fires that sweep them almost yearly. Their thick bark protects them from all but the hottest fires. With little ground cover except for saw palmetto and wiregrass, they approach a pure stand situation except in swampy areas. Neither humans nor animals useful to humans could find much subsistance in this "green desert," as it has been termed. While the majority of the fires that created and maintain these pine barrens are probably set by lightning, the Indians in the past contributed to the situation by systematic burning, largely in the form of game drives.

Along streams and lakes, or wherever there is more moisture, much of northern Florida is characterized by the hardwood hammocks found in so much of the southeastern coastal plain. These are mixed dense forests of hardwoods of which magnolia is perhaps the most obvious, although many other species such as oak and hickory are present. Characterized by a broad spectrum of plants and a dense understory of shrubs and vines, these plant communities offered shelter and food for a broad range of animals. Thus they provided excellent plant and animal foods for the Indians. Prehistoric communities, in nearly all periods, are much more common in areas that are or were hardwood hammock. When taken in conjunction with the many lakes and streams of Florida, the hardwood hammocks, like the coastal lagoon systems, provided ideal environments for people.

There were, of course, many more ecological niches in Florida. Those briefly mentioned here are only the larger, more obvious ones and those which affected in major ways the human use of the area's resources. Other local habitats will be mentioned in the following chapters. That humans did adapt to these ecological niches is indicated by the numbers of Indians present at the time of discovery and exploration.

Demography

It is difficult to arrive at useful figures for the aboriginal population of Florida, or any other region. Early students seem to have underestimated populations greatly. While this was in part because early explorers simply did not know where the Indians were or their numbers, much error was introduced by the heavy loss of life in the very early years of European conquest and settlement. New diseases spread ahead of the explorers and settlers decimating populations. Smallpox, measles, dysentery, the common cold—all were deadly to the Indians who had not developed partial immunity to these newly imported pestilences. Taking into account this factor of early loss through disease, it appears that the aboriginal population of Florida amounted to at least 100,000, perhaps several times that. The most heavily populated area was clearly the eastern panhandle where the Apalachee numbered at least 25,000. Next in size were the various Timucua groups in the northern quadrant of the state, numbering at least 40,000. The remainder were more thinly spread along the southeastern and southwestern coasts, where the lagoon systems offered some subsistence, and through interior portions of the state south of Orange County. The interior of the southern tip of Florida, the Everglades, did have some aboriginal population, but it seems not to have been very dense.

It is interesting that some areas of heavy population in the present expanding economy of the state were very slightly used by the Indians. The southeastern "Gold Coast" centering around Miami was thinly populated. Evidently the attractions for modern populations were not the same as those of the Indians. In the same fashion the expanding Central Florida lake district centered on Orlando seems not to have had much aboriginal population, although that region is poorly known archaeologically. Tampa Bay with its busy port and satellite retirement communities was less populated in relation to the Apalachee and Timucua areas northward where Tallahassee, Pensacola, and Jacksonville are now located. Certainly the culture and technology of modern Florida uses very different resources in many different ways than did the Indians.

Culture Stages

The gradual growth and development of Indian cultures in Florida can be briefly summarized in a few major stages. Whereas each area differed to some extent in the style of culture, each passed through most if not all of these major evolutionary stages. They can be briefly summarized as: Paleo-Indian, Archaic, Formative, Mississippian, and Acculturative.

The earliest evidence of human occupation so far known from the state dates from what has been called the Paleo-Indian period or stage. Characterized by skilled hunting of big game with supplementary foraging for smaller game and plant foods, it represents the earliest migrants to Florida. Highly nomadic as they followed the game herds, these people left few distinctive sites, although we do find their characteristic tools and weapons, mostly at riverine sites where they killed game. Their presence certainly began as early as 12,000 B.C. and continued for more than 5000 years.

In the following period, the so-called Archaic stage, the Paleo-Indian hunters probably gradually changed their adaptation to that of the increasingly sedentary collectors and gatherers. The Archaic peoples did not hunt the then extinct big-game animals which had been characteristic of the closing years of the Ice Age. They slowly developed an increasingly precise adaptation to a much broader range of plant and animal sources of subsistence. In much of the state this involved the use of shellfish, either from the freshwater streams and lakes or from the coastal lagoons. The evidence of their tools and weapons suggests that hunting, especially of deer, was still a major concern, but learning where and how to acquire many different foods allowed them to remain settled in one camp for at least part of the year. By about 2000 B.C. they acquired, or developed themselves, the techniques of making pottery, often a sign of at least partially sedentary existence. Most archaeologists believe that within the next millennium they also began to cultivate some plants, perhaps first the gourd, at least in a small way. Their increasingly broad adaptation is suggested by larger and a greater number of archaeological sites, clearly a measure of their success and of their increasing population.

After 1200 B.C. new styles of artifacts, perhaps most clearly shown in pottery, and new technological skills made their appearance and ushered in the Formative stage. We are almost certain that agriculture was known by these people who were, at least in part, the descendents of the earlier Archaic and perhaps of the still older Paleo-Indian peoples. There is some evidence to suggest that the extreme southern third of Florida (outside of the Lake Okeechobee Basin) remained in what was basically an Archaic stage until the coming of the Spanish. The Formative stage, denoting a beginning of formal, settled communities, with the gradual development of more complex forms of political and religious community organization, is marked by a great deal more regional diversity than the earlier stages. Largely due to more precise adaptation to differing local ecological conditions, the Formative stage is much more complex. Elaboration of cultural traits, especially in ceramics and in burial rituals, has probably made Formative stage sites more eagerly sought than sites from any other period of Florida's prehistory. Certainly many of the Formative stage cultures left descendants who became known as the historic tribes of the peninsula.

The Mississippian stage represents a further complexity of culture resulting in part from the intrusion of new ideas and ways of organizing communities that first appeared in the panhandle portion of Florida. Among these was a greater dependence on the growing of corn, beans, and squash as well as more centralized political governance. Our knowledge of the development of the Florida Mississippian cultures has increased greatly in the last few years as a result of recent excavations together with new interpretations derived in great part from other studies of southeastern Mississippian cultures.

The arrival of the Spanish, first as explorers and then as colonizers, ushered in the stage of acculturation. Just as this was a period of tremendous loss of population so it was also a time in which great changes were imposed on the native cultures. Much of the old way of life was lost and much of the remaining culture was highly modified through the acquisition of Spanish traits or adaptation to the presence of a new and dominant culture in the area. Often called the Mission period, from its most obvious feature, it also involved culture contact with the garrison at St. Augustine and the cattle ranches established in Alachua and Apalachee. By 1710 the native population was almost completely destroyed by disease and especially by the slaving raids from South Carolina. At about the same time, Guale Indians from the Georgia coast began to be a major element in and around St. Augustine. Their interaction with the Spaniards lasted until the British occupation in 1763, when the few remaining Florida Indians left for Cuba with the residents of St. Augustine. Already the inland parts of Florida were being infiltrated by Creek Indians from central and western Georgia. These new migrants, after adapting to the new conditions, became known as the Seminole, whose descendants still reside in the state. All these historic groups and their changing cultures make up the highly interesting and informative Acculturative stage. Archaeologists dealing with this period are involved in understanding the Indians, the Spaniards, the British, and the many changes in culture that are characteristic of the period. Historic archaeology not only amplifies the written documents of the times but also offers many insights into the processes that take place when cultures come into intimate contact with each other.

Culture Areas

These changes and developments in the cultures of Florida were played out in the various ecological zones of the state, producing somewhat different expressions in each of the culture areas of the state (Figure 1 and Table 1). Although these archaeological areas are largely expressed in geographic terms, they are really expressions of the varied ecological factors: cultural traditions, contacts or lack of them with other peoples, plants available and their seasonal frequency, and animals that could be procured once the necessary technology was learned or developed. Temperature, rainfall, amount of sunshine, and other such climatic factors seem not to have been major determinants of the regional differences, perhaps because these factors in all of Florida are so benign and impose so few limits on human activity. Soils, plants, animals, and cultural factors were the major factors determining change and the lives of Florida peoples in the past, just as they do today.

NORTHWEST FLORIDA

The Northwest Florida area comprises all those lands from Mobile Bay on the west through Apalachee Bay and the Aucilla River at the east and extending from the Gulf of Mexico to the Alabama and Georgia boundaries. Generally, open beaches, often with quite high dunes, line much of the coast and are usually without any archaeological sites. The shallow waters of the Gulf cover sites that have been submerged by the rising level of the water during the postglacial period. Lagoons are usually found back of the dune ridge, with Santa Rosa Sound and Choctawhatchee Bay being especially notable for archaeological sites. Inland there are often clay or loam remnant hills, and the whole area seems to have been thickly settled by Indians especially during Fort Walton times. Much of the rest of the inland area, excepting the river systems and the Tallahassee Red

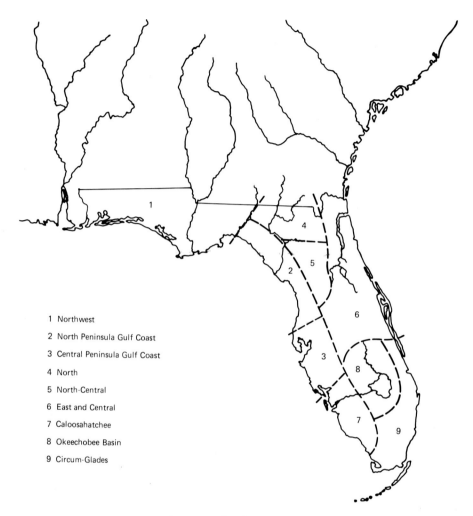

1 Northwest

2 North Peninsula Gulf Coast

3 Central Peninsula Gulf Coast

4 North

5 North-Central

6 East and Central

7 Caloosahatchee

8 Okeechobee Basin

9 Circum-Glades

FIGURE 1. *Florida culture areas.*

Hills, is barren with few if any evidences of former communities. The Mobile and Apalachicola — Flint — Chattahoochee river systems offered easy access to more northward areas, as far as the southern end of the Appalachian Mountains. There is good evidence that cultural influences, and perhaps peoples, moved up and down these great river systems and that at least the Weeden Island culture spread up the Apalachicola into what is now Georgia and Alabama soon after the Swift Creek culture spread southward. The long open coast, while not especially attractive

TABLE 1

Culture Periods in Florida

Years	Northwest	North	North-central	East and Central lake district	North peninsula Gulf coast	Central peninsula Gulf coast	Circum-Glades	Okeechobee Basin
AD 1800	Seminole Leon-Jefferson	Seminole Leon-Jefferson	Seminole Potano	Seminole	Seminole	Safety Harbor	Seminole	Seminole
AD 1500	Fort Walton	?	Alachua		?		Glades III	Belle Glade Plain pottery
AD 1300			Hickory Pond late	St. Johns II	Weeden Island related late	Weeden Island late	Glades II	
AD 1000	Weeden Island	Weeden Island	Cades Pond early / late			Manasota early		sand tempered pottery
AD 800								Belle Glade sand and fiber tempered pottery
AD 500	Swift Creek			St. Johns I	Deptford		Glades I some fiber tempered pottery	
AD 100	Deptford	Deptford	Deptford					
500 BC	Transitional	Transitional	Transitional	Transitional	Transitional	Transitional		
1000 BC	Norwood Late Archaic	Orange Late Archaic	Orange Late Archaic	Orange Mount Taylor	Norwood Late Archaic	Norwood Late Archaic		
2000 BC								
3000 BC	Middle Archaic	Middle Archaic	Middle Archaic		Middle Archaic	Middle Archaic		
5000 BC	Early Archaic	Early Archaic	Early Archaic	Middle Archaic Early Archaic	Early Archaic	Early Archaic		
6500 BC	Paleo-Indian late	Paleo-Indian late	Paleo-Indian late	Paleo-Indian late	Paleo-Indian late	Paleo-Indian late		
12000 BC	early	early	early	early	early	early		

2,800 YEARS

11,000 YEARS

for settlement, made access toward the west and the Mississippi River possible.

Historically, the most important group in the Northwest region was the powerful Apalachee, settled on the red clay hills near where Tallahassee now stands. The fertile clay and loam soils of the hills supported the heaviest, most concentrated population in the state. The area between the Apalachicola and the Mobile rivers seems to have been depopulated at the beginning of the historic period. Indian occupation apparently began with scattered groups of Archaic peoples, although fossil Pleistocene mammals are known from the St. Marks River at the eastern edge of the area and Paleo-Indian kill sites have been found in the Aucilla River. It is possible that further research will reveal Paleo-Indian evidences further west in the area. In spite of a continuing interest in the archaeology of the area from the middle of the nineteenth century to the present and the completion of a number of good excavations, many areas of the Northwest Gulf Coast remain virtually unknown and numerous problems await solution.

PENINSULA GULF COAST

The peninsula Gulf Coast from Apalachee Bay southward to Charlotte Harbor can be divided into two areas that are closely related ecologically and culturally. First is the North Peninsula Gulf Coast, an area stretching from the Big Bend—Apalachee Bay region southward to Pasco County north of Tampa Bay. The second is the Central Peninsula Gulf Coast from Pasco County southward to Charlotte Harbor. Along both these portions of the Gulf Coast the open sandy beaches farther west are replaced by much more muddy shores with vegetation extending right down to the water. Inland low, old dune lines run parallel to the coast in gradually rising tiers until the ubiquitous flatwoods are reached. The interior extent of the cultural distribution is not clear, as most of the work has been done along the coast. Except for the area around Tampa Bay and a few other localities, this is generally one of the less occupied regions of the state where great stretches of swamp persist. Once occupied by great stands of bald cypress, these regions are now mainly covered with slash pine. A number of rivers, including the Suwannee, cross the area, although they seem not to have been used as avenues of trade and communication to any extent. Most of the known sites occur at points where streams enter the Gulf. There, several ecological niches could be exploited within a short distance. Although agriculture was certainly practiced, the poorly drained soils seem not to be very favorable for agriculture, and it is likely that fish, shellfish, and upland game were major items of subsistence.

Particularly around Tampa Bay, at Crystal River, and near Cedar Key there has been extensive archaeological investigations dating from the time of Clarence B. Moore. Later, J. W. Fewkes and Gordon R. Willey contributed substantial understandings of the cultural sequence. Again, it is certain that after glacial times the rise of the relative level of the Gulf has drowned sites, which now lie offshore. Because of the relatively heavy silt load in the area, it seems unlikely that successful examination of these submerged sites will be possible. The outstanding sites are the Weeden Island and Safety Harbor localities on the western edge of Tampa Bay, the Crystal River site (now a state park) in the middle of the area, and a few sites farther north. At a relatively early time (the Deptford period), Crystal River seems to have been a major center for trade with the elaborate Hopewellian centers far to the north. It is also possible, though by no means proven, that Crystal River had some sort of sporadic contact across the Gulf of Mexico with the high culture centers of Mesoamerica. The Northern Peninsula Gulf Coast, despite a number of large prehistoric sites, seems not to have been heavily occupied during the early historic period. Perhaps this can be taken as evidence of the decimation of Indians by introduced diseases brought by the early Spanish expeditions such as that of Hernando de Soto who came through the region in the early sixteenth century.

Human occupation of the peninsula Gulf Coast area began during the Paleo-Indian period, as scattered early spear points have been found as well as extinct mammal bones in some of the more northerly rivers. Additionally, recent investigations by underwater archaeologists in two cenotes (naturally formed sinkholes) in Sarasota County have revealed Paleo-Indian materials. Again, other very early sites may be out in the Gulf, having been submerged by rising sea levels. Archaic stemmed points have been recovered from the Gulf, and a growing number of Archaic land sites are known. The Deptford culture (see Chapter 4) is represented by a number of sites as well as by at least some levels at the large Crystal River site.

The Weeden Island period (see Table 1) of the Formative stage is well represented at a number of sites in the area. Burial mounds are virtually the only Weeden Island period sites that have been studied, although quite large village middens are known. Mississippian influences are represented by the Safety Harbor culture, which seems to represent some sort of blending of Weeden Island elements with those spreading southward from the Fort Walton culture. Toward the end of the Safety Harbor period, there are European artifacts in the mounds, and the archaeological complex at that time level must represent the Tocobaga Indians. In the later period it is clear that Seminole were in the area, but sites are difficult to identify. The Oven Hill site on the Suwannee has revealed the best collection known of Seminole ceramics. In most post-Archaic periods, the Indian occupation seems to have been more concentrated along the coastal lagoons than on inland sites.

The southern portion of the Central Peninsula Gulf Coast represents a geographical and cultural transition zone between the Deptford, Weeden Island-related, and Safety Harbor cultures to the north and the cultures of South Florida. A similar transitional region is present on the Atlantic Coast where the cultures of northern Florida and those of South Florida came into geographical contact. In rethinking the 500 B.C. to A.D. 800 period, Luer and Almy (1979) have given the name Manasota to the culture of this area during that 1300-year range. The Manasota culture is followed by Late Weeden Island and Safety Harbor occupations. The Englewood ceramic series represented at several sites in Manatee and Sarasota counties seems to be a late development out of Weeden Island, probably influenced by and contemporary with Safety Harbor.

SOUTH FLORIDA

The southern one-third of the state, from south of Cape Canaveral, on the east coast and Charlotte Harbor on the west coast, can be divided into three areas: Caloosahatchee, Glades, and Okeechobee. The Caloosahatchee area extends from Charlotte Harbor to Cape Sable, where the Glades (or Circum-Glades) area begins, extending east and north along the coast into Brevard County. The Keys are included in the Glades region. Lake Okeechobee and the adjacent wet savannah comprises the Okeechobee area. There is some evidence that the poorly known Kissimmee drainage should be included within the Okeechobee area. Burial mounds, earthworks, and ceramics as far north as Lake Tohopekaliga bear affinities to those of the latter area. Jointly these related areas comprise the vast region often referred to as South Florida, and together they correspond to the tropical floral zone of the state. The animals of the region do not share this tropical character and are generally somewhat smaller specimens of those common to the northward. Nevertheless, the Indians had to develop special technologies and social systems to efficiently exploit this tropical setting.

The major feature of South Florida is the Everglades, the "River of Grass" as it has been called. A vast plain sloping gently toward the south, it is largely resting on peat or muck soils that are tremendously fertile if drained but are waterlogged through much of the year. Along the east coast are open sand beaches backed by low dunes and often a linear lagoon system. The lower west coast is cut by very numerous islands, bays, and lagoons where it is often difficult to draw a line between land and sea. Mangrove swamps are extending the line of the "land" seaward, as the sea level is still rising and silting patterns are changing. The Florida Keys extend southward from Biscayne Bay, differing from the coastal barrier islands farther to the north mainly in their isolation and lack of fresh water.

There is a strong suggestion that the Glades area was the last in the state to be occupied by Indians, probably because the major route by which they entered the state was from the north. It probably follows that cultures in the Glades, especially the Florida Keys, are somewhat later than related ones to the north. The necessity of making cultural adaptations to the special ecological conditions in the area also means that change was slow within the area. Once the Indians had found solutions to living in the Glades, they tended to adopt new elements very slowly.

Scarce finds of fiber-tempered pottery, which are interestingly sometimes associated with steatite sherds that originated far to the north in the lower Appalachian Piedmont province, are known for South Florida. Perhaps 1000 B.C., within the Formative stage, is an average date for the first major occupations in that region, although some earlier dates have come from Marco Island. Most likely, even earlier sites will eventually be found. Beginning about 500 B.C. in the Glades area we find the long sequence of the Glades culture, defined almost solely on the basis of ceramic changes. In Dade County and the Keys the period is marked by small black earth middens that may have been occupied only part of each year as the population moved about to exploit seasonal resources. The sea offered the most usable resources, and marine foods, including sea mammals and shark remains, are commonly found in the middens. Certainly plant foods were extensively gathered, but they have left little evidence except the humic soil found at the camp sites.

The Okeechobee and Caloosahatchee areas show a number of similarities in that the Indians in those areas built large, elaborate mounds and linear embankments at sites that may have been continuously occupied. On the coast these constructions were usually made of shell, as at Mound Key, Joccelyn Island, and Key Marco. In the Basin these mounds and embankments were made of earth. Investigation at one such Basin site, Fort Center, indicates some earthworks were mounds erected for ritual purposes whereas others functioned as raised fields or house mounds. Corn pollen has been identified from the Fort Center site (Sears and Sears 1976), as have burned shell deposits which Sears thinks is evidence of preparation of hominy by the use of lime. Such evidence is the earliest in Florida and serves to set the Okeechobee area apart from the rest of

South Florida. One puzzling question is why was maize agriculture stopped in South Florida; we know corn was not being cultivated in that area at the time of the arrival of the Spaniards in the sixteenth century.

At the beginning of the historic period, the Okeechobee and Caloosahatchee areas were occupied by the Calusa or people under their political control. There are indications that the Calusa maintained a complex political system despite their being a nonagricultural, fishing, and foraging culture. This is an excellent indication of their successful adaptation to the environment of South Florida. On the lower east coast the Tequesta were in possession of the area until decimated by European disease and military actions. They fished, foraged, and salvaged materials from Spanish wrecks to furnish an extremely meager living along the coastal strand. The great majority of the Indians had disappeared by the end of the First Spanish Dominion in 1763. The area served as a refuge for the Seminole, who refused to be uprooted to Oklahoma during the Second Seminole War, and their descendants remain there today. Little professional excavation of Seminole sites has been done, although looters have dug a number of Seminole graves, often placed in earlier sand burial mounds.

EAST FLORIDA

The East Florida or St. Johns area, extending from south of Cape Canaveral to the St. Marys contains the coast, the lagoon system, and the drainage of the St. Johns River. Goggin divided it into several subareas, but there is little actual variation in them. Evidence from Orange and Lake counties suggest that Central Florida, a region of many lakes and prairies, should be included with East Florida since similar cultures inhabited both areas. As a whole the area consists of hardwood hammocks or swamps along the river with pine barrens on higher ground. A large number of lakes are found in Central Florida; perhaps more acreage of aquatic habitats and wet prairies is to be found in this area than any other within the state. Along the Atlantic Coast below Cape Canaveral, the Formative and post-Formative cultures of the St. Johns area blend into those of the Circum-Glades region at about Indian River County. Rouse (1951) referred to the transition zone as the Indian River area.

The earliest Spanish settlement was in the area of St. Augustine, and the earliest systematic archaeology was also undertaken on the St. Johns River bank. Research has been intense there, and we probably know more about the St. Johns area than any other in the state. C. B. Moore followed Jeffries Wyman along the St. Johns, and both professional and avocational archaeologists have been busy there during the twentieth century. The many tall shell middens and impressive earthworks along the river have attracted many workers, although a number of sites still remain to be examined scientifically and there are still unresolved problems in the cultural evolution of the region.

Because many of the shell middens along the river are free of ceramics in their lower levels, it is clear that a preceramic Archaic people settled there very early. The coast and lagoon system was not exploited as early as the river basin. This preceramic culture shows clear but not well-understood relationships with the Middle Archaic culture to the west, perhaps indicating seasonal movement from the interior to the river and even to the coastal lagoon system, or a population shift. A broad continental shelf may contain early sites that have been inundated by rising sea levels. At least the late stages of this Archaic period culture gradually developed into the Orange period in which fiber-tempered ceramics appeared. Shell middens along the river, and to some extent along the coastal lagoons, are often very deep during this period, and there is every reason to believe that they represent an increasing sedentism and an increasing population as the Indians learned to cope with the rather lush resources. Along the coastal lagoons, oyster or the tiny coquina was a major food. Inland, periwinkles and apple snails were harvested along with a broad spectrum of fish, birds, mammals, and reptiles.

During the post-Orange, Transitional period of the Formative stage, new ideas entered East Florida. By 500 B.C. the St. Johns culture was formed. Sporadic instances of northern intrusions of the Deptford culture and later, other northern complexes appear, especially in the northern and western parts of East Florida. Trade with South Florida also occurred. Influences from the west are seen in copies of the ceramic styles of the Weeden Island culture. In the St. Johns II period there are also sporadic influences of Mississippian traits such as the Long-Nosed God masks and a few platform mounds. The Mississippian life style never became dominant in the St. Johns basin, however, perhaps because the soils in the area were poorly suited for the full agriculture characteristic of that expanding culture.

The historic period saw the final phases of the St. Johns II complex with a great deal of check-stamped pottery on the familiar chalky paste. These remains clearly belong to the historic Timucua tribes who occupied the region when French and Spanish colonists arrived. A few mission sites are known for the following hundred years but have not been extensively investigated. Virtually extinct by the end of the seventeenth century, the local Timucuans have left little except scattered remains in the state. They were followed by migrant Guale Indians from the central Georgia coast who were fleeing British aggression. Sites containing their distinctive San Marcos Stamped pottery are thinly scattered throughout the northeastern quadrant of the state but are especially abundant within the ancient city of St. Augustine. Guale ceramics make up about 75% of the pottery on Spanish sites until the Indians were removed to Cuba with the cession of Florida to England in 1763.

The historic archaeology of Florida as a whole is just beginning and is mainly concentrated in St. Augustine where combined excavations under several sponsors are proceeding annually. At present little evidence of Seminole occupation has been found, although the one good site of these migrants into Florida is known on the St. Johns River at Spalding's Lower Store just south of Palatka. The St. Johns area has been heavily occupied since at least 4000 B.C. and presents a number of extremely interesting archaeological problems that need additional scientific investigation.

NORTH-CENTRAL FLORIDA

Another area to be considered is that of North-Central Florida, extending from northern Lake County on the south to the Santa Fe River. On the west it abuts on the Northern Peninsula Gulf Coast area in a region of low pine woods. On the east it adjoins the St. Johns area in extreme eastern Alachua County. It might be expected that such an internally marginal region would simply reflect influences from the surrounding areas. While this is to some extent true, North-Central Florida has distinctive complexes and presents many interesting problems. It is predominantly either pine barrens or hardwood hammocks, with numerous lakes, ponds, and sinkholes present. The soils are mainly loose sands overlying a karst topography and tend to be poor agricultural lands, although expanses of good soils are known.

The area, with North Florida, probably has the best claim to Paleo-Indian remains of any regions in the state. Along the Silver Springs Run and portions of the Oklawaha, distinctive projectile points of Simpson and Suwannee types have been found. As in North Florida, the majority of these tools have been discovered at shallow fords on the rivers, evidently where early Indians ambushed large Pleistocene animals crossing the streams. Distinctive bone points are also found at the same place. So far, few land sites of the camps of these early hunters have been located; this remains one of the more urgent archaeological tasks for the future.

Following the Paleo-Indian period there is a long, poorly known Archaic period which can be divided into Early, Middle, and Late times. Archaic styles are typically represented by stone tools and large amounts of debitage deposited as a result of working chert. It seems probable that the North-Central Florida Archaic peoples frequently moved out from their central bases and may well have moved across lines that later marked cultural boundaries. Only the Newnan's complex is at all well known, consisting of long narrow blade knives and broad points with small finely chipped stems. There are certainly derivations of this Archaic culture from the earlier Paleo-Indian complex, although the details of the evolution are still to be worked out. The closing aspects of the Late Archaic, when fiber-tempered pottery and a somewhat more sedentary life way appear in the St. Johns basin, are not at present well known in the North-Central area. The distinctive Orange fiber-tempered ceramics do appear, however, at a few camp sites.

With the appearance of grit-tempered and chalky wares to the east, the central region seems to have experienced the appearance of Formative stage ceramic complexes related to Deptford, probably deposited by peoples from the Gulf Coast who were occupying small camps. These scattered remains are often overlain by the Cades Pond complex with simple burial mounds and sand-tempered, predominately plain pottery. Subsistence seems to have been largely by hunting, fishing, and foraging, especially of aquatic resources. There was a heavy dependence on hickory nuts and probably considerable use of other plant foods. The Cades Pond people evidently occupied the area throughout the year.

In the following period, the Alachua tradition represents a movement of populations down from the river valleys of the Georgia coastal plain. These groups brought with them distinctive cord-marked pottery. That the Alachua tradition was agricultural is clearly shown by the pottery marked with overall malleating of pots with a dried corncob and by the selection of fertile loamy soils for their sites. Through time, cob-marked pottery increased in popularity at the expense of cord-marked. Evidently these changes represent the change of the tool used in shaping the pot from a cord-wrapped paddle to the corncob. Burial mounds were built, perhaps for lineage use. Some Mississippian traits, such as the small triangular Pinellas projectile points, are part of the complex, but no temple mounds or elaborate incised pottery are known from the area. It is evident that the Alachua adaptation to North-Central Florida was sufficiently successful to resist intrusion by new ideas or peoples during the Mississippian stage.

The Alachua tradition persisted until the arrival of Spanish missionaries and ranchers in the seventeenth century. New crops such as peaches, wheat, and probably others were added to the agricultural base of corn, beans, and pumpkins. Spanish ceramics are present but seem not to have heavily influenced Indian techniques. Missionary activity did not involve any massive resettlement of native villages or the sort of massive influx of trade objects that were characteristic of British early settlement situations. Changes in religious practices took place, as the Spaniards claimed to have made many converts. The practice of burial in mounds stopped completely and church buildings replaced aboriginal temples. The major effects were a rapid decline in size and number of communities, as introduced diseases and harsh treatment reduced the native population. By the very early 1700s, the native population was eliminated as far as any organized communities were concerned. There was some appearance of Georgia coastal artifacts and some western traits in the mission sites as the Spaniards brought in Indians from outlying regions.

With the disappearance of the local Timucuan population, due in large part to raids from South Carolina, a temporary population void appeared in North-Central Florida. This was penetrated after 1725 by Creek Indians from central and western Georgia, moving away from areas of increased British pressure. Eventually these people became the Seminole Nation whose descendents still live in the southern part of the state. These migrant Creeks took up cattle herding of feral cows from the abandoned Spanish ranches, mainly in the Alachua area. This involved adoption of a more dispersed settlement pattern; they did not build the compact towns with squaregrounds that had been characteristic of their Georgia settlements. Their ceramics, however, remained virtually identical with those they had made to the north and offer valuable evidence as to their origin. Traders from Georgia and South Carolina followed the Creeks into Florida, and the few sites that have been examined show considerable quantities of trade goods, including guns which the Spaniards had been reluctant to give the Indians. The explanation of the process by which Creeks became Seminoles and adapted to new environmental conditions and subsistence strategies remains very largely to be defined by a combination of archaeological and historic research. By the end of the Second Seminole War the North-Central Florida area was thoroughly in the hands of Anglo-American settlers, and the Indian occupation was over.

NORTH FLORIDA

The last area, North Florida, has only recently been defined and is still poorly known archaeologically. Certainly the rivers of North Florida—the Suwannee, Withlacoochee, Ichetucknee, and Santa Fe—have produced more Paleo-Indian projectile points and examples of late Pleistocene animal bone, some exhibiting butchering marks, than any other portion of the state. The Paleo-Indian period is followed by the Archaic. However, we have no information, other than a very few surface collections, from Early and Middle Archaic sites, or from the fiber-tempered and Deptford sites that follow. The few Deptford sites located appear to be small camps like those in North-Central Florida.

As early as A.D. 300 the area, which is characterized by mixed pine — hardwood forests with many lakes and prairies, was occupied by a Weeden Island culture closely related to that of Northwest Florida. One major early site has been excavated and a number of early and late sites have been located and tested. The complex burial ceremonialism associated with Weeden Island peoples elsewhere is represented by the numerous mounds that dot northern Columbia and Suwannee counties. We know that the area was occupied by the Utina Indians during the historic period, and three Spanish missions have been located, all with aboriginal ceramic assemblages like those present in Northwest Florida. As yet, however, we cannot document the evolution of the Weeden Island culture into that associated with the Mission Utina Indians.

As Florida, including the panhandle, is certainly marginal geographically to the rest of the Southeast, it exhibits a number of clear-cut local developments. Beginning in the Paleo-Indian period, there is definite evidence of adaptation to the peculiar environmental features of the peninsula, as there is during the subsequent Archaic periods. However, uniformity of some Early Archaic projectile points with those from other southeastern states must indicate that populations were moving about and ideas were being exchanged over wide areas. At the close of the Archaic, the appearance of fiber-tempered ceramics may be regarded as an importation from the Georgia coastal plain.

Cultures of South Florida, however, clearly represent a new adaptation to tropical situations and resources. While Hopewellian "elements" are certainly present at such sites as Fort Center, they do not detract from the uniqueness of the Belle Glade culture as a highly stable adaptation. The St. Johns region, also, represents a cultural development with a good deal of stability over a long period of time. Again, this must in large part be because it represented a successful adaptation of a subsistence pattern to local conditions. The complexity of burial ritual in Northwest and North Florida is perhaps the best example of a case where new ideas diffused into Florida to be modified and recombined with older local traits into a new, persisting entity. The Florida Mission period, as most periods before it, represents a unique cultural process not exactly comparable to other examples of Spanish colonization. In each case, Florida represents an instructive laboratory for comparison and study of the processes by which human societies adapt to specific natural and cultural environments.

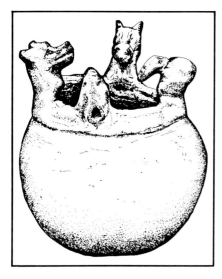

3

Early Hunters and Foragers: Paleo-Indian and Archaic Peoples

The first Floridians were hunters and gatherers who entered the state near the end of the Pleistocene epoch, the great Ice Age that was drawing to a close about 12,000 years ago. Archaeological evidence from Little Salt Spring, a cenote (sinkhole) in Sarasota County, documents the existence in Florida of these early people, called Paleo-Indians, at 10,000 – 12,000 B.C. It is very likely that Paleo-Indians were in Florida at least several thousand years prior to that time, perhaps as early as 15,000 B.C. Relative to the people who lived in later times in Florida, our knowledge of the early hunter—foragers is exceedingly limited. But archaeological projects presently underway promise to make significant new contributions to our knowledge. Figure 2 shows the location of some of the Paleo-Indian and Archaic period sites.

Paleo-Indians

Past archaeological interpretations viewed the Florida Paleo-Indians as residents of the northern portion of the state who hunted large game, several species of which became extinct at the end of the Pleistocene. Animals were slain with darts or spears tipped with lanceolate stone projectile points similar in shape to Clovis and other Paleo-Indian points found elsewhere in the United States. The typical Florida Paleo-Indian point, the Suwannee point, is widely distributed along the beds of a number of North Florida rivers, including the Aucilla, Withlacoochee,

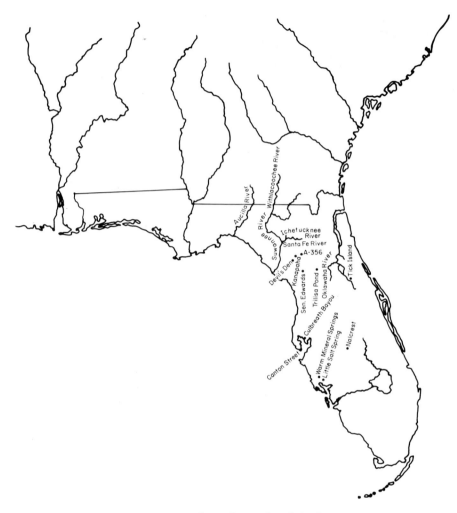

FIGURE 2. *Paleo-Indian and Archaic sites.*

Suwannee, Santa Fe, Ichetucknee, and Oklawaha, where scuba divers have found literally hundreds of them. It was believed that bands of Paleo-Indians hunted game along the rivers, ambushing the animals at shallow crossings (Waller 1970). Almost nothing else was known about other activities of these peoples and archaeologists were not able to isolate well-dated and documented Paleo-Indian components in land sites, although a variety of tools found in the rivers and from several land sites were thought to belong to the Paleo-Indian tool kit (an exception is the undated Silver Springs site [Neill 1958; Hemmings 1975b]). The riverine materials, however, were generally found in poor contexts— Paleo-Indian points and tools similar to known Paleo-Indian tool types outside of Florida were recovered along with more recent stone tools and even modern beer cans and other refuse.

In the last decade, underwater archaeologists, employing new data-recovery techniques, and paleontologists, both working side by side with amateur archaeologists and hobbyist divers, have gradually been clarify-ing and adding new knowledge to our understanding of Paleo-Indians and how and when they lived. Although our old perspectives were par-tially correct, work in Little Salt Spring and in another Sarasota County cenote, Warm Mineral Springs, is producing types of data, including human remains, which most archaeologists would have thought were impossible in the past. Carl J. Clausen, Wilburn Cockrell, and their asso-ciates are almost daily producing new information; they have even ver-ified the discovery by Col. William Royal (Royal and Clark 1960) that some early Archaic and possibly Paleo-Indian human skulls still retain brain tissue. A sophisticated interdisciplinary project spearheaded by Clausen at Little Salt Spring, and originally made possible through the generosity of the General Development Corporation, promises to produce even more new information in the future. Much of the data on Holocene climatic changes included in this chapter comes from the Little Salt Spring project.

At the present time we surmise that small groups of Paleo-Indians must have entered Florida from the north as a result of the natural expansion of human populations and the presumed nomadic nature of the Paleo-Indian bands. During the last stages of the Pleistocene, Flori-da's environment was different than that present in modern times. The level of the sea surrounding the peninsula was much lower during the periods of Pleistocene glaciation—perhaps as much as 100 m lower dur-ing the peaks of glaciations—and cooler temperatures and semi-arid conditions prevailed over land. Water must have been in more limited supply on the peninsula, and the rivers, springs, and cenotes of North Florida and the cenotes of southern Florida served both animal and human populations. Forested regions were less in extent than at later times, and more savannahs and grasslands were present. Oaks and other hardwoods predominated in the stands of forest that were present. With lower sea levels, the coasts were much farther out than they are at pres-ent, and during glaciations the Florida peninsula doubled in geograph-ical extent. At the time human populations were entering Florida, the sea levels were still as much as 35 m below present levels; Paleo-Indian sites must exist below the surface of the Gulf of Mexico and off the Atlantic coast, but we do not as yet have the technology to locate or investigate such sites scientifically. Consequently, our view of the Florida Paleo-Indians does not include data regarding probable estuarine or littoral cultural adaptations.

During Paleo-Indian times, at least 12,000 B.C. to about 6500 B.C., life must have been more difficult for these peoples than previously thought. Upland Florida was not a lush, tropical haven; human populations were severely limited by the freshwater sources. Populations must have been quite small since all Paleo-Indian camp sites are represented by only scatterings of tools and debris. None of the dense or large Paleo-Indian sites like those known for other areas of the Eastern United States—Thunderbird in Virginia (Gardner 1974:3), Wells Creek in Tennessee (Dragoo 1973), Plenge in New Jersey (Kraft 1973)—have yet been found.

Small bands probably moved almost continuously from water source to water source, hunting and foraging. Hunting and butchering of large game such as mammoths, horses, and deer occurred at what are now rivers, but which in the past may have been ponds or drainage systems—water holes about which the Indians camped. In addition to the large game just listed, hunting and gathering of a host of other animals also probably took place. At Little Salt Spring (Clausen *et al.* 1979:609– 610), an extinct giant land tortoise (*Geochelone crassiscutata*) was found which is believed to have been killed by being impaled with a wooden stake. Other faunal species associated with the tortoise and possibly eaten by humans include an extinct box turtle (*Terrapene carolina putnami*), an extinct sloth (*Megalonyx* sp.), portions of an immature mammoth or mastodon, and an extinct bison. Extant species include freshwater turtle (*Chrysemys nelsoni* and *C. floridana*), gopher tortoise, diamondback rattlesnake, rabbit, and wood ibis (Clausen *et al.* 1979:610). Later in time, but still within the Paleo-Indian period, the white-tailed deer seems to have been a major meat source. Within Warm Mineral Springs (Cockrell and Murphy 1978:6) extant species have also been identified—panther, opossum, raccoon, frog, and turtles—and were probably eaten by Paleo-Indian peoples. Most likely the Paleo-Indians hunted or collected most of the animals within their environment as well as collecting a number of plant foods. Perhaps they camped for short periods of time around water sources after making a kill. Animals could be surprised at river crossings as well as at cenotes and other water holes. Foraging for smaller game and for plants, as well as refurbishing tool kits, may have also occurred while camping. Once food became hard to find, hunters might have gone out to surprise game at other water sources and the camp was subsequently moved In such a fashion, small groups would have made use of huge tracts of land to support themselves. No doubt this accounts for the relative uniformity of the Paleo-Indian tool kit in Florida, which however, is still poorly known.

The most characteristic Paleo-Indian tool is the Suwannee point (Figure 3b−d). Bullen (1975:55) describes the point as "slightly waisted . . . with concave base, basal ears, and basal grinding of bottom and waisted parts of sides." Hundreds of the points have come from springs and rivers where they were perhaps lost during game ambushes. Some (if not all of the points) were hafted in a two-piece bone foreshaft which was attached to a wooden shaft. The foreshaft was composed of a round bone shaft (at least some of which were manufactured out of elephant ivory) beveled at both ends. One end of the shaft fit into the wooden shaft while the other was roughened to serve as one side of a clamp which held the base of the stone point. The other side of the clamp was usually a small double pointed piece of bone. Pitch and tightly wrapped sinew were possibly used to bind the clamp together. A number of such foreshaft pieces have been found in Florida (Figure 3g, h).

Another stone point found in Paleo-Indian contexts in Florida is the Simpson point (Bullen 1975:56). Simpson points are possibly Suwannee points which were snapped at the base and later reworked (Figure 3e, f). Clovis points are also occasionally found in Florida (Figure 3a).

Although other stone tools in the Paleo-Indian tool kit have not been well documented, excavations at the Silver Springs (also called Paradise Park) site in Marion County (Neill 1958) and typological similarities between Florida tools and those from known Paleo-Indian contexts elsewhere indicate that thumbnail scrapers, blade knives, flake knives, gravers, sandstone hones or abraders, and bifacial knives were used (Figure 4a, b−d, f, g). The latter generally had flat bases with rounded corners and measured 10−15 cm in length. Another type of knife, the Waller knife or hafted flake knife, is more limited in distribution; Waller (1971) reports that they are common in and around the Santa Fe River. The knives appear to be made from flakes; one side displays flake scars while the other, the side that came off the core, is smooth and slightly convex or concave. Two side notches near one end were apparently used to haft the tool. Most are 31.5−58 mm in length and less than 36 mm wide and all are unifacially retouched on the edges.

Another possible addition to the Paleo-Indian tool kit are oval ground stone weights the shape and size of eggs with one end flattened (Neill 1971). Most likely these were bolas weights, which were attached by thongs and used to bring down water birds and other game (Figure 4e).

In addition to foreshafts, another type of bone tool common at kill sites is the double-pointed bone "point." Made of ground splinters of bone, these tools are sharpened on both ends and generally are round in cross

FIGURE 3. *Paleo-Indian artifacts;* **a,** *Clovis point;* **b — d,** *Suwannee points;* **e — f,** *Simpson points;* **g — h,** *beveled bone foreshaft and bone "clamp." All artifacts in Figures 3 through 44 are shown full-size unless otherwise noted; the artifacts reproduced in this book are from the collections of the Florida State Museum and the Department of Anthropology, University of Florida.*

40

FIGURE 4. *Paleo-Indian lithic artifacts;* **a**, *bifacial knife;* **b**–**d**, **f**–**g**, *unifacial blade and flake knives;* **e**, *possible bola weight.*

section, about 10 cm long. More than 100 of these have been found with one elephant kill in the Aucilla River. Waller (1976) has suggested that these "points" are actually pins used to hold back tissue while the animal was being butchered. Literally thousands of the tools have been found in North Florida rivers at kill sites. Some were perhaps used as leisters (barbed fishing spears) and still others as tools with uncertain use (Figure 5c–f, Figure 6a, b).

Underwater excavations have also revealed Paleo-Indian tools. At Warm Mineral Springs (Cockrell and Murphy 1978: Figs. 4 and 5) several bone and shell tools have been recovered which are indicative of use by Paleo-Indians of the spear-thrower (atlatl). A shell spur or "trigger" which fitted over the end of the atlatl and provided the surface for the base of the shaft or dart to butt against was found in a Late Paleo-Indian context. A possible atlatl weight was also recovered. Other tools include a worked fossil shark's tooth, a bone eyed-needle, a socketed antler point, and a socketed bone handle (Cockrell and Murphy 1978: Fig. 5). The latter two tools are also very common in later Archaic contexts (Figure 5b, g, h; Figure 6c).

From Little Salt Spring, Clausen (Clausen *et al.* 1979: Fig. 2, 611) recovered a similar socketed antler projectile point and a portion of what appears to be a carved oak log mortar, perhaps used to grind seeds or nuts. One of the most dramatic artifacts is the head of a nonreturnable, wooden boomerang. Carved from oak, the tool is very similar to boomerangs used by the Australian aborigines.

During Late Paleo-Indian times, after about 7500 B.C. (a period which encompasses what some archaeologists call the Dalton period), wetter conditions prevailed in Florida. Late Paleo-Indian hunter–gatherers were possibly able to make use of a larger number of water sources and to alter somewhat their hunting and foraging strategies. However, we are only beginning to be able to document these environmental changes and have almost no understanding of the cultural processes that were taking place.

We know even less about these peoples than about the aborigines of the earlier portion of the Paleo-Indian period. We can surmise that with wetter conditions the hunter–gatherers increased in population and, consequently, used greater amounts of floral and faunal resources. Certainly the life-style of these people was similar to that of their Paleo-Indian ancestors. They continued to hunt horses, mastodon, and especially deer along with other animals. It was not until about 6500 B.C. that many animal species present in Florida during the Pleistocene disappeared. Martin and Webb (1974) report the following animals from a cenote (Devil's Den) in eastern Levy County dating from that period, all of

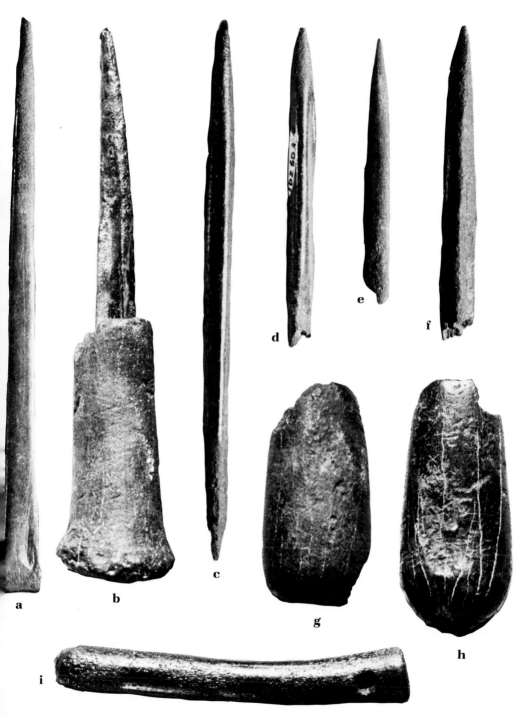

FIGURE 5. *Bone tools used during the Paleo-Indian and Archaic periods; all were recovered from the Ichetucknee River;* **a,** *expanded head pin;* **b,** *tool placed in hollowed socket handle (hypothetical);* **c−f,** *bone "points," probably leisters and/or tools;* **g−h,** *hollowed antler sockets believed used as handles;* **i,** *antler "flaker" with perforation (for suspension?).*

FIGURE 6. *Bone tools used during the Paleo-Indian and Archaic periods; all were recovered from the Ichetucknee River;* **a−b**, *bone "points,"* **a** *has roughening for hafting on base;* **c**, *hollowed antler projectile point;* **d−e**, *deer ulna awls;* **f−g**, *antler "gouges" or punches.*

which could have been hunted by Paleo-Indian and Early Archaic peoples: sloth (*Megalonyx* sp.), southern bog lemming (*Synaptomys australis*), dire wolf (*Canis dirus*), North American spectacled bear (*Tremarctos floridanus*), sabercat (*Smilodon floridanus*), American mastodon (*Mammut americanum*), Pleistocene horse (*Equus* sp.), and extinct peccary (*Platygonus compressus*). From the site, however, deer was the most prevalent animal and undoubtedly provided the major source of meat for the Late Paleo-Indian hunters as it did for almost all later Florida peoples.

The correlation between the larger Late Paleo-Indian period human populations in Florida and the subsequent extinction of several species of Pleistocene animals may not be coincidental. Human predation as well as the optimal humid conditions that prevailed after 7500 B.C. may have been jointly responsible for the extinctions. It is tempting to speculate, however, that species such as horses would have thrived with the better-watered conditions and that increased hunting by larger human populations led to at least some of the animals' demise.

Although we do not have good stratigraphic data from Florida, it is likely that during the Late Paleo-Indian period Suwannee and Simpson points were replaced by smaller points, which still were lanceolate-shaped with concave bases, usually with waisting and with basal grinding (Figure 7e–l). Such points include Tallahassee, Santa Fe, and Beaver Lake types (Bullen 1975:45–47; Bullen's chronology is not strictly adhered to here). Dalton points of several varieties and a number of other points also are believed to date from this period—Gilchrist, Greenbriar, Hardaway Side-Notched, and Bolen Plain and Bolen Beveled (Bullen 1975:44, 49–53)—all of which appear to be "transitional" stylistically from Paleo-Indian to Archaic points (Figure 7a–d; Figure 8). Some or all of these latter points may be hafted knives. Measurements of the two Bolen varieties indicate that they are quite the same; the only difference is that the beveled type have a right-hand bevel (97%) or left-hand bevel (3%). Possibly these were originally Bolen Plain knives that were resharpened while hafted, resulting in beveling.

With the exception of one remarkable site, almost nothing else is known about the tool kit of these Late Paleo-Indian peoples. Their points and/or knives, like their hunter–gatherer ancestors, are known best from springs and riverine localities where they have been recovered by divers. As would be expected with larger populations still organized in small bands, their points appear to be more common at land sites than earlier Paleo-Indian types. However, these observations need to be further investigated and quantified.

The remarkable site just mentioned is located on Lake Weohyakapka in Polk County. Bullen and Beilman (1973) have reported on the microlithic

FIGURE 7. *Late Paleo-Indian points and/or knives;* **a—d,** *Bolen* (**c** *is not beveled*); **e—h,** *Santa Fe;* **i—j,** *Beaver Lake;* **k—l,** *Tallahassee.*

FIGURE 8. *Late Paleo-Indian points and/or knives; a − b, Nuckolls variety of Dalton; c − d, Colbert variety of Dalton; e − f, Greenbriar; g − j, Bolen (i − j are not beveled).*

tool complex that was actually recovered from underwater around the edge of the lake. Although the largest number of projectile points from this Nalcrest site are of Archaic types, the remarkable microlith complex is typologically very similar to such assemblages associated with Bolen points elsewhere. It may be that materials were used and deposited over a long period of time after 7500 B.C. Although the levels of many Florida lakes vary with local ground water conditions, it is likely that the bulk of the microlith assemblage was deposited during drier conditions than those of today.

The Nalcrest tools are unique in Florida; no other single site has produced such a large number and variety of microliths, although single or multiple specimens are found at a number of sites in later Archaic times. Bullen and Beilman's analysis involved only a portion of the very large total collection now housed at the Florida State Museum. The microlith assemblage, the tools of which measure from 1 — 4 cm in length, includes tiny stemmed points, twisted drills and scrapers, side scrapers or drills, spurred chips, small spurred cores, small cores, small concave end scrapers, long concave end scrapers, small ovate scrapers, spurred scrapers, small hafted scrapers, medium sized trianguloid engraving tools, flake drills, and small Waller knives (Bullen and Beilman 1973:4 — 9, Figs. 2,3,6 — 10). Some of these tools are shown in Figure 9. Certainly Nalcrest was a special use site, perhaps used by various peoples for the same purpose over many generations. Possibly a single resource was exploited at the site and specialized tools whose types did not change through time were used. For instance, the processing of cane and grasses might have required a microlith assemblage. We can speculate that peoples occasionally camped beside the then lower lake to collect, cut, scrape, and weave baskets, mats, and other artifacts. Although not found at early sites in Florida because of poor preservation conditions, such items, along with cordage, are common in dry cave sites in the southwestern United States.

Early Archaic Peoples

After 6500 B.C. changes in settlement patterns and, most likely, subsistence patterns occurred. These changes are highly visible in the archaeological record, although they remain to be further investigated and verified. They mark the beginning of the Early Archaic period, a time of further cultural transitions from the nomadic life-style of the Paleo-Indians to the new ways of life present during the Archaic period.

The beginning of the Early Archaic period is marked by dryer condi-

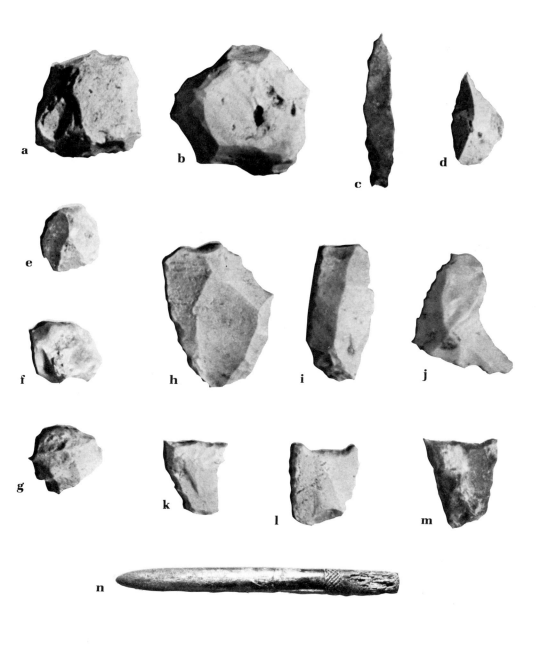

FIGURE 9. *Microlith assemblage from the Nalcrest site, Polk County, and Archaic period incised bone pins;* **a – b,** *cores;* **c – d,** *drills;* **e – g,** *thumb-nail scrapers;* **h – j,** *flake knives;* **k – m,** *end scrapers;* **n – o,** *incised bone pins (Ichetucknee River).*

tions in Florida. The land size of Florida would have been reduced as the sea level continued to rise, inundating coastal lands, especially along the Gulf of Mexico. Oak-hardwood forests covered areas of the state that now are characterized by pine or mixed pine forests.

Human populations must have been in increased competition with one another for dietary resources. Less land area, extinction of some animal species, and a drier climate would have combined to cause population pressure that probably resulted in increased use of certain old food sources and first use of new ones. We can surmise that acorns and hardwood nuts, because they were abundant and accessible, were one old source that became more important, at least on a seasonal basis. Freshwater snails appear to be first exploited along the inland rivers at this time and, perhaps, oysters were harvested in large numbers along the Gulf Coast. These oyster shell middens were inundated by subsequent sea-level rises and have received little study by archaeologists, although it has been recognized for more than 15 years that Paleo-Indian and Archaic period shell middens exist offshore, especially in the vicinity of Tampa Bay (Warren 1964; Warren and Bullen 1965; Warren 1970; Goodyear and Warren 1972).

Social changes might also have taken place, changes which allowed more efficient exploitation of food resources. Such changes may have been combined with shifts in settlement patterning; social groups would come together to form larger populations at certain times of the year and break up into small family groups at other times, according to the resources being collected or hunted and the need for sharing or nonsharing. That larger social groupings did occur is apparently reflected in the increased size of some Early Archaic sites which cover more than 2.6 ha and produce hundreds of stone tools when surface collected. These "central bases," some near chert outcroppings where stone could be quarried, contrast with the riverine kill sites and small "camps" found throughout almost all of the state north of the central portion of Lake Okeechobee. Separate quarry sites are also present from this period and a variety of stone tools were manufactured. Thousands of such tools have been found, attesting to the density of occupation left by what must have been much larger populations than those present prior to 6500 B.C. The forests of the Florida Central Highlands and the Tallahassee Red Hills region, both characterized by hardwoods during the Early Archaic period, are dotted with small Archaic sites interspersed with deposits that are much larger in extent and probably represent central bases.

The larger variety of projectile point (and knife?) types present in Early Archaic times may reflect ethnicity or, more likely, different site functions. Some of the points and related tool complexes are like those found in adjoining states, suggesting that communication over large areas was occurring or that populations were still entering (and leaving?) Florida as part of the yearly subsistence round.

The point (or knife) types from this period include both stemmed and nonstemmed varieties. Typological evidence, as yet unconfirmed in Florida by stratigraphic excavations, suggests that early in the Archaic period the prevalent point types were Arredondos and Hamiltons (Bullen 1975:38–39). Some of these points were used to tip projectiles while others were actually knives that were probably hafted. Later projectile point types (Figures 10, 11) include Florida Spike, Thonotosassa, Hardee Beveled, Kirk Serrated, Savannah River, Florida Morrow Mountain, and Sumter (Bullen 1975:33–37, 40–41). Stemmed points with broad, Christmas-tree-shaped blades came to predominate by the end of the period and were the most prevalent point type during the Middle Archaic period. These stemmed Archaic points are the most numerous types found in Florida.

A variety of stone tools is found with Early Archaic projectile points. Although some come from excavated contexts, such as Trilisa Pond where Arredondo points were recovered (Neill 1964), the largest numbers are from surface collections made in northern Florida. Like Paleo-Indian sites, sites of this period tend to be buried under several feet of aeolian sands, or they occur as surface finds where the soil matrix has been eroded away by wind and water action. Many small sites were apparently originally situated on slopes that have eroded due to modern land-clearing activities that increase erosion.

Perhaps the greatest differences between tools of this period and those of Paleo-Indian times are in the larger number of Archaic tools and the lesser degree of workmanship evidenced in tools of the Archaic period. Nearly all Middle Archaic tools are percussion flaked and some are cores or large flakes that received only enough shaping to make them usable. Tools used for more than one purpose (e.g., both scraping and chopping) also seem to be common as do many large core and flake tools, some weighing several pounds. The implication is that the users of the tools were performing many more tasks besides simply butchering meat and processing food. Some of the large choppers might well have been used in working wood. Large flake and core tools include planes, hammerstones, bifacial scrapers, bifacial knives, unifacial scrapers, end scrapers, flake knives, flake scrapers, and choppers as well as composite tools. Hafted end scrapers, some knapped intentionally and others probably reworked broken projectile points or knives, are also known, along with expanded-base drills and hafted drills.

Undoubtedly many tools were made from bone, but because of the acid

FIGURE 10. *Early Archaic points and/or knives;* **a – c,** *Arredondo;* **d – f,** *Hamilton.*

FIGURE 11. *Early Archaic points and/or knives;* **a,** *Florida Morrow Mountain;* **b,** *Florida Spike;* **c,** *Savannah River;* **d – e,** *Kirk Serrated;* **f,** *Sumter.*

nature of Florida soils, none have been found in excavated sites. Large numbers of bone tools have been recovered, however, from Florida rivers, especially the Ichetucknee River in North Florida, where they were collected by the Simpson family of High Springs. These bone tools cannot absolutely be attributed to the Early Archaic period, but the large numbers of projectile points from that and later Archaic times found with them strongly suggest that such tools were used throughout the entire Archaic period. The variety of bone tools preserved in the water almost equals that of the stone tools. Double-pointed points (also called bipointed or simple points) are the most prevalent. They were probably used as spears or several were hafted on a shaft to make a gig for fish. Several have been found with a small bone barb attached to the tip with pitch. Carved barbed points, some with multiple barbs, and bone pins are less common, and socketed antler points still rarer. Purdy's (1973) summary of distributional data regarding all of the bone tools just referred to implies that they were probably used throughout the Archaic period in northern Florida and even later in South Florida.

Other bone tools in the collections of the Florida State Museum are fish hooks, atlatl weights, socketed antler handles, "triggers" (curving L-shaped spurs), believed to have been used on throwing sticks to rest the butt of the dart or spear shaft on, splinter awls, deer-ulna awls, beaver teeth which show evidence of being hafted, and antler punches (Figures 5, 6). It should be stressed again that all of these could have been and probably were used throughout the Archaic period.

Middle Archaic Peoples

The date of 5000 B.C. used here as the division between the Early and Middle Archaic period is based on radiocarbon dates obtained for Middle Archaic archaeological assemblages at three sites. The dates and locations of these sites, all of which have produced Newnan projectile points, are: two dates averaging about 4850 B.C. calendar years from site 8-A-356 in Alachua County (Clausen *et al.* 1975:28); three dates averaging about 5000 B.C. calendar years from Little Salt Spring (Clausen *et al.* 1979:611); and three dates averaging about 4200 B.C. calendar years from the Tick Island site in Volusia County (Jahn and Bullen 1978:22 n.1).

The Middle Archaic archaeological assemblage is characterized by several varieties of stemmed, broad blade, projectile points of which the Newnan point (Clausen 1964:8 – 11; Bullen 1975:31) is perhaps the most distinctive and most widespread (Figure 12a – c,g). The Hillsborough point appears to be a Newnan variety (Figure 12d – f). Other types of

FIGURE 12. *Middle Archaic points and/or knives;* **a − c, g,** *Newnan;* **d − f,** *Hillsborough.*

a

b

c

d

e

f

g

h

i

stemmed points (Figure 13a—f) are Putnam, Levy, Marion, and Alachua (Bullen 1975:32). Some of the earlier stemmed point types, such as Morrow Mountain and Savannah, continued to be manufactured, perhaps as knives. There are more stemmed Middle Archaic points found in Florida than any other types of points.

A number of Middle Archaic sites have been excavated and an even larger number located and collected or tested as a result of surveys. Small, special-use camp sites predominate. We can guess that these sites were used for hunting and foraging of certain, perhaps seasonal resources, by small groups. Such sites are characterized by lithic debitage and a smaller amount of tools, including points, knives, scrapers, and a few larger chopping or hammering tools. An excellent report documenting an area containing several of these special-use camps has been produced by Hemmings and Kohler (1974) for the Kanapaha area in Alachua County. Larger sites believed to be central-base villages for larger groups (e.g., the Alachua Field site, 8-A-166, in Alachua County) may cover several hectares and contain tens of thousands of pieces of flint debitage and tools. Other sites, apparently occupied for shorter periods of time, contain fewer artifacts but are still spread over several hectares.

The tools collected from the central-base sites include all of the types listed above for the Early Archaic period and more, including blades at some sites. Although archaeologists, on the basis of shape, can separate tool collections in macro-categories—flake knives, bifacial knives, scraper knives, choppers, hammerstones, and so on—typologies based on other criteria, such as use-chipping, produce many more types. If the Middle Archaic peoples were performing the same types of activities at their villages and camps as their Early Archaic ancestors, they must have been using a much greater variety of tools to do them. The implication is that increased sedentism, most likely on a seasonal basis, led to the acquiring of more, specialized tools. At least some of the tools, perhaps those used for woodworking, are quite large and would not have been easily transportable in large numbers. As yet we do not have a good comparative analysis of lithic collections from camps versus central-bases or even analyses of collections among camps or central-bases. Such analyses may provide us with information on the uses of different sites.

Nor do we have bone preservation at these large sites. However, we can speculate that all of the bone and antler tools described for the Early Archaic period continued to be manufactured and used.

FIGURE 13. *Middle and Late Archaic points and/or knives; a—b, Levy; c—e, Marion; f, Putnam; g, i, Lafayette; h, Clay.*

Quarry sites are also known for the Middle Archaic period, both large sites in localities of major outcroppings where chert was mined and tools manufactured, and very small sites where smaller outcroppings are present, such as along rivers or around lakes where erosion has cut through the soil to the chert deposits in the underlying limestone. Quarrying activity was probably often carried out in conjunction with other activities at camps. An excellent example of a large quarry-manufacturing site is the Senator Edwards site in Marion County (Purdy 1975) dating from the Early and Middle Archaic periods. Limited excavation of the site using mechanical equipment has produced more than 500 tools, 50,000 flakes, 4600 utilized flakes, and 6000 blades. A second large workshop site which possibly also functioned as a central base is the Johnson Lake site in Marion County (Bullen and Dolan 1959).

Still another type of site, one known only from a very few examples, is caves. The best known example is Dixie Lime Cave No. 1 (Bullen and Benson 1964), although other such sites have been located in the panhandle. The excavations in the Dixie Lime Cave produced a modest assortment of points and other tools which suggest that the cave was lived in, perhaps functioning as a camp for hunting deer and opossum which were brought back to the cave and butchered. The deer hides might also have been at least partially processed for tanning within the cave, since scraping tools were common. Analysis of the bones of animals used for food which were found preserved in the cave deposit (with the minimum number of individuals present listed) include: opossum (62), mole (2), pocket gopher (5), cotton rat (9), rabbit (2), bear (6), raccoon (1), gray fox (4), mink (1), bobcat (4), panther (1), gopher tortoise (22), unidentified bird (6), and deer (196). The moles, rats, and pocket gophers may have been deposited by predators other than humans.

We would be remiss in this discussion of the Middle Archaic peoples if we did not mention two very important sites both characterized by Newnan points. These sites illustrate some of the differing activities of these early peoples. The first is the type-site for the Newnan point, site 8-A-356, which was excavated in the 1960s and led to our recognition of the widespread nature of the archaeological assemblage (Clausen 1964). The second is Little Salt Spring, which is presently being investigated and which holds the potential to provide a very large amount of new data on beliefs, burial ceremonialism, and other aspects of culture relevant to perhaps a regional variation of the same culture (Clausen *et al.* 1979).

The 8-A-356 site is located just east of Gainesville on high ground that separates Newnan's Lake from Payne's Prairie. Excavations revealed a lithic assemblage which resembles neither that found at a small, special-use camp nor the assemblage found at the large, central-base sites, even though the site is itself rather large in extent, covering more than 2.5 ha. Out of the 186 Archaic stemmed projectile points recovered, 95% were Newnan points. Other tools, which occurred in small quantities, were ovate blanks, probably brought from quarry sites used in the manufacture of the points, bifacial knives with rounded or squared bottoms, sandstone hones, hammerstones, and cruciform drills. The most numerous artifacts were blades, flakes, and cores associated with a well-developed blade industry which functioned at the site. Many of the blades, though less than a majority, were also used as cutting tools. Although blades are found occasionally at Middle Archaic sites, the 8-A-356 site with its hundreds of blades is unique. Whatever was being killed or cut or worked with the points (some of which are knives) and the blades was apparently not preserved in the archaeological record. But the specialized nature of the site leads to speculation that some specialized resource was being worked or processed at the site in large quantities. Could it have been that the points or blades were used to hunt and butcher animals on nearby Paynes Prairie?

A hiatus in the human occupation of Little Salt Spring seems to have occurred just after the end of the Late Paleo-Indian times (6000 B.C.), during the drier period present during the Early Archaic (Clausen *et al.* 1979). However, by 5000 B.C. Middle Archaic peoples bearing Newnan points began once again to utilize the spring and adjacent areas. Clausen's investigations have revealed an as yet largely unexplored village area 6.2 to 12 ha in extent which bordered a slough connecting with the cenote. Human burials were made in the wet peat or muck of the slough. Evidently the burials were placed just adjacent to and above the water edge. As the water level dropped, the burials were moved closer to the cenote, following the retreating edge of the water. Clausen estimates that the cemetery covered approximately 3.7 ha in extent and that the densely placed burials may number in excess of 1000. Individuals were interred in extended position on branches or biers of wax myrtle and portions of the body were wrapped in grass. Wooden, bone, stone, and shell artifacts were placed with burials, including one wooden, oak digging stick sharpened on one end. A carved wooden tablet was also found with one burial in the now inundated spring basin. The carved tablet is very similar to examples of tenoned tablets recovered from the famed Key Marco site in Collier County (see Chapter 9) and appears to have a bird carved on it. Preservation of the burials and the grave goods in the muck is so good that even brain tissue is still present in skulls (Clausen *et al.* 1979:612).

In his preliminary report on the Little Salt Spring Archaic burials, Clausen notes that the practice of interment in areas close to water is similar to the pattern present several thousand years later at the Belle Glade culture, Fort Center site (see Chapter 7). Evidently certain of the Archaic cultural patterns (as well as tools, as evidenced by the Key Marco materials) lasted in South Florida for many thousands of years.

Palynological analysis from Florida and South-Central Georgia (Watts 1969, 1971) indicates that increasingly moist conditions appeared during the Middle Archaic period after about 4000 B.C. and a gradual change in forest cover took place, with oaks in some regions giving way to pines or mixed forests. The resulting vegetation communities are essentially those found in modern times. These vegetative changes may or may not be related to shifts in settlement patterning that occurred during the Middle Archaic period, the first major occupation by Archaic peoples of the St. Johns River Valley. The large shell middens that began to accumulate about 4000 B.C. in that region, especially along the river adjacent to modern Volusia County, suggest that significant amounts of people began to live in that region for at least a portion of the year. The resulting Mount Taylor culture, the Middle Archaic culture of East Florida, is discussed in Chapter 6 along with the later cultures of that region.

Late Archaic Peoples and the Early Ceramic-Manufacturing Cultures

The start of the Late Archaic period is not well documented, and the date of 3000 B.C. given here is little more than a guess. Generally, the end of the Late Archaic is signaled by the first appearance of peoples who manufactured and fired clay pottery. The date of this technological innovation appears to vary in different parts of the state, but ranges from about 2000 B.C. to 1000 B.C. Here we will include these first ceramic-making cultures within the Late Archaic period since it is recognized that they had an Archaic-like hunting—foraging subsistence pattern, although this included villages that served as central-bases, perhaps throughout the year.

The earliest pottery-manufacturing culture in East Florida is the Orange culture (see Chapter 6) as it is on the Gulf Coast from Tampa Bay north. Within Northwest Florida it is referred to either as Norwood or Orange. In South Florida, especially south of Lake Okeechobee, the evidence for Late Archaic or second millennium B.C. pottery-making cultures is almost nonexistent at this time. We do know that by about 1000 B.C. pottery-making cultures were present in the Lake Okeechobee Basin (see Chapter 7) and that shortly after this date a few sites were occupied along the lower southeastern coast. Excavations on Marco Island on the southwestern coast by archaeologists from the State Division of Archives, History and Records Management have provided some documentation for early ceramic-bearing cultures in that locality by 1500 B.C. (Division of Archives, History and Records Management 1970). In all of these regions of the state, the earliest pottery had vegetable fibers or a mixture of vegetable fibers and sand as temper. Fiber-tempered pottery thus serves as a convenient horizon marker for temporal comparisons.

Between 1200 B.C. and 500 B.C. significant changes occurred among all of these cultures: Tool types changed; fiber-tempered pottery disappeared and was replaced by other types; dense village middens began to accumulate. These changes are thought to be due to a combination of factors, including larger populations, the first experimentation with agriculture (although this remains to be proved), and increased regional interaction among different groups within and outside of Florida. However, all of these causal factors remain to be more thoroughly investigated and proven. The period between 1200 B.C. to 500 B.C., which Bullen (1959) has referred to as the Transitional period, was certainly a period of cultural transition from the hunting—gathering Archaic cultures to the many post-500 B.C. regional cultures that receive most of the attention of the remainder of this book.

Cultural events occurring during the Late Archaic period present a puzzle. On the one hand, we have in land portions of northern Florida a large number of Middle Archaic sites, as typified by Newnan's and other types of stemmed Archaic points. Yet there does not appear to be any significant number of sites that we can point to as being from the Late Archaic period; there are only very small sites or components within sites which have fiber-tempered pottery. All of the latter were probably hunting or other special-use camps occupied for very short periods of time. On the other hand, such fiber-tempered pottery sites do occur in some frequency within the St. Johns-Oklawaha drainage and along the Gulf Coast from Tampa Bay north. Interior portions of the northern part of the state appear to have been used only sparingly by aboriginal peoples during Late Archaic times, including the Orange and Norwood periods. The changes in floral communities that occurred in Middle Archaic times as a result of wetter conditions may have resulted in populations formerly accustomed to spending most of the year in the interior forests and moving to the Gulf Coast or St. Johns drainage for short periods of time, altering this pattern and spending a greater portion of the year outside of the interior highlands. This shift, which as previously noted may have led to the Mount Taylor culture, left the interior forest largely unpopulated. It was not until after A.D. 1 that significant numbers of peoples returned to those regions.

The Late Archaic cultures along the Gulf Coast are known both from shell middens adjacent to the Gulf and from sites back from the coast proper, although the largest sites are the shell middens. Sites such as Culbreath Bayou on Tampa Bay (Warren *et al.* 1967) contain preceramic Late Archaic components and indicate that the dominate projectile point types are Culbreath (most common), Clay, and Lafayette (Bullen 1975:26 — 28), all of which are stemmed and corner notched (Figure 13g — i). From the Culbreath Bayou site a number of hafted scrapers, end scrapers, and ovate and trianguloid knives were recovered. Some of the points were asymmetrical, evidently from being resharpened on one edge of the blade and probably were used as hafted knives.

Warren (1968) has reported on materials dredged from Apollo Beach, another site on Tampa Bay, which also contained large numbers of Late Archaic points and associated materials. The Culbreath Bayou site contained a great deal of oyster shell midden, while the Apollo Beach dredged material did not.

At other sites in the Tampa Bay area, such as Canton Street (Bullen *et al.* 1978), occupation appears to begin at about the time of the first appearance of pottery-making cultures or slightly after and last up into the immediate post-500 B.C. period. As would be expected, such sites represent a continuum with those of the preceramic Late Archaic period. Culbreath points are found in fewer quantities and Lafayette points are more popular. Hernando and Citrus points, popular at later times in Northwest Florida, appear (Bullen 1975:24 — 25). Crudely knapped, stemmed knives resembling Archaic stemmed points are also present.

Other tools from Canton Street include pottery tempered with vegetable fibers, sand, or limestone; steatite sherds and ornaments; sandstone sherds from vessels; an imitation carnivore jaw made from slate; bone awls; *Busycon* shell hammers and picks; and stone cleavers, perhaps also used as scraping tools. The variety of stone tools at the Late Archaic and the post-1200 B.C. Gulf Coast sites seems less than the variety present in Middle Archaic times, although this may be a sampling error.

During the Transitional period, the Florida Indians certainly had contact with the Poverty Point culture populations living in the Lower Mississippi Valley and some adjacent portions of Louisiana and Mississippi. Webb (1977:4 — 5) has reviewed the radiocarbon and thermoluminescence dates of the Poverty Point culture and suggests that the culture began about 1800 B.C. and was fully developed by 1200 — 1000 B.C., lasting until about 500 B.C. Artifacts associated with the culture, possibly manufactured at the Poverty Point sites, were traded far and wide within the Southeast, including to Tick Island on the St. Johns River (Jahn and Bullen 1978:Figs. 21, 46, 50) and Canton Street, both Transitional sites, and to several sites in Walton and Okaloosa counties where the objects were first recognized (Lazarus 1958; Fairbanks 1959). William Lazarus (1958:28) originally gave the name Elliot's Point Complex to Poverty Point-type clay balls in Florida, a name that might now be applied to the entire assemblage of Poverty Point-related objects in Florida.

The Transitional period marks the end of the hunting—foraging style of life that lasted in Florida for more than 10 millennia. Although some populations in South Florida evidently continued to live as their Archaic ancestors, most populations would combine the cultivation of plant crops with hunting and foraging. But subsistence changes were only one facet of the cultural changes that occurred among the Florida Indians during the next 3000 years. They began to put to use new ideas, some undoubtedly obtained through the same communication routes that brought the Poverty Point materials into Florida, and to solve new problems related to increasing populations and a growing dependence on agriculture. The cultures evolved, eventually developing into those systems observed and ultimately destroyed by explorers and colonists from the Old World.

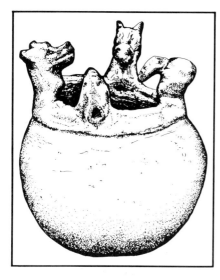

4

Deptford:
Life on the
West Coast Marshes

The fact that the Late Archaic peoples of Florida learned to make fired-clay pottery is almost as important to the modern archaeologist as it was to the prehistoric Indians. It is pottery that initially allows the archaeologist to distinguish the variety and geographical range of the post-Archaic cultures, since different cultures tended to manufacture their own distinctive ceramic types. The Deptford culture, which inhabited the Gulf Coast of Florida and the Atlantic Coast of Georgia and South Carolina, is one of the first widely spread post-Archaic cultures to be recognized by archaeologists. Much of the Deptford pottery was decorated by stamping the vessel surfaces with carved wooden paddles before the vessels were fired. The carved designs appear on the pots as indented linear grooves (simple stamping), small rectangles or squares (check stamping), or small rectangles or squares that have two parallel sides more raised than the other two sides (linear check stamping). Other pottery has the surfaces roughened by malleating them with a wooden paddle wrapped with cord, and some vessels have plain, smoothed surfaces. Pastes of all of these types contain various sizes of quartz sand particles and, occasionally, clay lumps. Deptford pottery is consequently easily distinguishable from the fiber-tempered pottery of the Late Archaic period.

The Deptford ceramic series was first discovered on the Georgia Coast and derives its name from the Deptford site located near Savannah. In the mid-1930s, research carried out by Willey and Woodbury in Northwest Florida (Willey and Woodbury 1942; Willey 1949a), showed that Deptford pottery was also present in that locality. Subsequent work by Willey demonstrated that the Deptford culture spanned almost the entire length of Florida's Gulf Coast (Milanich 1973:51 − 52). In the intervening three decades since the early work of Willey in Florida and Joseph Caldwell and others on the Georgia Coast, additional research into the Deptford culture now makes it possible to describe many details about the coastal way of life and to understand the position of Deptford relative to other Southeast cultures.

The geographical region of Deptford in the Southeast stretches along the Atlantic Coast from Cape Fear, North Carolina, southward to the mouth of the St. Johns River near Jacksonville, Florida, and along the Gulf Coast from the Alabama − Florida state line eastward and southward to below Tampa Bay, Florida (Figure 14). Deptford was a coastal-dwelling culture whose subsistence centered on the exploitation of coastal resources such as fish, shellfish, deer, plants, and other wild foods. Occasionally, perhaps seasonally, small groups of Deptford peoples moved inland up the river valleys of the coastal plain and into North-Central Florida. This is basically the same pattern as was practiced earlier during the Late Archaic period. Sites occupied during these journeys are found up to 80 km or slightly more from the coast. Most likely these trips were made to gather specific types of nuts, berries, and other river valley products. Trade and cultural contact with noncoastal cultures would have been possible at this time.

The temporal range of the Deptford culture is not as well known as its spatial distribution. A date of 500 B.C. is generally accepted for the invention of Deptford carved-paddle-malleated pottery on the coast (or the diffusion of such techniques to the coast), an event which marks the beginning of the Deptford period. This date is supported by three radiocarbon dates, two from the Georgia Coast of 270 B.C. and 400 B.C., and one from the Florida Gulf Coast of 625 B.C. There are also three radiocarbon dates for the Deptford component at the Gulf Coast Crystal River site which range from 30 B.C. to A.D. 200. These are matched by three from the Georgia Coast ranging from A.D. 55 to A.D. 520. Together, these dates show that along the Atlantic Coast the Deptford period lasted several hundred years later than on the Gulf Coast, about A.D. 600 for the Atlantic subregion as compared to A.D. 100 − 200 for the Gulf subregion. This separate developmental sequence for the two subregions is also apparent from other archaeological evidence which is discussed later in this chapter.

The Archaic cultures from which the Deptford peoples are descended are St. Simons on the Georgia Coast and Orange − Norwood on the Gulf. The major differences in these geographically diverse Archaic cultures are the presence in the former of both donut-shaped shell middens and

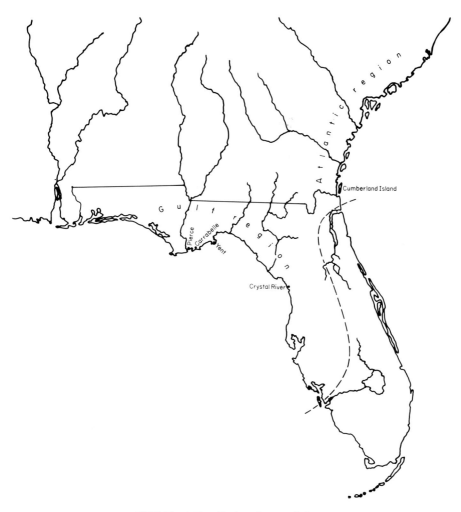

FIGURE 14. *Deptford regions and sites.*

large, linear shell middens. The donut-shaped rings do not appear to be present in the Gulf subregion. Decorations on the fiber-tempered pottery of the two regions also vary. On the Gulf Coast, Norwood pottery is either plain or impressed with sticks, whereas the St. Simons pottery is either plain, punctated, or incised and punctated. Further north along the South Carolina Coast, the unnamed pre-Deptford Archaic culture manufactured a high percentage of sand-tempered pottery that was decorated with a variety of punctation motifs. The Archaic shell rings are not found along the North Carolina or northern South Carolina coasts.

Deptford coastal sites are rarely deeply stratified or large in horizontal extent. It hardly seems possible that the more than 1000 years of Deptford occupation on the Georgia and Carolinas coasts and 600 – 700 years on the Gulf Coast would have left such relatively little evidence of occupation. Either the populations were small or it is possible that many sites have been destroyed or inundated by a rise in sea level since and, perhaps, during Deptford times. The small quantity of Deptford cultural remains, as evidenced by shell middens, is probably the result of both of these explanations, although inundation may be the more significant factor. Research on St. Simons Island, Georgia, carried out by the University of Florida, has yielded evidence of an apparent 1 m rise in the Atlantic sea level since approximately 1000 B.C. Many of the Georgia coastal Deptford sites today extend to the edge of the high tide line, indicating that, in the past, portions of the shell middens have been destroyed either by erosion or by inundation.

Along the Gulf Coast the evidence for the inundation of Deptford sites is more dramatic. There, certain factors, including the weight of the sediments deposited by the rivers flowing into the Gulf, are causing a subsidence of the land relative to the sea. This subsidence rate has been calculated at about 2.5 cm each 25 years (Fairbridge 1960). Thus, from A.D. 1 to 1980, the Gulf has risen roughly 2 m relative to the land. Although such data are, of course, not uniform for the entire Gulf, archaeological evidence tends generally to support such a rise off the coast of peninsular Florida. A submerged archaeological site spanning the temporal range from the end of the Archaic period to the beginning of the Deptford period has been located .8 km out into the Gulf off New Port Richey under nearly 2 m of water (Lazarus 1965). Excavations by Ripley and Adelaide Bullen conducted at three Gulf Coast sites—Johns Island in Chassahowitzka Bay, Wash Island in Crystal River, and the Battery Point site near Bayport—also confirm a Deptford relative rise in sea level (Bullen and Bullen 1950, 1953, 1963).

Settlement Traits, Subsistence, and Social Organization

Deptford coastal villages were nearly always located in live oak – magnolia hammocks that are adjacent to the salt marshes. These hammocks are present on both the Atlantic offshore barrier islands and the Gulf keys as well as on the mainland proper. No doubt many of the sites that today are immediately beside the salt marshes were farther away from the high tide line and the marshes when they were occupied originally. This is due to the rise in sea level and to the subsequent shifting of the marshes.

Probably, the acorns from the live oaks and the palm berries from the sabal palms and the saw palmetto, all of which are found in the oak—magnolia hammocks, were important to the Deptford peoples as seasonal foods. It is significant that the northern limit of the Deptford culture on the Atlantic Coast corresponds with the northern extent of the live oak and the sabal palm.

Wild foodstuffs from the hammocks which were used by the Deptford peoples were many and varied. Although plant remains usually are not preserved in archaeological sites unless they are charred, we can hypothesize some of the foods that were eaten by analogy with Southeast Indians known from the historic period. The bones of the animals killed and eaten by the Deptford peoples, and the remains of shellfish, last thousands of years in middens, making the meat diet of the Deptford culture more easily reconstructable.

Edible plants probably used for food growing near Deptford coastal sites include pignut hickory; several species of *Smilax* from which the roots are dug, prepared, and then eaten; blueberry; persimmon; and muscadine. Leaves of the cassina plant, *Ilex vomitoria*, which is found in large quantities in the coastal hammocks, were used by many Southeast Indians to make a sacred tea called "black drink." The drink, also used as an everyday beverage because of its caffeine content, was made by brewing the roasted leaves of the plant. The use of the plant appears to have had a long history in the Southeast and, quite likely, it was drunk by the Deptford coastal peoples.

Many animal species can today be observed in the coastal hammock areas. The Deptford Indians hunted or gathered nearly all of them, especially the white-tailed deer which, in terms of meat consumed, was the largest single source of food. Animal bones from various Deptford sites represent the following land animals: deer, raccoon, opossum, rabbit, pocket gopher, bear, bobcat, gopher tortoise, box turtle, and Florida panther. Bones from birds indicate that the red-breasted merganser, lesser scaup, and loon were caught for food.

Although the hammocks offered the Deptford Indians a large number of food resources, it was not the hammocks alone that drew both the Deptford peoples and their Archaic predecessors to the coast. Rather, it was the availability of many diverse environmental habitats, each supporting communities of potential plant and animal food sources. Within easy walking or canoe distance of the Deptford camps, there were a number of such habitats—the hammock itself, the beach, the salt marshes and tidal streams which drain them at low tide, the lagoon, the delta areas where freshwater rivers empty into the Gulf or Atlantic, and the sea or Gulf itself. All of these separate habitats are distributed longitudinally along the coastal strand. The strand itself varies in width from about 1.5 km to as much as 25 km, the greatest width being near deltas where brackish water extends up the rivers that flow down to the sea through the coastal plain. These same rivers deposit silt out into the sea, causing the shallowness that is a prerequisite for marsh and stream formation. At these delta areas, the marsh is distributed both farther inland and farther out to the sea than at other places along the coast.

If one of the habitats were to be chosen as most important in terms of variety and quantity of food resources, it would be the marsh and tidal streams. The marshes are composed of several species of grasses which grow only where there are shallow mud flats to lessen the eroding force of the tidal change. These flats are found along the Gulf Coast and the Atlantic Coast north of Jacksonville. Here, sediments brought down the coastal plain by rivers are deposited. Along the Gulf, these rivers include the Mississippi, Mobile, Apalachicola, Ocklocknee, Suwannee, and others. On the Atlantic, they are the St. Marys, Altamaha, Savannah, Edisto, Santee, and many others. There is no large build-up of similar sediments and, hence, no extensive salt marshes on much of the east coast of Florida south of St. Augustine simply because there are no rivers that flow from the interior of the peninsula into the Atlantic Ocean. The salt-marsh-dwelling Deptford peoples never permanently expanded into the St. Johns area because they were not adapted to the riverine-type environment there, which was being exploited by the St. Johns peoples. Because of such environmental factors, the east and west coasts of Florida developed different aboriginal cultures. Even today, the modern settlements of the two areas differ because of the same basic reason: the presence of the beach and lagoon of the Atlantic in contrast to the keys, salt marsh, and lagoon of the Gulf.

Just as East Florida was not well suited to the Deptford subsistence pattern, so did the mangrove swamps of South Florida present an inhospitable environmental situation to peoples acquainted with the salt marsh. For this reason, Tampa Bay or a point slightly south marks the southern limit of the Deptford culture.

The salt marsh provides an almost inexhaustible food supply of shellfish, fish, sea mammals (otter, porpoise, seal, whale), and raccoons. There is no archaeological evidence that the Deptford peoples overused any of the marsh resources; they were assured of a rich harvest of foodstuffs nearly all year round except for, perhaps, the coldest winter months when changes in sea temperature occurred, affecting shellfish and fish distribution. Today, however, we are aware that unrestricted commercial fishing and water pollution can ruin the ecology of the coastal strand and what seemed to be an inexhaustible source of food. Seals and whales (meat providers, prehistorically) are no longer found along the Southeast coasts due to human predation. Some ecologists also feel that because of pollution and commercial fishing the quantities of fish available on the coast are much less than they were even several decades ago. The coastal strand was probably a lusher environment in the past than it is today in terms of quantities of animals present.

On the Atlantic Coast, oysters constitute about 95% of the total shellfish used by the Deptford peoples, whereas on the Gulf Coast at some panhandle coastal sites clams comprise the majority of shellfish species collected for food. Other shellfish include ribbed mussel, several species of *Tagelus*, and several species of whelk *(Busycon)*.

Raccoons, ordinarily nocturnal predators, hunt according to the tides when they hunt in the marshes. They can be taken in relatively large numbers when the tide is out, or at extreme high tide when they are stranded. A variety of fish can be caught in the marsh tidal streams and in the adjacent lagoon. Fish were extremely important in the Deptford diet. Generally, the fish caught were bottom scavengers which fed near shellfish beds. Bones from several species of shark, ray, and catfish have been identified in large numbers from Deptford sites along with drum, channel bass, sheepshead, snook, snapper, jack, trout, flounder, mullet, blowfish, and other saltwater species in lesser numbers. The salt marsh terrapin, *Malaclemmys terrapin*, also was used in relatively large numbers for food and could be collected from the marshes.

The beach habitat has never been an important source of food to Southeast Indians who did not have an offshore deep-sea fishing technology. However, during the late summer months, the large sea turtles, *Cheloniidae*, nest on the beaches. These massive creatures, some of which weigh 225 kg provided a seasonal meat source and have been recovered from nearly all of the coastal Deptford sites excavated.

Bones from a number of freshwater turtle species have been recovered at many sites, indicating widespread gathering of these amphibians from ponds and streams. Such freshwater sources are often present on the offshore islands and the mainland and are formed by the collection of rainfall. The freshwater fish inhabiting these ponds evidently were not eaten; their remains have not, as yet, been identified in the Deptford middens.

Although the Deptford peoples maintained their main villages in the coastal strand, the presence of small sites inland from the coasts suggests occasional movements of peoples to the coastal plain. Whether or not such sites were occupied on a seasonal basis or just haphazardly on an irregular schedule is unknown at this time. The size of the inland sites relative to the coastal villages does suggest short-term occupations by small groups of people, perhaps separate nuclear families. It is conceivable that short-term excursions by canoe were made up the river valleys to harvest nuts, berries, and other nonmarine resources during the late summer and early fall. These products could then be brought back to the coast for winter use. Also, at this time of the year the deer congregate in the coastal-plain hardwood hammocks, since fall is the time of both the rutting season and the nut fall. Deer are most successfully hunted at this time, thus hunting excursions may have taken place.

Evidence for the types of activities occurring at these inland sites is lacking from most Deptford localities, except North-Central Florida where such sites have been excavated (e.g. Sunday Bluff and Colby sites) both on the Oklawaha River in Marion County. These latter two sites show that the same riverine locations were occupied by both Deptford and St. Johns peoples at various times. The two cultures must have occasionally practiced similar patterns of exploitation of inland riverine-hammock resources. Contact and trade between the two groups would have been possible at this time.

Nearly all archaeological excavations in Alachua County, where the most inland archaeology has been carried out, reveal sparse Deptford occupations, probably camps, on top of Archaic or under Alachua tradition components. It appears that the inland habitats were utilized less by the Deptford peoples than by their Archaic predecessors. This is, perhaps, due to increased exploitation of the coastal resources by the more specialized Deptford hunters and gatherers in comparison with the generalized Early and Middle Archaic hunters and gatherers who might have moved between broad environmental zones more frequently. Much more research is needed to determine whether the paucity of inland Deptford sites relative to preceramic Archaic sites reflects such a subsistence change or whether it is simply due to a greater occupational time span for the preceramic Archaic period.

As stated before, Deptford sites are neither deeply stratified nor do they cover a large horizontal area. Such sites are generally shell middens containing sherds, food bones, and other refuse from living activities. In sites that have not been disturbed by recent activities (such as by plowing), circular, often overlapping, shell middens 6 m to about 9 m in diameter are usually discernible on the ground surface. These separate circular piles probably represent the natural accumulation of refuse next to individual house locations. Often, closer to the marsh, a larger, possibly communal, dump is also present. It appears that when houses or fire pits were cleaned, or when there were large quantities of shellfish remains to be thrown away, the refuse was carried a short distance away from the village area.

At sites which have been occupied over a long period of time, the individual midden piles might overlap one another, making individual house locations difficult to spot. Where certain local conditions of soil strata are present, these small middens may be covered under one or more layers of soil deposited either as humus formed by rotting organic matter (such as leaves and branches in forests) or as topsoil that is eroding toward the marsh from higher adjacent areas. Some sites may be entirely covered in this manner while still other site locations may be buried under debris and shell left by subsequent cultures. Deptford sites cannot always be located by simple surface observation.

Surveys and excavations of single-component Deptford sites on the Georgia Coast and the Gulf Coast show that usually about 15 to 25 separate circular shell middens are present. Assuming that these are associated with individual houses, it can be postulated that villages consisted of no more than this number of houses. Since some houses may have been rebuilt and new ones constructed through time, a guess of 5 to 10 houses per village at any one time seems reasonable. Some later Deptford sites, especially those on the Gulf Coast, were larger, reflecting larger, later village populations. Within the villages, the houses were linearly arranged parallel to the marsh as opposed to a circular or semicircular arrangement as is common at many post-Deptford period villages in the Southeast.

One complete Deptford house and portions of another structure, both on the Georgia Coast, have been excavated. The two structures were of a size sufficient to house one nuclear family of 5 or 6 persons. This figure combined with the houses per village figure yields a village population of 25 to 60 persons. Such an estimate is very reasonable when compared to other hunting—gathering groups.

Investigation of one of the Deptford houses, a presumed winter house on Cumberland Island, Georgia, showed the structure to be oval, approximately 6.7 by 9.8 m. Walls of the house were formed by placing the butt ends of posts in a trench dug for that purpose. The trench varied in width at the top from 1.2 m to about .6 m and tapered to a width of .3 m at the bottom. Depth averaged 36 cm. Humic stains and depressions from individual posts 15 to 24 cm in diameter were apparent in the bottom of the trench. Posts were placed side by side several centimeters apart. The cracks between posts were probably caulked with brush, clay, or mud. This rather substantial structure must have been repeatedly occupied over a several-year period or more. The closed nature of the house suggests that it was used during the winter months.

One end of the house was not walled with posts. Possibly hides or reed mats were placed at that end. These could be raised or lowered as the weather or cooking smoke from inside of the house dictated. An entranceway was present on one long side of the structure. A small slot trench, which probably anchored an intrahouse partition, divided the house into two "rooms," one containing a long, bathtub-shaped cooking pit and the other the presumed sleeping area. This partition had evidently been repaired or replaced at least once during the lifetime of the house. A large post set in a trenchlike post hole in the fire-pit room probably helped to support the roof. Shells were packed around the base of the wall posts and the support post to help anchor them.

The center post and other posts found at the Deptford sites on Cumberland Island were raised into place by digging a sloping, linear trench or slot; then the horizontal post was slid into the trench butt first, braced against the end of the trench, and raised to an upright position. Such posts must have been large, and the cooking area post, for example, could have supported a considerable number of large roof beams covered with heavy roofing materials including earth packed over grass or reeds.

Shellfish, fish, deer, and other foods were prepared for eating in the central fire pit. Refuse was dumped beside the house, forming a small, circular shell midden. Careful excavation of the house showed that the floor was occasionally scraped clean and the refuse dumped both outside the house and pushed up against the inside house walls.

Trenching excavations by Bullen (1969:17–20) at the Sunday Bluff site southeast of Ocala, Florida, intersected what seems to have been the wall trench of a similar Deptford structure. As yet, none have been reported from the Gulf Coast. Perhaps future excavations will yield evidence of other "winter" houses built by the Deptford peoples.

A second house, an open structure, was also excavated on Cumberland Island, Georgia, at a second Deptford site. The house was also oval and measured 6.7 by 4.3 m. Widely spaced support posts held up the roof which was probably thatched with palmetto fronds. Whether or not the sides were similarly covered is uncertain. The floor of the house was slightly depressed; possibly the old ground surface was scraped clean before the structure was built. A small, bell-shaped storage pit had been dug in the house floor and extended down through earlier strata. No hearth was found within the confines of the house; one might have been outside.

Two structures alone do not represent all the possible structures built by the Deptford peoples. But they do give us information on family size and the types of households established by the Deptford peoples. The presence of the two different types of structures does seem to indicate that the coastal occupation was year-round, spanning both the cold and warm seasons, a pattern already suggested.

Deptford society was probably originally organized into bands — groups of interrelated families. Descent was most likely (although not necessarily) traced through the males of the family, a trait common in band social organization. Separate bands inhabited separate villages, and nuclear families evidently occupied their own houses within the village. Thus, two or more adult brothers, their spouses, and their married sons and their families together could form one village. There was probably no elected chief. Rather, the most respected male, usually the oldest, assumed leadership.

The growth of ceremonialism during the late Deptford period on the Gulf Coast is generally viewed as indicative of the growth of more complex village forms and more complex social organization such as the organization of families into clans. Clan groups are bound together by the belief that the members of the family are descended from the same mythical ancestor. Children belong to the same clan as either their father or mother, depending on whether membership is reckoned through the male or female line. Within the villages, clans are united under one or more village chiefs whose position is determined by patterns of birth, not by simple selection. In such societies, special religious practitioners perform the ceremonies and provide the guidance necessary for the well-being of the society, especially the perpetuation of religious beliefs and ceremonies that reinforce the basic economic system. Sites such as Crystal River, which was first occupied by late Deptford peoples, reflect such sociopolitical and religious organization.

Technology

Very little is known about Deptford subsistence and tool technology. Because of the absence of stone on the coast, wood must have been worked into a variety of tool types. Only under special conditions is wood preserved at archaeological sites in Florida, thus our knowledge of Deptford technology is based on supposition and a small number of stone, bone, and shell artifacts. A few impressions of basketry and cordage on fired-clay pots have also been found.

That the Deptford peoples worked wood is shown by their pottery designs, which were applied with carved wooden paddles. Probably, most weapons and tools were manufactured from wood. Medium-sized triangular projectile points have been found at Deptford sites, but whether they were used to tip the shafts of spears or arrows is unknown. If the bow were present, it was probably less important in food-collecting activities than were snares and nets. Cord impressions on Deptford pottery indicate that cordage was in use. Snares and nets could have been used to collect a variety of small hammock-dwelling game as well as fish and birds. Such techniques were in use during the historic period by the Indians of Florida and Georgia and certainly had a history dating well back into the Late Archaic in the Deptford region.

The techniques used to hunt deer are not well known, although deer seem to have been an important meat source in the Deptford diet. Due to the large number of acorn-bearing oaks in the coastal strand, the area is capable of supporting a relatively large deer population. This is true even today in isolated areas. During the fall rutting season the deer group together and are more easily hunted than at other times of the year, and hunting was probably most important at that time. Several bannerstones (throwing-stick weights) have been recovered at Deptford village sites; thus the throwing stick might have been employed along with the bow and arrow and snares to hunt deer. Knowledge of the throwing stick was passed on to the Deptford peoples by their Archaic predecessors. Some of the large, stemmed, Christmas-tree-shaped points found at Gulf sites were probably used to tip the throwing-stick darts.

Fishing was carried out by using nets and, perhaps, basketry weirs. Impressions of netting and basketry have been found on Deptford pottery vessels. Thus far, archaeologists have not found any Deptford fishhooks. If hooks were made out of wood rather than bone, however, they would not be preserved.

The manner in which the large sea mammals—seals, porpoises, and whales—were caught is not known. Nets or weirs would have been incapable of containing these agile and strong swimmers. They may have been hunted with leisters, and a few bone points have been found at coastal sites.

As among the Archaic peoples, canoes, baskets, and some sort of rakes must have been employed to gather shellfish in large enough quantities to make eating them worthwhile. So that they would open, oysters and clams were heated or steamed over fires. Because of the nature of their remains—a modern oyster roast leaves quite a pile of shell midden— shellfish are often thought to have been a more important part of the Deptford diet than they actually were. Deer, fish, and plant foods were probably more important.

Wooden knives, scrapers, and other tools were probably used in preparing foods for eating. A few such stone tools have been found at Gulf sites. No stone grinding tools have been found and, most likely, wooden pestles and mortars were used to grind seeds and acorn and other nut meats. Stone celts, hammerstones, and hones or whetstones, all present in very small quantities within the Deptford region, were employed to shape the large and small wooden implements.

Other than wood, the raw material most available on the coast was shell, which was also shaped into various tools. It is often difficult, however, to separate shell tools from midden shell during the course of an archaeological field excavation, and many shell tools probably go unnoticed. Oyster and clam shells could be used as ladles or spoonlike instruments. Dippers or cups were manufactured from the various conch shell species *(Busycon)* which are found on the Atlantic and Gulf coasts. Shell picks or hammers were made by simply punching one or two holes in the crown of the conch shell and hafting the shell on a stick. Awls or gouges were made from the conch columella.

Bone tools other than occasional points are extremely rare at Deptford sites, and the only specimens known were used as awls or as basket fids. Compared to the tool industries of later coastal Indians, as well as to contemporary, noncoastal Indians, the Deptford stone, bone, and shell complexes were poorly developed. Even if such specimens had been reshaped and reused many times over, the final expended tool fragments would be found in the middens associated with the villages. This is not the case, however, and the contention that wooden tools were very important seems correct.

A comparison of the quantity of stone tools within the two Deptford subregions shows that stone was utilized more frequently in the Gulf villages than in the Atlantic Coast villages. This is due to the fact that flint, or chert from which the vast majority of stone tools was manufactured, can be quarried in the Northwest and North-Central Florida highlands which are only 65 or so kilometers inland from the coastal sites. On the Atlantic Coast, such lithic outcroppings are much farther inland, almost to the fall line.

The Florida stone most prevalent at Deptford sites is a low grade, whitish chert which usually turns a light pink to red when thermally treated. Sandstone, limestone, and agatized coral were also used as a raw material for tools.

Items of personal adornment were made and used by the Deptford peoples, but these are also found only rarely. Several limestone or siltstone plummets and several shell beads made from *Oliva* shells or *Busycon* columella comprise the total known inventory of such everyday artifacts.

By far the best known Deptford artifact complex is the fired-clay pottery. Potsherds last almost indefinitely, and constitute the artifact found in the largest quantities at Deptford sites. The Deptford type of paddle-malleated ceramics is not unique to the Deptford culture and their presence or absence cannot be used as the sole determinant of whether or not a Deptford component is present at a specific site. On the Atlantic Coast especially, such ceramics types continued to be made until almost the historic period.

The Deptford ceramic complex represents the diffusion to the Southeast coasts, or more likely, the local invention of wooden paddles to compact coiled pots. The coiling technique, itself, may have diffused from the piedmont cultures. While the earlier Archaic period pottery was tempered with vegetable fibers and (at times) sand, Deptford pottery was mainly tempered with sand and grit, much of which probably occurred naturally in the clays of the coastal regions. Also, the Deptford vessels were built up by stacking coils of clay, whereas the Archaic pots were formed by hand-molding large lumps of clay, much as modern pie crusts are shaped.

The replacement of fiber-tempering by sand, clay, and other modes of tempering was not sudden. Information from the Georgia Coast indicates that fiber-tempering was still used sparingly as late as about A.D. 1. On both the Atlantic and Gulf coasts, fibers are present in potsherds which were malleated with Deptford carved wooden paddles. Likewise, some sand- and grit-tempered sherds display Archaic styles of decoration such as punctations or stick impressions. This gradual replacement of Archaic styles of pottery by the Deptford ceramic series clearly demonstrates the cultural continuum between Late Archaic and Deptford peoples.

Reasons for the invention or adoption of Deptford ceramic-making techniques are not certain. The best explanation seems to be that the coiling—paddle-malleating method of manufacturing is superior to the old method of hand-molding. With the new method there was a change to the deep, cylindrical-shaped vessels so common throughout the woodland areas of the eastern United States. Such pots may have served more useful functions than the flatter, broader bowl-shaped vessels of the Late Archaic period.

As noted before, the most common vessel shape is a deep, cylindrical pot with a rounded or conoidal bottom. Some pots also may be short and somewhat stubby, though still having the general cylindrical shape. Bowls occur rarely. In a few instances the rim of the vessel is slightly flared; in most others the rim is straight. The lips are generally simple rounded or flattened, and all appear to have been scraped with a stick or other similar tool to remove excess clay. Some specimens have this excess clay pushed down over the outside of the lip, forming a folded lip. A few vessels from the Gulf Coast have notched or scalloped lips.

Paste mixtures vary almost by site. The Gulf subregion Deptford sherds, however, tend not to have the large quartz inclusions found in the Atlantic subregion specimens, but are tempered instead with smaller quartz particles. Size of the particles in Atlantic subregion sherds ranges from sand grains to larger pieces of quartz up to 15 mm in diameter. Also, the sherds from the Atlantic Coast and Northwest Florida Coast tend to have some mica in the paste, while those of the peninsula Gulf Coast do not. Mica is brought down from the piedmont in river-deposited sediments and is found in panhandle clays and soils.

Color of the fired Deptford pots ranges from an orange-buff to dirty brown. Usually the core is uniform in color and dark, though occasionally light-surfaced sherds have a dark central core—probably the result of low-temperature firing. Smoke clouds are frequent. Together, these characteristics indicate that the pots were fired in open fires with oxidation of the pot surfaces occurring.

Another characteristic of Deptford pottery is the presence of tetrapods. Such tetrapods are also found in contemporary Woodland cultures in the piedmont as well as in the Tchefuncte and Bayou La Batre coastal plain cultures to the west. Their origin is, therefore, uncertain. Pot bottoms on which tetrapods are found are squared and flat or slightly curved, rather than rounded or conoidal. Tetrapodal pots, which are able to stand up, may have served a function different from other non-free-standing vessels.

Surface treatment on Deptford vessels was either plain, cord-wrapped- or carved-paddle-malleated, brushed, or punctated. The latter two types are localized on the Atlantic Coast in the Savannah area and probably represent late Deptford minority types. Some plain vessels appear to have been malleated and then smoothed over.

The majority of Deptford vessels are stamped with the well-known cord-wrapped or carved paddles. Cord-marking is present on both coasts throughout the temporal range of Deptford culture, increasing in popularity late in the Deptford period on the Atlantic Coast. At no time, however, does it ever reach the popularity of carved-paddle ceramics. The cords are generally 25–30 mm in diameter and are either closely spaced or spread about, with inconsistency being their most notable characteristic. Although clay-tempered, cord-marked pottery is one characteristic artifact of the succeeding Wilmington culture on the Atlantic Coast, it should be stressed that these ceramic surface treatment and paste types were present on the Atlantic Coast for as much as 2000 years and, alone, they are very poor temporal indicators.

Deptford check-stamped sherds (Figure 15a–f) can be divided into two types on the basis of size—Deptford Bold Check Stamped (larger) and Deptford Check Stamped (smaller). These types have never been quan-

FIGURE 15. *Deptford pottery; a–f, Deptford Check Stamped; g, Deptford Simple Stamped.*

tified by measurements, however, and the range in check size seems to be a continuum from large to small. Attempts to find temporal differences related to check size have proved fruitless, although such measurements show that in extremely large samples, Gulf checks are smaller than Atlantic checks. Check size, however, is not a useful analytical tool for establishing either geographical or temporal origins.

The manner in which the carved check-stamped design is applied to the pot varies from extremely carefully, which produces a continuous check-stamped design over the entire surface, to hitting the surface randomly, producing a sloppy, overlapping pattern. The large checks often appear to have been carved with much less care than the smaller checks, reflecting (perhaps) the skill of the wood carver. Some of the large checks appear to have been carved separately, one land at a time. Lands of the small checks are carved in long rows, a technique that produces neat and uniform check size and rows.

A variant of check-stamping is the type Deptford Linear Check Stamped (Figure 16d – h). As with check-stamping, both crude and well-carved examples of linear check-stamping are known. Plasticene impressions of crude check-stamped sherds show them to be attempts at mass producing a check-stamped design rather than attempts to imitate a stab-and-drag motif. Vertical lands are carved deeply into the wood. Then the horizontal lands are added. These are not always carved to the same exact depth as the others, producing a surface with lands in one direction being more prominent than those in the other. Such inconsistencies in the paddle carving result in some sherds with sections that appear to be linear in one direction in one place and in another direction in another place. Crude linear stamping is not roulette stamping as suggested by some prehistorians.

Although much linear check-stamping is crudely carved, other examples are extremely well done and appear to be intentional. At times, both degrees of skill are present on the same vessel. Generally, linear check-stamping as a decorative motif decreases in popularity through time.

The second major form of carved-paddle-malleated ware is the type Deptford Simple Stamped which occurs less frequently than linear check-stamping during the early portion of the Deptford period, but which is found throughout the temporal range of the culture. A variation of this motif is stick-impressing which is restricted to the Gulf Coast and is a type obviously descended from the similar Archaic Norwood stick-impressed pottery.

The Deptford Simple Stamped paddle has the same long vertical grooves as the linear stamped paddle, but without the cross grooves. At times, the paddle lands and grooves are very uniform in width and are

FIGURE 16. *Deptford pottery;* **a–c,** *Deptford Simple Stamped;* **d–h,** *Deptford Linear Check Stamped.*

carefully applied, producing an impression on the pot which is almost continuous. As with the other types of carved-paddle stamping, there is also a carelessly carved and applied form of simple stamping with grooves of different thicknesses and overlapping stamp impressions. The latter variant is more common than the more "skillfully" carved and applied variant. Again, these contrasting forms appear on the total range of Deptford pastes and temper, and may reflect work by potters with different levels of expertise.

Two other carved-paddle types occur in the Deptford series—Deptford Geometric Stamped and Deptford Complicated Stamped. The latter is probably a local attempt to copy the intricate carved-paddle stamps found elsewhere in the Southeast at the same time as the Deptford culture. The type occurs rarely at Deptford sites and seems to be most popular after A.D. 1. Deptford Geometric Stamped is also thinly distributed throughout the Deptford region, having been noted only near the mouth of the Savannah River and on Cumberland Island. Most frequently, this motif is a series of carved triangles rather than squares. In other cases, the stamp is made up of connected rows of diamonds with a dot in the center of each diamond. These motifs may have been reserved for special vessels, since there is evidence that complicated stamped vessels in the Southeast were valued as trade items by some cultures and often were assigned ceremonial usage by the cultures that received them through trade.

The Growth of Complex Ceremonialism in West Florida

The reconstruction from archaeological evidence of religious beliefs, rituals, and religious-related social stratification is always tenuous. Archaeologists can, however, derive some information from such things as earthworks, remains of ceremonial structures, burial forms, grave goods, and religious paraphernalia. Although these phenomena may reflect only a portion of a culture's total religious system, they seem to be good indicators of the level of socioreligious complexity in a culture. In the case of the Deptford culture, these criteria also point out the differences in the development of the two subregions. By A.D. 1 changes were occurring in the Gulf area that did not appear on the Atlantic Coast; two distinct groups were emerging. Either these two Deptford cultures had little contact with each other, or more likely, because of specific environmental, geographical, and cultural factors, the Atlantic Deptford peoples did not readily adopt the new traits that were being incorporated into

Gulf Deptford culture. The stimuli presented to the Gulf peoples were different from those in the Atlantic subregion. The separate development of the two subregions is apparent when the evolution of their respective cultures is viewed over the millennium following A.D. 1. In the Gulf area major changes occurred that led to the coastal Weeden Island culture, whereas in the Atlantic area there were few major changes until at least A.D. 1000.

One of the major stimuli for change in the Gulf region seems to have been the geographical location which allowed the Gulf Deptford peoples to act as "middle men" in the trade exchange that was occurring among the relatively more complex Gulf coastal plain cultures (e.g., Tchefuncte), the Woodland peoples to the north (e.g., Adena, Hopewell, Cartersville, Copena), and the South Florida peoples. This fortuitous position, which was not available to the more isolated Atlantic Deptford peoples, may have been a major causal factor in the evolution of the Gulf area cultures.

The exact processes involved in the Gulf Deptford culture's evolution have not been thoroughly investigated and cannot be described with certainty at this time. It seems likely, however, that originally there was an exchange of marine products—especially conch shells and perhaps cassina leaves and marine foods—for Woodland copper, stone, and ceramic exotic items. The desire for more trade goods and their associated status, coupled with a natural population increase, possibly led to more formalized or complex social organization. This was, in turn, reinforced by more complex and binding religious beliefs and activities. In short, the stimulus for cultural evolution occurred as a result of concrete factors of the same sort that were leading to changes in the Southern Appalachian Piedmont cultures and in the Ohio River Valley and Illinois Hopewell cultures.

Perhaps later research will allow these cultural processes to be delineated in more detail. Some evidence, however, is available on the types of goods traded and the changes in Deptford ceremonial and social life—the latter reflected in the specialized religious objects buried with certain individuals, suggesting status differences. These changes indicate that previous to about A.D. 1, growth of ceremonial life took place apart from major changes in village life (i.e., only minor changes in the basic economic pattern are associated with more intense changes in ceremonial life). Between 100 B.C. and A.D. 100−200, there appear to have been changes in village life, most notably the movement of peoples away from the coast to inland areas more suitable for horticulture. Ceremonial centers and villages were established in North-Central Florida and in the inland tri-state area of Alabama—Florida—Georgia. These subsistence changes, along with the accompanying apparent development of even more complex ceremonialism, mark the end of the Deptford culture. The A.D. 100−200 time is a transitional period when new patterns of life were established. Although the coastal way of life was continued by post-Deptford Swift Creek and Weeden Island peoples on the West Coast lagoons, new cultural patterns evolved within the inland cultures which affected the coastal peoples. The story of these post-Deptford cultures is reserved for the next chapter.

Sears (1962) has described some aspects of the ceremonial life associated with the post-100 B.C. Deptford culture on the Gulf Coast. He groups certain of these traits into an archaeologically recognizable complex called Yent. Just as Deptford village life evolved into the post-Deptford cultures, so did Yent ceremonialism gradually develop into other types of ceremonialism after the end of the Deptford period. The two main archaeologically recognizable post-Yent "religions" are the Green Point complex, also defined by Sears, and the Weeden Island ceremonial complex. According to Sears, Green Point seems to be a regional complex which in Northwest Florida bridged the gap between the Yent complex and the Weeden Island ceremonial complex. The Green Point and Weeden Island ceremonial complexes are discussed in the following chapter.

Nothing is known about the forms of pre-Yent, early Deptford ceremonialism. Certainly, some developmental sequence exists. Knowledge of the Yent "religion" among Deptford peoples may have been partially due to the diffusion of ideas and beliefs to the Gulf area from the cultures with whom the Deptford peoples were involved in trade.

The Yent complex was defined on the basis of information from three Florida mounds—Crystal River, Yent, and Pierce. Much of the information from the mounds was gathered by C. B. Moore more than 50 years ago and was not collected by the more rigorous field methodologies employed today. Consequently, later research may show the need for redefining the Yent complex, especially regarding whether specific artifact types are Yent or post-Yent in origin.

At the present time, Northwest Florida seems to have been the locality where the Yent complex developed. The center of the later Green Point complex also seems to be in Northwest Florida. This can tentatively be explained by noting that Northwest Florida is geographically much closer to other complex Southeast aboriginal cultures than was the peninsular Gulf Coast.

Trade items found in Yent mounds which are exotic to the Gulf Coast region include stone, metal, ceramic, and (perhaps) some bone artifacts. Many of these artifacts resemble items found elsewhere in the Southeast during the Hopewell period. Some of the Yent nonceramic artifacts appear to be ornamental in use or elaborated forms of utilitarian artifacts (such as gorgets) and were perhaps worn or used by political or religious specialists. These artifacts include copper panpipes, rectangular copper plates, and copper ear spools, both single and double-sided. Silver-plated copper ear spools, one inset with a pearl on each side, were excavated from the Crystal River mound.

Elongate plummets and double-ended plummets, both made from either copper, stone, or shell, are also represented in the Yent complex artifact inventory, as are two-hole bar gorgets of stone. Shell ornaments of various shapes and sizes, including gorgets, are common. These include many circular ornaments, some perforated, and one unique flower-shaped ornament. More research is needed to determine if such items had symbolic significance or were simply valued objects buried with important individuals.

In the Yent complex, cut carnivore teeth, including puma, bear, and wolf are found in mounds, as are shell and bone imitations of canine teeth. Several porpoise teeth have also been recovered. One cut puma jaw came from the Crystal River Mound.

Most of the ceramic vessels found in Yent mounds and associated with Yent religious paraphernalia seem to be vessels especially constructed or acquired through trade for ceremonial usage. Many seem to have symbolic significance. Ceremonial pottery comes in many unique shapes and sizes, including spherical pots—one pot in the shape of a ram's horn—a vessel with three pouring spouts, two four-lobed pots with tetrapodal feet, and one compound jar-shaped vessel (see Sears 1962). Other vessels are of more conventional shapes—cylindrical jars, globular bowls, and deep conical vessels with flaring rims whose shape is common among southeastern Woodland peoples. Many of the vessels have large amounts of mica in the paste, indicating that they were made in northern Florida or farther north, and traded southward to the Deptford peoples. Designs on Yent vessels include cord-marking, check-stamping, zoned punctations, and zoned painting. Miniature vessels, usually tetrapodal cylindrical pots or bowls, occur in relatively large numbers in the mounds. Many are small replicas of Deptford vessels.

The Yent vessels are not found in the village middens of the late Deptford peoples, confirming that the vessels had special significance. Their use or deposition was evidently restricted to sacred areas such as the ceremonial mounds.

Yent complex mounds are of the type described by Sears as continual use (i.e., the mounds were continually added to, new burials and other items were placed in the mound through time). Burials, probably initiating the construction of the original portion of the mound, are often found near the mound base. Types of burials from the mounds include flexed, bundled, extended, and single skull interments. Burial form may be indicative of status differences, or it may reflect the manner in which bodies of the dead were cleaned and stored.

The purpose of the ceremonial pottery associated with late Deptford culture is not certain. One explanation is that the vessels were used to serve special sacred teas or medicines. Often the vessels are found in association with conch-shell drinking dippers of the type known to have been used during the Mississippian period for black drink, suggesting that the ceremonial pots were used for the other sacred teas. The Creek tribes are known to have had four separate teas, and the use of sacred medicines was widespread in the Southeast at the time of contact. It is quite possible that the origins of this trait lie on a time level comparable to the Yent complex, and that the sacred Yent vessels and shell dippers were used during ceremonies which continued in various forms until the historic period in the Southeast. Shell cups have been found at all three of the Yent complex mounds. Fifty-three were taken from Crystal River; one clay effigy of a *Busycon* shell was recovered from the Yent Mound.

This, however, does not explain the presence of the pots in burial mounds where they occur with burials as grave goods and in separate deposits. Nor does it explain why some of the ceremonial vessels from the mounds appear to have been "killed" by having their bottoms knocked out. It is generally thought by archaeologists that this was done in an effort to "free the spirit" of the pot to allow it to accompany the spirit of the individual buried in the mound. An alternative explanation is that the vessels were intentionally broken and placed in the mound to prevent their reuse by persons who were not qualified religious practitioners. If the vessels had been used in sacred tea ceremonies, both those involving black drink and other medicines, they may have been ritually placed in the mounds after their function was fulfilled. This might have been at the same time as when the bodies, previously prepared for burial and stored in a charnel house, were interred in the mound. Sacred vessels, then, may have been used and stored elsewhere. Periodically the sacred structures were cleaned out and the religious items in them were placed in consecrated special areas, such as mounds, which were intended to receive such items. This periodic purging of religious paraphernalia might have been related to one or more calendrically determined ceremonies.

There is also some evidence that a black drink ceremony was involved with the construction or consecration of Yent mounds. At the Pierce Mound A in Franklin County, shell cups and minature sacred vessels were found on the ground surface on which the mound was built. These objects were placed around a fire hearth, and food bones, one wolf and one puma tooth were scattered around the fire. Perhaps black drink was brewed on the spot and drunk before the mound was built.

From this information on the Yent complex, we can suppose that the late Deptford peoples had special religious practitioners who oversaw the preparation and carrying out of ceremonies associated with mound-building, the deposition of sacred objects in mounds, and the cleaning and interment of burials. Charnel houses for the cleaning and storage of burials were probably also present. Various ceremonies in which sacred medicines were taken might also have been a part of late Deptford religious life. Together, these traits suggest that many aspects of Southeast Indian religions recorded during the early historic period by Europeans, had their beginnings during the period of general growth of Southeast ceremonial life after 100 B.C.

It should be noted that not all individuals were interred in burial mounds. A very few burials have been found in Deptford village sites on the Gulf Coast. At the Carrabelle site in Franklin County, two cremation burials were found in the village midden. A cache of purposefully de-stroyed pottery was found nearby. Perhaps this was a sacred area used before the knowledge of burial mounds was incorporated in Deptford religious beliefs. Flexed primary burials have also been found in at least one Deptford village.

On the Atlantic Coast, burial mounds seem to have become a part of Deptford life early on, shortly after 400 B.C. But the complex social and ceremonial life begun during the Deptford period on the Gulf Coast and elaborated during the later Weeden Island period did not occur in the Atlantic subregion until after A.D. 1000 and, perhaps, even later. The isola-tion of the Atlantic Coast and the lack of significant changes in economic production left the area relatively unchanged for nearly 1500 years follow-ing the beginning of the Deptford period. Comparisons of the two Deptford subregions are helpful in pointing out the types of cultural pro-cesses responsible for the cultural evolution of the Florida Indians.

5

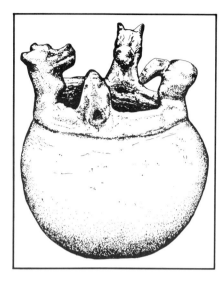

Weeden Island Period Cultures and Their Predecessors

In 1949 Gordon R. Willey published his monumental *Archeology of the Florida Gulf Coast* which contained a description of Weeden Island culture as reconstructed from information gathered by a number of researchers over the previous half-century. The Weeden Island culture derives its name from Weeden Island located at the mouth of Old Tampa Bay where Jesse W. Fewkes carried out research in the early 1920s. Since the date of the publication of the Gulf Coast volume, there has been, until recently, a relatively small amount of new data made available concerning the post-Deptford, Weeden Island culture. There have been, however, new interpretations of the data presented by Willey, and new information from noncoastal areas. This change in perspective is due largely to new theoretical emphases in the field of archaeology. In the 1940s Florida archaeologists were concerned with establishing the sequences of cultures for the various culture areas such as the Gulf Coast. Today, using these culture histories as a basis, researchers are beginning to fill out the framework and reconstruct the general cultural processes which were involved in the development of the Florida cultures. Research projects underway in North and Northwest Florida are now beginning to yield new data which enable archaeologists to test ideas derived from previous work.

Formerly the pre-Mississippian sequence of West Florida was defined as Deptford, Santa Rosa-Swift Creek, and Weeden Island. Deptford culture, described in Chapter 4, is recognizable primarily by the presence of check-stamped and simple-stamped pottery in the village middens. The

Santa Rosa-Swift Creek culture, as defined by Willey (1949a:366–368), is represented on the coast by only a relatively few village sites which are largely confined to the area from northern Taylor County westward. It is recognizable by the presence of complicated-stamped pottery and other minority decorative techniques. Complicated stamping is a pottery decorative technique similar to Deptford carved, wooden paddle-malleating. With complicated stamping, the design carved on the paddle is an intricate curvilinear or rectilinear motif. Today we know that the majority of Swift Creek village sites are found in the panhandle highland forests and seem to be restricted to the area east of a line drawn northward from Pensacola. The little known Santa Rosa culture, which has been separated from Swift Creek, lies west of this line and appears to be related to other non-Florida developments (Phelps 1969:17–18).

Willey divided the period of the succeeding Weeden Island culture into two divisions. The earlier Weeden Island I period was characterized by the presence of complicated-stamped pottery along with plain pottery, and pottery with punctated and incised decorations. These latter plain and decorated vessels, when used for ceremonial purposes, often displayed ornate designs, were shaped into animal effigy forms, or had effigy adornos. Such decorative motifs were applied to a wide range of vessel shapes. Weeden Island pottery is still recognized today as the best-made, most ornate aboriginal pottery in Florida.

The Weeden Island II period, according to Willey, was characterized by a decrease in popularity of complicated-stamped pottery and the presence of a new type, Wakulla Check Stamped. During this period the Weeden Island plain and effigy types continued to be manufactured.

The culture sequence of Deptford, Santa Rosa-Swift Creek, Weeden Island I, and Weeden Island II remained relatively unquestioned for 2 decades following the publication of *Archeology of the Florida Gulf Coast*, and it served as a basis to which other culture sequences in the Southeast, especially areas adjacent to the Gulf Coast in Florida, Georgia, and Alabama, were correlated. The Gulf tradition, defined by Goggin (1949:34–39) to encompass the Santa Rosa-Swift Creek and Weeden Island cultures, was seen as a major culture center from which influences were felt throughout the Southeast. Contact with the Troyville and Coles Creek cultures of the Gulf Coast west of Northwest Florida, and contact with the Hopewell culture of the Ohio River valley and adjacent areas, were suggested. The concept of a Gulf tradition, and the culture sequence represented by that tradition, became firmly ingrained in published literature on Florida and the Southeast.

Today, application of different archaeological concepts to the Gulf Coast data, and the presence of new archaeological information from sites in North-Central, Northwest and North Florida, and the coastal plain of Georgia and Alabama, have led to a refining of the previously accepted Gulf coastal sequence. The taxonomic term, "Weeden Island," has taken on new meanings and now refers to several distinct, regional cultures that shared the same basic ceremonial complex (Figure 17). This complex may have been associated with specific patterns of sociopolitical behavior. However, some of the basic Weeden Island traits are not found on the peninsula Gulf Coast nor in North-Central Florida, and the

FIGURE 17. *Weeden Island and Weeden Island-related regions with sites discussed in text.*

Weeden Island cultures of these regions are now referred to as Weeden Island-related or Weeden Island period cultures.

Not all of these Weeden Island cultures inhabited the coastal strand. In fact, the major Weeden Island developments probably were centered at inland sites in southwestern Georgia, northern Florida, and southeastern Alabama. Likewise, Swift Creek seems to be primarily an inland, woodland culture. Although some coastal villages exist, these were probably occupied seasonally for the purpose of fishing and oystering. Swift Creek village sites also are not present in large numbers on the Gulf Coast of peninsular Florida or in extreme western Florida—the location of the Mississippi Valley-related Santa Rosa culture. The major distribution of Swift Creek seems to be within Georgia, extending down into inland Northwest Florida. Complicated-stamped pottery, however, has a much wider distribution, extending up into the Georgia piedmont and over to the Georgia Atlantic Coast.

Because these various cultures, formerly grouped together as the Gulf tradition, did not share a basic pattern of subsistence or "life-style"—a pattern described as a coastal adaptation very similar to that of the Deptford peoples, but with more emphasis on horticulture—there can be no Gulf cultural tradition, and that concept should be discarded. On the other hand there is, as described later in this chapter, a Weeden Island ceremonial complex which developed out of Yent and Green Point and, perhaps, other localized ceremonial complexes, and which climaxed in the ceremonialism associated with the various late Weeden Island cultures. It is this continuum that should be referred to by the taxonomic term, "Gulf tradition." The Weeden Island I and II periods have also recently been revised as they apply to a portion of Northwest Florida. The peninsular cultures, discussed later in this chapter, differ in several ways from North and Northwest Florida, thus it appears best to apply a separate chronology to that geographical region. Eventually, it may be recognized that other taxonomic terms are needed to refer to the Weeden Island period cultures of the peninsula.

Although the Weeden Island period cultures, both in northern Florida and those in the peninsula, practiced different types of subsistence patterns within their respective environmental zones, they did share some similar ceremonial activities, as reconstructed from mounds and suggested by the presence of similar religious objects, including pottery. Trade or other contact between the cultures must have been extensive. This separate development of secular and sacred traits, recognized and delineated by Sears (1971b:60, 1973:31–42), was not restricted to Florida or the Weeden Island cultures. Rather, such a trend was common throughout the eastern United States; many different groups shared similar religious–sociopolitical systems while maintaining different basic subsistence adaptations. By the second millennium A.D. a distinctive Southeast religious–sociopolitical complex evolved, culminating in the well-known southeastern pattern present in the historic period. This Southeast pattern cross-cut many different cultures. For example, at the time of historic contact in the sixteenth century, the Saturiwa, a Timucuan-speaking group inhabiting the lower St. Johns River Valley and adjacent coastal lagoon, shared similar social and political systems, as well as many religious beliefs, with the various Creek tribes living on the fall line.

One unfortunate result (for the archaeologist) of the separation of sacred and secular activities and paraphernalia by the various Weeden Island period peoples is that, for most of the cultures, village utilitarian pottery was quite different from the sacred ceremonial pottery. In some cultures, such as the peninsular Gulf Coast Weeden Island period cultures, the village pottery was undecorated. The same plain pottery, with minor variations in temper, continued to be manufactured from the end of the Deptford period until the proto-historic period, from A.D. 100–200 to about 1500. As a consequence, changes in utilitarian pottery decoration are not always available for use as indicators of temporal change, leaving the archaeologist with the ornate ceremonial pottery types and vessel shapes as a means to construct temporal seriations. However, there is a further complication. Since some of the mounds were used over long periods of time, and since ceremonial vessels were apparently kept for many generations, it is often difficult to tell which vessel types and decorative motifs were in vogue at which times.

Weeden Island Chronologies

Percy and Brose (1974) have offered a revised relative chronology, based on secular ceramic changes, for the upper Apalachicola River region Swift Creek and Weeden Island cultures. Percy and Brose's period designations for the time span from approximately A.D. 200 to A.D. 1000 or 1200 are as follows: Swift Creek period; Weeden Island 1 period, characterized by the presence of Weeden Island series pottery in small amounts (the types Carrabelle Incised, Carrabelle Punctated, Keith Incised, and Weeden Island Incised and Punctated); Weeden Island 2 period, characterized by an increase in the just-mentioned Weeden Island ceramics, a decrease in complicated-stamped ceramics, and the appearance of other Weeden Island types; Weeden Island 3 period, characterized by the appearance of Wakulla Check Stamped pottery and a slight decline in complicated stamping; Weeden Island 4 period, characterized by a decline in the previous Weeden Island types, an increase in Wakulla Check Stamped pottery, and the disappearance of complicated-stamped ceramics; Weeden Island 5, characterized by Wakulla Check Stamped as the dominant secular ware (about 55% of all pottery, with 40% of that number usually plain undecorated), the appearance of corncob-marked pottery as a minority ware, and the very limited occurrence of Weeden Island incised and punctated types. Weeden Island 5 develops into the Fort Walton culture. This sequence may apply only to the upper Apalachicola River Valley where it was derived.

An alternative culture sequence for the post-Deptford period in a portion of Northwest Florida has been offered by Sears based on his excavations at the Tucker site in Franklin County, a coastal site occupied from the Norwood period through late Weeden Island times. In *The Tucker Site on Alligator Harbor, Franklin County, Florida* (1963), Sears offers convincing evidence for the existence of a post-Deptford, pre-Weeden Island occupation in Northwest Florida which is contemporary with, but separate from, the Swift Creek culture. This period of occupation, referred to by Sears as the "Middle Period" at Tucker, is approximately contemporary with the late Deptford and early Weeden Island periods (described later in this chapter) for peninsular Florida, where a Swift Creek occupation is also absent.

The "Middle Period," which is well represented archaeologically at Tucker, is characterized ceramically by a decrease (from Deptford) in check-stamped pottery (to about 10%) and a concomitant increase in plain ware (to more than 50%) and complicated-stamped motifs (less than 19%). The Weeden Island series secular ceramics (about 15%) are also present. This ceramic inventory differs greatly from contemporary inventories excavated at Swift Creek culture sites such as Bird Hammock (described later in this chapter), or at Georgia Swift Creek sites. After A.D. 800 at Tucker, as at other Weeden Island sites, check-stamping again rises in popularity, becoming the primary form of surface decoration for secular pottery.

It is strongly suspected that other areal chronologies exist for portions of northern Florida during the post-Deptford period. It also appears that the chronology for the Weeden Island– Fort Walton continuum may also differ across Northwest Florida, with the dates for the end of Weeden Island (and the beginning of Fort Walton) earlier in the Apalachicola River Valley than farther east.

As noted before, the chronology for the peninsular Weeden Island period cultures is different from both of those just described for Northwest Florida. Because there have been few attempts to work out a temporal seriation for the sand- and limestone-tempered, undecorated secular pottery manufactured at the peninsular villages, the chronology for those cultures must be based almost enitrely on changes in ceremonial traits. The results of this exercise suggest three main periods. The first period is late Deptford (or proto-Weeden Island) dating from A.D. 100–300. During this period, Deptford paddle-stamped ceramics decline in popularity and plain undecorated pottery is manufactured in increased amounts for utilitarian use. It is also late in this period that some inland highland areas are first occupied on a sedentary basis rather than on a sporadic—perhaps seasonal—basis as was true during the Deptford period. Populations continue to occupy the old coastal areas, although there seems to be a slight shift in the location of some sites to areas where shellfish, especially oysters, are not found in as large quantities as in other areas. Trade between these coastal and inland villages was continuous throughout the late Deptford period.

In peninsular Florida during this time, vessels in mounds tend to be of three main types: St. Johns Plain, Dunns Creek Red (actually St. Johns Plain with a red slip on the vessel exterior), and plain, undecorated, sand-tempered vessels. Some complicated-stamped vessels are also present but, generally, their frequency is very low, relative to these other types. Pottery caches are never found in these mounds. The ceremonial vessels appear to have been broken and the large sherds scattered randomly throughout the mound fill. In peninsular Florida, burials are usually secondary bundled burials, suggesting use of charnel houses. Some primary burials which presumably initiated the building of the mound may be present toward the mound's center.

Early Weeden Island period burial mounds in peninsula Florida dating A.D. 300/400–800 contain examples of the ornate Weeden Island effigy vessels. In these mounds secondary burials are most common. Other mounds, with no burials but rather serving as perhaps platforms for structures, are also present. During the late Weeden Island period, A.D. 800–1200, check-stamped vessels appear in the mounds, along with examples of the earlier ornate forms. This may indicate that mounds were reused. The quantity of ornate wares in both early and late mounds never approaches that of Northwest or North Florida, nor are caches of vessels found on the east sides of mounds.

Additional research is certainly needed to refine and give additional meaning to these three periods. The present nomenclature of early Weeden Island and late Weeden Island is not completely satisfactory and also needs to be revised as more information is made available.

Weeden Island Cultures

Regional Weeden Island or Weeden Island-related cultures which can presently be defined are: (1) the Cades Pond culture in North-Central Florida; (2) the Central Peninsular Gulf Coast culture now encompassed within the Manasota culture; (3) the Northern Peninsular Gulf Coast culture; (4) the panhandle coastal Weeden Island culture; (5) the Apalachicola–Flint–Chattahoochee rivers tri-state area Weeden Island culture, also referred to as Wakulla Weeden Island; (6) the North Florida McKeithen Weeden Island culture; and (7) the coastal plain, inland culture(s) of North Florida, Georgia, and Alabama. This latter culture, which excludes the tri-state area delineated in the fifth culture listed, has been little-studied in Florida. The latter four are recognized as being "heartland" Weeden Island cultures. The first three bear many or few Weeden Island traits and are designated Weeden Island-related or Weeden Island period cultures. Future research will no doubt demonstrate several different coastal plain Weeden Island period cultures, as well as provide the needed information for defining phases within each of these cultures.

The remainder of this chapter will examine the peninsular Weeden Island period cultures as well as the Swift Creek and "classic" Weeden Island cultures of North and Northwest Florida, and, where possible, will focus on their respective or collective forms of village life. The inland, Southeast coastal plain Weeden Island cultures will be largely ignored in this discussion since they are outside of Florida and, more importantly, since very little is known about them other than ceramic typologies and the location of some sites. Also, the Alabama Gulf Coast Weeden Island culture variant—located east of Mobile Bay—is not dealt with for the same reasons. However, it is likely that much of the information concerning the coastal cultures is applicable to the latter area. Weeden Island ceremonialism and its relationships to the forms of Weeden Island village life and the sociopolitical system are summarized at the end of the chapter.

Cades Pond: A Late Deptford and Early Weeden Island Period Culture

The Cades Pond culture, named for a burial mound near Lake Santa Fe excavated in the 1870s, was originally defined by Goggin (1949:25). Goggin recognized the presence of burial and ceremonial mounds in North-Central Florida that contained ceramics bearing resemblances to both the St. Johns culture in East Florida and the Weeden Island period cultures in West Florida. At these inland sites Goggin noted that, through time, the St. Johns ceramics seemed to become more plentiful—indicating, perhaps, increased contact with East Florida.

Goggin's original research dealt almost solely with the Cades Pond mounds; no recognized Cades Pond village sites were excavated. Since "classic" Weeden Island ceramic types (i.e., ceremonial vessels) were not present in the mounds, Cades Pond was correctly interpreted as dating from the late St. Johns I or post-Deptford period. According to the chronology presented here, this would be late Deptford and early Weeden Island, from as early as A.D. 200 to A.D. 800.

In 1951 Goggin excavated an important Cades Pond village in Alachua County, the Melton site. Because the dominant ceramic type (more than 90% of the 12,000 total sherds) was a dark brown or grey, undecorated, sand-tempered type, and not St. Johns ware, Goggin felt that the site did not correlate temporally with nearby Cades Pond mounds. The concept of secular and sacred ceramic series had not yet been introduced, and Goggin did not realize that a culture's village ceramics could be widely divergent from their mound ceramics. Thus, he assigned the site to a different time period than the mounds. Because Goggin felt that St. Johns pottery increased in frequency through time in North-Central Florida, and because there was so little St. Johns pottery at the site, he reasoned that the village pre-dated the mounds and called the new temporal period Pre-Cades Pond. The culture sequence for North-Central Florida was then given as Archaic, Pre-Cades Pond (affiliation with Gulf Coast), and Cades Pond (affiliation with East Florida). The Cades Pond occupation was terminated by the entrance of the Alachua tradition to the area.

Today we can revise the North-Central Florida culture sequence. The term "Pre-Cades Pond" is no longer useful or meaningful, since the Melton village is now recognized as being associated with the Cades Pond culture dating from the late Deptford and early Weeden Island periods. Like the contemporary cultures of the Florida Gulf Coast, the Cades Pond culture village pottery is largely plain while the early ceremonial vessels appear to be St. Johns Plain and Dunns Creek Red, either traded from East Florida or manufactured locally. The undecorated, sand-tempered pottery accounts for as much as 85–95% of the secular, village pottery found at late Deptford and early Weeden Island peninsula villages, both those inland and those on the Gulf Coast. Similarities between the Cades Pond ceremonial traits and those of contemporary cultures on the peninsular coast also demonstrate that the Cades Pond culture dates during those periods. When this is acknowledged, the culture sequence for North-Central Florida is: Paleo-Indian, Early, Middle, and Late Archaic, Deptford, Cades Pond (late Deptford and early Weeden Island periods), and the Alachua tradition.

The Archaic and Deptford peoples occupied the area only on a seasonal or occasional basis, as described in the preceding chapters. After approximately A.D. 200, late Deptford peoples began to move inland, perhaps to take advantage of the inland aquatic and hardwood hammocks which could provide a year-round source of food. The role of agriculture in influencing this change in subsistence emphasis from the coast to the interior was inconsequential, if, indeed, agriculture was present.

Most of our knowledge of Cades Pond village life comes from the 1971 reexcavation of the Melton village site by the University of Florida. While a graduate student in anthropology at the University of Florida, Stephen L. Cumbaa provided a detailed analysis of Cades Pond subsistence activities in his master's thesis entitled "An Intensive Harvest Economy in North-central Florida" (1972). In the summer of 1974, another Cades Pond village site, A-346, located just west of Newnan's Lake, was also excavated by the University of Florida, and a third was excavated in 1976 (Milanich 1978a). Cumbaa's research was preceded by the thesis of another University of Florida graduate student, Samuel D. Smith, who studied the ceremonial mounds associated with the Cades Pond culture. Smith's thesis, "A Reinterpretation of the Cades Pond Archeological Period" (1971a), draws on data from a mound excavated by Sears (1956b), as well as information gathered by University of Florida excavations carried out in 1957, 1964, and 1970 at the Cross Creek and Melton mound areas in North-Central Florida. The discussion of Cades Pond which follows is based almost entirely on the excellent and thorough research of Smith and Cumbaa and on papers by Hemmings (1978) and Milanich (1978a).

The Cades Pond culture, tentatively dated to ca. A.D. 200 to A.D. 800, occupied a very restricted geographical and physiographic region in North-Central Florida. All of the sites thus far located are in the region bounded on the north by the Santa Fe River, and the south by Orange Lake slightly south of the Alachua–Marion county line. None of the sites are found in western Alachua County and most are located in the wetter regions of eastern Alachua and western Clay and Putnam counties. Future surveys will probably extend the Cades Pond distribution even farther east. All known villages are adjacent to extensive swamp areas and/or to large lakes.

The largest number of Cades Pond village and mound complex sites located to date are located either between Newnan's Lake and Paynes Prairie, or adjacent to Orange and Lochloosa lakes. Analysis of floral and faunal remains from the Cades Pond village sites thus far excavated clearly demonstrates the importance to the village inhabitants of the natural resources available in the hardwood oak and hickory hammocks, and especially the lakes and adjacent marshes.

The hammock forests provided deer, nuts, and other lesser important floral and faunal species. Deer was the most important single meat source while hickory nuts were, perhaps, the most important plant resource in terms of economic value. Of the more than 1500 separate animal individuals represented in the analyzed faunal collections from the Melton village site, almost 90% were taken from either the lake or marsh habitats. Thus, although the hammocks were important for a few major resources (and perhaps the largest amount of meat protein), the aquatic habitats provided the larger number of animal species for food. The choice of locations for Cades Pond villages (i.e., in hammocks adjacent to extensive aquatic habitats) was no accident. This is why sites are clustered around Paynes Prairie, Levy Lake, Orange Lake, Lake Lochloosa, and Newnan's Lake. The presence of loamy soils, which are excellent for agriculture, may have been a factor in the selection of village site locations, although no evidence of agriculture has been found at this time.

Cumbaa has demonstrated that the Cades Pond people practiced an intensive harvest subsistence pattern. High yield resources were selectively utilized. Hunting and collecting technologies, both knowledge of food sources and of equipment and tools, must have been well adapted to the specialized exploitation of the hammock, and lake and marsh habitats. This knowledge must have begun to be accumulated by the Archaic and Deptford peoples, ancestors to the Cades Pond population, during their occasional hunting and foraging trips into North-Central Florida. Certainly, more knowledge developed during the period of year-round Cades Pond occupation, thus increasing the efficiency of the intensive harvest methods.

The tools and methods used by the Cades Pond people in acquiring the large range of animals and plants utilized for food resemble those of more northerly Southeast Woodland peoples. Hickory, pine, and oak nuts were gathered, stored, and eaten as needed. The most popular nut was the mockernut hickory (*Carya tomentosa*) which contains about twice as much meat as the next most frequently used nut, the pignut hickory. Acorns and pine nuts, the latter from both slash and long-leaf pines, were used to a lesser extent. Methods used to process the nuts for eating were probably much the same as those employed by the Southeast Indians of the historic period. Nut meats were crushed and mixed with water to form a white "milk" which was drunk, and crushed nuts were mixed in with broths made from various vegetables. Nuts were also boiled in water, and the nut oil or fat was scooped off and eaten. In any of their prepared forms, nuts provided a compact source of protein and calories.

Other wild plant-fruits collected for food were the Chickasaw plum, wild cherry, and persimmon. These could be collected, dried, and stored for future eating.

Other than the large animals such as deer, black bear, and panther, most of the mammals—muskrat, opossum, mole, rabbits (two species), squirrels (two species), skunk, rat (two species), grey fox, red wolf, pocket gopher—could have been taken with snares or traps. The large mammals could also have been trapped with various devices, although a variety of flint projectile points large enough to have tipped atlatl darts or spears for hunting were recovered at the Melton village (Figure 18a—g, j—m). These points, all of which are stemmed and relatively crudely made, can be classified as Columbia, Jackson, and Bradford types (Bullen 1975:19, 21, 14). Battering on the edges of some of the specimens indicates use of hafted knives. Small triangular points, probably used to tip arrows, appear at late Cades Pond sites (Milanich 1978a:165). If, indeed, these are arrow points, they will constitute the earliest evidence for bows and arrows in the eastern United States (Figure 18h,i). A number of double-pointed bone points showing marks and discoloration from hafting were also recovered and were available for hunting (Figure 19d,e). The discoloration is probably from pitch used to glue the points within a shaft.

The large amount of deer bone present at the Melton village allows some of the butchering techniques to be reconstructed. These can be summarized by saying that most of the butchering was done at the kill site. Many of the metacarpals and metatarsals showed evidence of cut marks made during the skinning process.

Various birds were also used for food. Cumbaa reports that large amounts of young bird bones were often found together, indicating that they were collected in large numbers from rookeries. Several of the birds—white ibis, sandhill crane, coot, egret, heron (two species)—normally establish nests next to lakes. Other birds were identified as bald eagle and turkey. These could have been utilized for feathers as well as meat, as could some of the water-dwelling species.

Several species of reptiles and amphibians, mostly snakes, frogs, and toads, could have been taken in the hammocks, although they are more plentiful and more easily collected near the lakes and marshes. A large variety of water reptiles—snakes and turtles of several species—were also used as food. The total list of amphibians and reptiles includes Southern toad, frog (*Rana* sp.), Southern leopard frog, amphiuma, greater siren, mud turtles (at least two species), musk turtles (several species), pond turtle, chicken turtle, box turtle, gopher tortoise (available in the hammocks and cleared fields), soft-shelled turtle, black snake, indigo snake, rat snake, mud snake, king snake, coach whip, water snake, brown water snake, cottonmouth moccasin, eastern diamond back rattlesnake, and

FIGURE 18. *Cades Pond lithic artifacts;* **a – e,** *stemmed points and/or knives;* **f – g,** *snapped tips of points and/or knives;* **h – i,** *triangular probable arrow points;* **j – m,** *snapped bases of points and/or knives.*

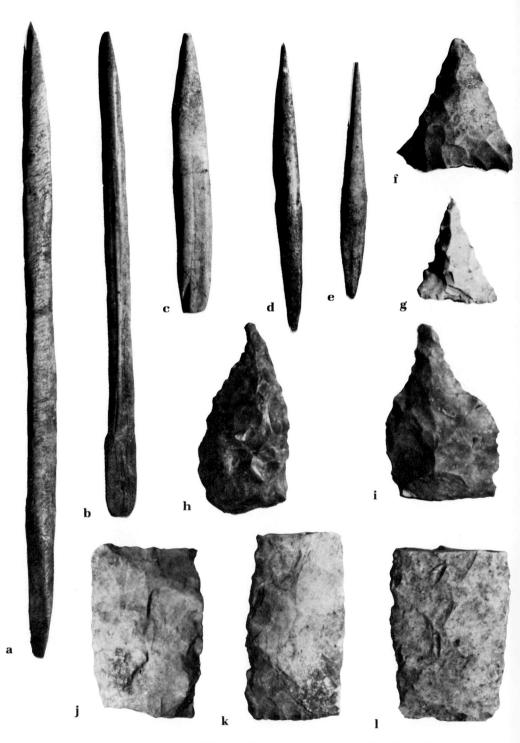

FIGURE 19. *Cades Pond bone and lithic artifacts;* **a**—**b**, *bone "points," perhaps leisters or tools;* **c**, *probable bone basketry awl;* **d**—**e**, *double-pointed bone "points," both show evidence of hafting on bases;* **f**—**g**, *Cross Creek perforators;* **h**—**i**, *perforators;* **j**—**l**, *snapped bases of lanceolate, bifacial knives.*

alligator. The water snake, cottonmouth, and mud snake were most frequently eaten.

Several intact turtle carapaces were found and appear to have been used as vessels. One box turtle plastron fragment was drilled, and originally the whole shell may have been used as a rattle, a common Southeast Indian trait.

Another food source provided by the lakes were freshwater pond snails (*Viviparus georgianus*) and clams. Snails were often found in huge quantities in the site, showing that they were mass-collected, processed (probably by boiling), and eaten, then the shells discarded.

The largest food source from the lake habitat was the fish. Altogether, 11 species of freshwater fish were identified from the midden remains: gar, mudfish, gizzard shad, chain pickerel, lake chubsucker, catfish, sunfish, warmouth, large-mouth bass, and speckled perch. All are common to the North-Central Florida lakes, and their frequency of occurrence at the Melton site approximates their natural population distribution in the lakes.

Size of the fish ranged from 10-cm long catfish to 3.5–4.5 kg large-mouth bass. The gar scales recovered indicate that some of these individuals were as much as 1 m in length. Although some of these fish, such as gar, were, no doubt, speared with bone leisters composed of three points hafted on the end of a shaft (Figure 19a,b), the most common technique was to use seining nets. The species and size of distribution of the fish demonstrates a total catch; that is, everything was collected in the same size and species distribution as occurred naturally in the lake. With hook-and-line fishing or with fish-spearing, such normal distributions are not obtained.

A variety of bone and stone tools other than those just mentioned were also in use (Figure 19): bone awls made from deer ulnae and from bone splinters, and a variety of bone tools including awls used for basket weaving, perforators, flakers, scrapers or fleshers, and punches. Fossil and nonfossil sharks' teeth were hafted by drilling, or by notching them on the upper edges, and used as cutting tools. Bone was also carved and decorated for use as gorgets and, possibly, other ornaments.

Lithic tools other than projectile points and nutting and seed-grinding equipment include medium-size triangular knives, stemmed and hafted drills, and triangular perforators. The triangular perforator, named the Cross Creek perforator by Smith, seems to be diagnostic of the Cades Pond culture.

Cumbaa's analysis of the floral and faunal remains from the Melton site leads him to conclude that the Cades Pond people maintained year-round villages in North-Central Florida. By employing their intensive harvest food-gathering and hunting techniques, sufficient food was available to support such an occupation. The range of animals exploited is far greater than for any other Florida culture except the inhabitants of the Lake Okeechobee Basin.

Thus far, no complete house patterns have been excavated at the Melton site or at any other Cades Pond village. At the former site, however, a large number of storage pits, which often overlapped one another, were excavated. The density of the pits suggests long-term occupation of the same structures. Most of the storage pits were basin-shaped, measuring about 1 m in depth. Smaller pits probably anchored large support posts for sturctures. The sides of structures were possibly covered with brush and smaller poles. Future research should produce a clearer picture of community and household settlement traits.

The Cades Pond people did not live in isolation. A variety of exotic artifacts and foods were acquired by trade. Most of the trade goods found in the villages were used in secular activities and, most likely, were obtained by trade with other early Weeden Island period peoples on the Gulf Coast and in northern Florida. The trade routes extending up into the piedmont Woodland cultures, which were established during the Deptford period, seem to have still been operating, since exotic stone and copper from that region are also present at the village. The St. Johns Plain and Dunns Creek Red vessels found in the Cades Pond ceremonial mounds are generally thought to have come from East Florida because of the similarities of their paste to the well-known St. Johns ceramic series. However, it is now known that many similar vessels are found on the Gulf Coast, also. When certain local clays containing sponge spicules are carefully washed clean of sand and other impurities, the resulting vessels exhibit the St. Johns chalky paste. The large number of such vessels in North-Central Florida and on the Gulf Coast lends support to the hypothesis that they were made locally. Many of the Cades Pond ceremonial vessels contain red inclusions in the clay not present in the east coast vessels of the same period.

Trade goods from the Gulf Coast found in North-Central Florida are mainly marine foods and shell items. Other exotic non-Florida items are tools and stone and metal ornaments. The marine foods from the coast included several species of sharks—white, mako, requiem, tiger, and hammerhead—and the large sea turtles. In addition, mullet and several species of mollusks were brought inland. An adze, or scraper, made from the shell of a Queen conch shell shows that trade with East Florida did occur, although the bulk of the trade goods come from the Gulf area.

The trade ornaments take the form of gorgets and plummets. These are generally manufactured of slate, sandstone, or greenstone. Rolled copper beads and a copper boatstone-shaped object also have been identified from the Melton village site. These are probably items of everyday personal adornment, as indicated by their presence in secular contexts, both in North-Central Florida and at a variety of Woodland culture sites in the Southeast.

In return for these goods, the Cades Pond traders had flint and other noncoastal resources to offer. Archaeologists are only now beginning to focus on aboriginal trade within Florida, and our understanding of trade items and trade routes will increase as this research progresses.

To date, four ceremonial Cades Pond mounds have been thoroughly excavated by the University of Florida. Two were burial mounds associated with the Melton village site. Another burial mound and platform mound excavated were associated with the Cross Creek site. In addition, several sand mounds containing few, if any, artifacts and only scattered remains of human teeth or other fragments of skeletons not destroyed by soil acids have been examined. These include the Wacahoota mounds on the west side of Paynes Prairie, and the Evinston mounds just south of Evinston in Marion County. An additional number of small sand mounds located between Paynes Prairie and Newnan's Lake have been completely destroyed by local collectors searching for artifacts. Still other mounds have only recently been located.

In 1971 Ripley P. Bullen excavated a late Deptford—early Cades Pond period ceremonial mound and embankment located just north of Orange Lake. This site, called the River Styx mound, is radiocarbon dated at A.D. 180 ± 85 and appears to be the earliest mound in North-Central Florida; it demonstrates the continuity between Deptford and Cades Pond secular and sacred activities.

Together, the five Cades Pond mounds from which the most data are available span the temporal range of the Cades Pond period. Arranged from the earliest to the most recent, these mounds are River Styx, Melton Mound No. 1, Melton Mound No. 3, Cross Creek Burial Mound (No. 2), and Cross Creek Platform Mound (No. 2). This seriation, however, is not completely satisfactory. When geographical and community patterning factors are taken into consideration, along with the location and form of other mounds, there seems to have been six or more or nexuses of mounds and villages which were occupied through the same period of time, with several nexuses being "founded" earlier than others. Milanich (1978a:166—171) has suggested that each geographically distinct nexus formed a distinct social group. The earliest nexuses have mounds surrounded by a horseshoe-shaped embankment like at River Styx. As villages and the associated "mound centers" were abandoned, others were established within the same nexus. As populations increased separate villages with no mounds were formed and occasionally a new nexus beginning with a village and mound or mound complex budded off from an older nexus. The most recent nexuses apparently contain ceremonial centers with both platform and burial mounds. Testing of this nexus model awaits additional research, but Cades Pond promises to be a worthwhile candidate for studies of prehistoric ethnicity and demography. Description of the best known of the Cades Pond mounds follows.

First occupants of the River Styx complex possibly were not year-round inhabitants of the North-Central Florida region. They might still have been moving seasonally from the peninsular Gulf Coast into the highlands during part of the year. Soon they remained all of the year inland. As these early Cades Pond peoples achieved sedentism based on their intensive harvest methods, their burial ceremonial practices, as evidenced by the mound excavations, diverged somewhat from those of the Gulf Coast proto-Weeden Island cultures. At about this time, the River Styx population abandoned their ceremonial area and moved the center of ceremonial activity to Cross Creek. The village at River Styx may have continued to be occupied after the Cross Creek center and village were established. Cross Creek is 5 km southeast of River Styx.

The River Styx site was, unfortunately, partially bulldozed before salvage excavations were undertaken by Bullen. A detailed map of the ceremonial earthworks has been made and, with Bullen's data, it allows some interpretations to be made. The complex consists of a burial mound constructed over a large number of cremation burials. Whether or not cremations or other types of burials were present in the mound fill is not certain. Digging by nonprofessional archaeologists has also turned up several cremations which appear to have been placed outside the area of the mound. This mound and burial area is enclosed on three sides by a horseshoe-shaped earth embankment. On the fourth side of the burial area is a kidney-shaped pond which is probably the borrow pit from which dirt was excavated for the construction of the mound and the embankment. A village is present on the opposite side of the pond from the mound. Axes of the embankment measure roughly 45 and 60 m.

Ceremonial vessels from the mound included Deptford and St. Johns wares and some sand-tempered plain ware. Some of the pottery is reminiscent of the coastal Yent complex. Also recovered from the mound were rolled copper beads which seem to be a popular trade item present in both Cades Pond villages and mounds.

The pattern of the River Styx site—a mound enclosed by a horseshoe-shaped embankment with a pond adjoining—is typical of the Crystal River site (as mentioned previously), as well as the Fort Center site in the

Lake Okeechobee Basin, and the Cross Creek site. At all of these sites these features date roughly within the period A.D. 100 to A.D. 400. River Styx was probably in use near the middle of this period. The construction of mound "centers" seems to have been common throughout the geographical and temporal range of Hopewellian, Weeden Island, and Mississippian-type cultures in Florida and the Southeast.

River Styx, like the other contemporary centers, contains a sacred area where bodies were prepared for burial or cremation. This area was enclosed and separated from the secular living area. From the small number of cremations found at River Styx, it seems likely that only certain individuals were afforded burial in the enclosed area. Probably bodies were stored in a charnel house until a specified time, perhaps simply until the structure was filled. Then they were cremated and the remains deposited within or around the mound. The cremations might also have taken place at the interment site. After the sacred area was determined to be "filled" with both burials and the sacred vessels and other items that were placed in the mound, the ceremonial portion of the site (and, perhaps, the entire village) was abandoned. Such a sequence of events is very typical of Southeast Indian religious ceremonialism.

Related in form to the River Styx center is the Cross Creek village and mound complex which consists of two ceremonial mounds placed roughly 185 m apart on a northeast—southeast axis. The village area is located between the two mounds and is closest to the southernmost mound. The more northerly mound, Cross Creek No. 1, is a conical, sand burial mound. A trench 2—2.4 m wide and 1.2 m deep, with an embankment thrown up on the south (interior) side, was dug around the burial mound in an arc at a distance of approximately 50 m from the mound. The trench and embankment run from almost due south of the mound to due north in a semicircle. In appearance, the enclosure is very similar to the River Styx enclosure except the latter did not have a trench beside it. Two borrow pits lie between the north side of the village and the burial mound. Dirt to build the mounds was probably taken from these pits.

The southern mound, Cross Creek No. 2, is a low, flat-topped structure, measuring 48 by 40 m at the base. The larger axis runs north and south. The village midden extends underneath the mound, indicating that the site was occupied before the mound was constructed. South of the mound is a large pond, possibly the borrow pit from which the mound fill was taken. The mound contained no intentionally deposited artifacts, and appears to have functioned as a platform for a temple or charnel house.

As with most North-Central Florida burial mounds, the burials excavated by the University of Florida in their 1964 research at the Cross

Creek site were in an extremely bad state of preservation due to the acidic soil. Sherds and lithic artifacts were found in the burial mound in relatively large quantities. Although some were certainly unintentionally deposited with the mound fill, several ceramic vessels appear to have been purposefully shattered and the sherds scattered throughout the mound fill.

More than 500 potsherds had been deposited in the mound fill; sand-tempered plain (48.8%), St. Johns Plain (11.0%), with various other types such as Weeden Island punctated and incised wares totaling the remaining number. These frequencies of presumed ceremonial pottery contrast sharply with the frequency of pottery types from the village area. In the village area, 82.5% of the sherds were a sand-tempered plain type like that found at the Melton village site. The remaining 17.5% were St. Johns Plain (10.5%), Weeden Island Plain (2.2%), and Dunns Creek Red (1.2%). Overall, the Cross Creek village ceramic inventory is like that of other known Cades Pond villages which postdate the River Styx site. And, as at other Cades Pond villages with mounds in association, the secular and ceremonial pottery types used vary greatly from one another.

Smith reports three other mounds near the Cross Creek site. These are found in a line extending south from the flat-topped mound at distances of 365, 460, and 915 m, respectively. All have been heavily disturbed by pothunting. Local collectors previously recovered a cache of greenstone celts either from one of these mounds or from the burial mound Cross Creek No. 1.

Several other small village areas have been found close to these three southern mounds, but none have been excavated. Surface collections indicate that they are Cades Ponds occupations.

The Cross Creek site appears to have been a planned village with a burial mound and a temple or charnel-house mound placed at the respective north and south ends of the village. A trench and dirt embankment about 100 m in length surrounded the sides of the burial mound that were away from the village. Perhaps a palisade of logs or a similar device originally enclosed the fourth side of the burial area, separating it from the village. At the River Styx site, the pond served this purpose.

Probably River Styx and then Cross Creek were sequentially occupied by the same group of Cades Pond peoples. Both are similar in having a burial area enclosed by a horseshoe-shaped embankment. Burials were generally placed in or under mounds built especially to receive them. Possibly a charnel house for preparation and storage of bodies before final disposition was present at both sites. The Cross Creek site is more elaborate and is larger than River Styx. At the former site the charnel house was, most likely, placed on a raised mound whereas at the River Styx site such a structure evidently was built at ground level in an unknown location.

In contrast to the River Styx and Cross Creek Cades Pond nexus is the Melton nexus which contained at least five ceremonial mounds and 10 villages and camps. Most have been destroyed. The three intact Melton mounds were located well to the west of the associated villages. Distance from the westernmost mound, Melton Mound No. 1, to the easternmost village, site 8-A-346, is about 4 km. The mounds and villages are strung out in an east–west line parallel to the north edge of Paynes Prairie at a distance of up to 1.5 km from the prairie edge. This pattern appears to be somewhat similar to that of the three southern Cross Creek mounds and village areas, which are in a line parallel to both Orange Lake and Lochloosa Lake. Probably at the time that the main Cross Creek ceremonial center was abandoned, both Melton and the south Cross Creek habitation areas were occupied contemporaneously.

Melton Mound No. 1 is a burial mound. Sand for the mound was taken from a borrow pit west of the mound. North about 70 m is another low sand burial mound believed to have been excavated in the 1880s by James Bell (1883:635–637). The mound contained a large number of secondary burials and what, evidently, were Weeden Island effigy vessels, a unique situation in North-Central Florida. No Cades Pond village area is evident anywhere in the immediate vicinity of these two Melton mounds. The nearest occupation areas are the Melton village site and site A-346 with which the mounds must have been associated.

Melton Mound No. 1 contained portions of 17 human burials, most of which were represented by only a few teeth. Again, the acidity of the soil destroyed all of the bone except for teeth which are somewhat more sturdy due to the enamel. As with all of the Cades Pond mounds, there was no eastside pottery deposit. Rather, ceramic vessels had been broken and placed in the mound fill during the construction process. Of the nearly 1600 sherds recovered from the mound, half were St. Johns plain, one-third were sand-tempered plain. Some Dunns Creek Red sherds (6%) had also been placed in the mound. The percentage of St. Johns paste vessels in the Melton mounds is significantly higher than at River Styx and Cross Creek, indicating perhaps differences in ceremonialism or, more likely, in temporal association.

Two burials in the east side of the mound seem to have secondary bundled burials, again indicating use of a charnel house as at other Cades Pond mounds. The mound appears to have been reused after its initial construction, and two primary burials, one a female in a flexed position, were interred in intrusive pits in the center of the mound.

Melton Mound No. 3, excavated by Sears, is smaller than the other Melton mounds, measuring only 15.2 m in diameter and 1.2 m in height. The distance between the two villages about equals the distance from Melton Mounds No. 1 and No. 2 to Melton Mound No. 3, suggesting that the former two mounds were associated with the Melton village site while No. 3 was associated with A-346. This, in turn, suggests that the Melton population moved east to A-346 for a period of time during which Mound No. 3 was built, and then returned. The mound dug by Bell, Mound No. 2, was constructed during this latter period of occupation. The depth and richness of the Melton village site suggest such a long occupation.

Although direct evidence was lacking, Sears felt, from the position of artifacts and burials in the mound, that it was constructed in two distinct stages. The primary mound, about 60 cm high and 9 m in diameter, contained a deposit of pottery sherds and several burials in its central portion. Later, before the second mound was added, a mass burial of 7 or 8 bundles was placed on the primary mound's surface near its center. Apparently, these burials had been stored together in a charnel house and were simply stacked on the mound previous to the second-stage construction. At this same time more bundled burials, perhaps as many as 20 were placed on the mound's surface. At least two cremations were also laid on the primary mound.

Just west of the central mass burial, an adult female was placed on the mound in a flexed position. The female had fragments of an infant skeleton in her abdominal area indicating, as Sears notes, that she died during pregnancy. Two sand-tempered plain vessels, one globular in shape with nonfunctional tetrapods and one with a pointed bottom and constricted mouth, were placed next to this evidently primary burial.

Between the female burial and the western edge of the mound, Sears uncovered a deposit of more than 1000 potsherds which had also been placed on the mound surface. This deposit of broken ceremonial vessels covered an area about 5 m in length, 1.5 m in width, and 15 cm in depth. Other sherds were scattered throughout the fill of both mound layers. St. Johns Plain sherds accounted for about 70% of the total recovered, a number significantly larger than in the other Cades Pond mounds and probably indicates that the mound postdates the River Styx, Cross Creek, and Melton Mound No. 1 mounds. More Weeden Island sherds were present in the mound than were in any of the other Cades Pond mounds, except Melton Mound No. 2 excavated by Bell.

Like the other Cades Pond mounds, Melton Mound No. 3 contained scattered sherds in the mound fill, only a very few intact vessels, and few, if any, grave goods. A charnel house must have been used to store the bundled burials before their interment in the mound. In some cases bodies were cremated before burial. Bodies must have been stripped of flesh and retained until it was determined that it was time to build a mound for their deposition. Such activities are fairly common in the Southeast and have been described for several historic tribes, including the Tocobaga of the Florida Gulf Coast.

The Cross Creek — River Styx and the Melton mound complexes share many traits. Sand-tempered plain, St. Johns Plain, and Dunns Creek Red vessels are the primary types of sacred vessels from which sherds are found in the mounds. Deptford and plain wares decrease in ceremonial usage through time while the Weeden Island and St. Johns wares increase. Perhaps this reflects the increased use of exotic vessels for ceremonial purposes. Presumably, these ceremonial vessels were used and broken elsewhere and then brought to the mounds for deposition. In all of the mounds except the earliest, the majority of burials were stored as bundles in a charnel house before interment in the mounds. Quantities of bones were buried at the same time by placing them on a sand surface, either the surface of a primary mound or a construction layer in a mound, and then covering them with a sand cap. A few cremations and flexed burials, the latter either primary burials or wrapped, secondary, flexed burials from which the flesh had not yet been removed, were also occasionally placed in the mounds.

Although the Cades Pond peoples certainly had cultural ties to the Gulf Coast cultures and were engaged in trade with that area, their burial ceremonialism began to diverge from that of the central Gulf Coast after A.D. 200. The Cades Pond culture overlaps temporally with Weeden Island, but it is quite distinct from the Weeden Island developments to the north. Thus, although it lies partially within the Weeden Island *period*, it is not a Weeden Island culture.

Coastal Weeden Island Period Populations and Their Predecessors

The region occupied by Weeden Island period coastal peoples discussed in the next few pages is about the same as that described previously for the Deptford culture — from south of Tampa Bay north and west to the Alabama — Florida state line, and includes the northwest coast and the northern and central peninsula coast. As previously stated, the culture sequence for peninsular Florida differs from that of northwestern Florida. The Deptford, Swift Creek, Weeden Island continuum found in parts of the panhandle does not hold true for the peninsular Gulf Coast or for North-Central Florida; few Swift Creek occupations are present in the peninsula. The late Deptford or proto-Weeden Island period fills the temporal gap between the end of Deptford (A.D. 100) and the later appearance of the Weeden Island period cultures (A.D. 300–400). Much more research is needed, however, to further refine the culture sequence along the Gulf Coast and to further define the cultures of the Weeden Island period. Luer and Almy (1979) have noted the uniformity in culture traits for the Central Peninsula Gulf Coast area from ca. 500 B.C. to A.D. 800 times. They cite evidence which demonstrates that Deptford and early Weeden Island ceramics occur only rarely; the majority of ceramics in mounds and villages are plain. To distinguish the archaeological complex from 500 B.C. to A.D. 800 from those cultures farther north they propose the name Manasota culture. Their work is a step in the right direction to clarify the cultural evolution of the coastal peoples. It is our hope that the future will see additional attempts to describe and interpret the Weeden Island period coastal cultures along the peninsula coast. It is clear that they were different from the cultures of the Weeden Island heartland to the north.

The evolution of Weeden Island period cultures along the Gulf Coast was a gradual process; the date of A.D. 200 seems to be an important cut-off date, marking the appearance of new traits both inland and on the peninsular coast as well as in Northwest Florida. This date also marks the end of the Deptford paddle-malleated ware and the increase of plain ware in the peninsular coastal middens. From ca. A.D. 200 up into the Safety Harbor period, the majority of village pottery along the peninsula coast north of Charlotte Harbor remained undecorated (usually 90% or more at any one site).

The coastal region can be divided into two other subregions in addition to the Manasota culture. Criteria for all of these divisions include settlement and subsistence traits, ceremonialism, and differences in village pottery. Subsistence and settlement differences between the inland cultures, such as Cades Pond discussed previously, and the tri-state area culture to be discussed, are obvious. Other less subtle differences can also be used to differentiate the Gulf coastal cultures.

The Northwest coast can be separated from the peninsular coast on the basis of differences in relative percentages of incised and punctated pottery during the post-A.D. 300–400 Weeden Island period. Incision, punctation, and, later, check-stamping were much more prevalent north and west of Taylor County than they were south along the northern or central peninsular coast where they generally comprise from 10% of collections in the north to less than 1% in the Manasota region. This panhandle–peninsula separation is also evident when ceremonialism is considered. Northwest Florida seems to have been the "heartland" of Weeden Island ceremonialism (along with North Florida and Southwest Georgia). The pre-Weeden Island Yent and Green Point complexes are almost solely restricted to coastal and inland sites outside of peninsular Florida. Also, the later Weeden Island patterned burial mounds with east-side pottery deposits are found only in Northwest and North Florida and not in the peninsula where the Weeden Island-related mortuary complex seems to be a "country cousin" of the more northerly complex, or, as south of Tampa Bay, where it is almost entirely absent until after A.D. 800. Many of the well-known Weeden Island ceremonial vessels, especially the elaborate effigy vessels, were probably made in northern Florida or in Georgia and traded south to the Gulf Coast below Taylor County. Future research on Weeden Island village life and ceremonialism should further define this panhandle—peninsula coastal division and refine our knowledge of the coastal Weeden Island period cultures. Later, during late Weeden Island times when check-stamping once again became popular in northern Florida, plain pottery remained the most popular ware on the peninsular Gulf Coast.

The peninsular Gulf Coast cultures of the post-A.D. 100 period can be further divided into the two main subcultural regions: the northern coast peninsula culture(s) and the central coast peninsula or Manasota culture. The secular ware along the northern coast above mid-Pasco County tends to be both the limestone-tempered Pasco series and sand-tempered wares. From mid-Pasco County southward, the village pottery complex contains less Pasco ware and more sand-tempered ware. There is considerable overlap of sand-tempered and limestone-tempered series along the entire peninsular Gulf Coast; however, Pasco County seems to be the central dividing line within the continuum. In addition to these two ceramic series, St. Johns ceramics also are found in quantities as high as 10% at some coastal Weeden Island period sites, both early and late. The origins of these vessels are uncertain. No tests have been carried out to ascertain whether the pottery represents items brought from East Florida or if they are locally made vessels.

Any syntheses of Gulf Coast village life are severely hampered by a lack of data. Very few extensive excavations have been carried out in post-Deptford middens, and information detailing subsistence activities or other aspects of village life is lacking. Also, there have been no widespread attempts to seriate secular pottery from a number of sites to establish a regional chronology. Exceptions are work by Bullen (1971) in Sarasota County, Sears (1971b) at the Weeden Island site in Pinellas County, Kohler (1975) at the Garden Patch site in Dixie County, Luer (1977a, 1977b) in Sarasota County, and Goggin, whose excavations at

Shired Island in Dixie County have been reported by Goldburt (1966), in a master's thesis at the University of Florida. Willey's *Archeology of the Florida Gulf Coast* also provides some information, although data on village life are limited. Percy and Brose (1974) have synthesized much of the data on Weeden Island in Northwest Florida. The work of all of these individuals is taken into account in the sections that follow.

Because detailed information on the coastal cultures is lacking, the panhandle, the northern peninsula, and the southern peninsula (late Manasota) coastal cultures will be discussed together. Important distinctions will be pointed out wherever possible. However, the small amount of information now available suggests that the Gulf coastal Weeden Island period cultures maintained very similar subsistence and settlement patterns, and the only differences documented well are ceramic technology and burial ceremonialism.

Coastal Predecessors: A.D. *100 – 300*

The late-Deptford (or pre-Weeden Island) period on the peninsula coast (roughly temporally comparable to the Swift Creek period in Northwest Florida) is almost totally unknown. No effort has been made in coastal excavations to isolate this component. From limited excavations at Shired Island and Garden Patch, it appears that the village pottery was sand-tempered plain (about 50%), sand-tempered cord-marked (about 20%), with the rest being about equal amounts of Deptford Check Stamped, Pasco Plain complicated stamped, and smoothed (or burnished) sand-tempered plain, although sand-tempered plain types constituted the majority of the utilitarian ware. The exact frequencies of limestone and sand-tempering vary almost by site, but together account for 90% or more of all utilitarian wares. In the Manasota region the pottery vessels are nearly all bowl forms with straight or incurving rims (Luer and Almy 1979).

Villagers lived much like their Deptford ancestors, collecting shellfish (mainly oysters), hunting deer, raccoon, bear, and opossum, collecting a variety of small mammals, wild plants, and a variety of marine, land, and freshwater turtles, and fishing in the Gulf for catfish, small sharks, mullet, jack, sheepshead, drum, and other fish. Kohler calculates that 75% of the total meat diet came from marsh and Gulf. A very few flint chips, shell picks or hammers, lithic tools, bone basketry fids, and fragments of worked bone, have been recovered. There seems to have been very few changes in either site location, midden distribution, or subsistence from the preceding Deptford period. The Shired Island and Garden Patch excavations clearly indicate the cultural continuity on the northern peninsula Coast between late Deptford and early Weeden Island periods.

A somewhat similar sequence is apparent in some localities on the panhandle coast during this time. Sears's (1963:21) research at the Tucker site in Franklin County demonstrates the decline in check-stamping and an increase in plain ware at the end of the Deptford period.

Perhaps these post-Deptford coastal peoples were horticulturalists, cultivating squash (and, less likely, corn) in small garden plots, either directly on the coast or away from the coast on plots of high ground within, or on the edge of the coastal flatlands. To date, however, there is no concrete evidence for agriculture, although there is meager evidence for *Cucurbit* cultivation during the Swift Creek period. The lack of such evidence is probably due to a lack of systematic excavations.

Coastal Populations: A.D. *300 – 1200*

During the Weeden Island period, populations increased, possibly reflecting increased importance of horticulture, and began to spread inland into portions of the state previously little occupied. The tri-state, Upper Apalachicola region was first heavily occupied during this period, and Weeden Island peoples moved into northern Florida at this time. Information from excavations by Sears at the Weeden Island site (which spanned the entire post-Deptford time period), from the Sarasota County mound investigated by Bullen, from the definition of the Manasota culture by Luer and Almy, and from surveys and some excavations from Northwest Florida, we can synthesize the following picture of Weeden Island period village life along the coasts.

Village sites along the Gulf consist of shell middens which were deposited beside or adjacent to houses. Generally, these middens are long embankments which are spread out laterally, parallel to the adjacent marsh, to the Gulf itself, or to a bay or estuary. The shell heaps appear to represent the overlapping of small, circular middens, each about 15 m or slightly less in diameter. At some sites the occupation period was not intense enough or long enough for a large number of these individual piles to be deposited on top of one another. In such cases the distinct individual piles are still visible.

Generally, these middens are composed almost entirely of oysters with other shellfish species accounting for less than 10% of the total quantity. An exception to this pattern is the Ocklocknee Bay where Percy and Brose (1974) have noted that *Rangia* are the majority shellfish. Shellfish were an important dietary source for these coastal dwellers, as were fish.

In Northwest Florida some villages of this period were placed away from the coast proper on the ecotone between the coastal scrub flatlands and the coastal strand. The nature of these sites is much the same as that described previously for the Swift Creek culture; that is, horseshoe-shaped shell middens.

With the presumed growing importance of horticulture and an increased reliance on proper rainfall and soil fertility, and knowing exactly when to plant and harvest, there must have been a growth in attempts to control nature or, at least, attempts to assure that the natural elements would provide the needed conditions for successful horticulture. Possibly such attempts are partially reflected in the change from Green Point to Weeden Island ceremonialism.

Excavations at Weeden Island coastal strand villages indicate heavy use of fish, deer, and turtle. The species of animals utilized for food were little changed from those of earlier periods. One change in the midden contents is the quantity of debris present. Excavations by Bullen at the Sarasota County mound gives evidence of an increase in material goods found in the middens. Relative to pre-Weeden Island period levels at the site, a larger quantity of plummets, bone and shell tools, stone points and knives, and various types of shell beads, was taken from the late Manasota (early Weeden Island period) component at the site. Although these artifacts are more plentiful than those found during earlier periods, they are the same types of artifacts manufactured previously; in all probability, there are simply more of them because there were more people.

During the later portion of the Weeden Island period in Northwest Florida, check-stamped pottery once again became popular for village use, as it had during the Deptford period. This phenomenon also occurred in the Upper Apalachicola River Valley. Percy and Brose (1974) suggest that at this time, individual coastal village sites remained the same approximate size although the number of villages increased dramatically, indicating increased populations. Also, villages appear to be clustered around a single shared burial mound. Most likely, mound burial was reserved for a certain group of individuals. During this period, villages appear to be of about equal size; there does not appear to be central-base villages as there were during the earlier periods.

Information for late Weeden Island period village life along the peninsular coast is sparse. Sears's work at Bayshore Homes and at Weeden Island demonstrates a continuum between the late Weeden Island period and the succeeding central coast Safety Harbor culture. There is not enough information to quantify the relative size and numbers of late versus early sites, except for a few hints that suggest many new sites were established during the late period; most of these were occupied up into the Safety Harbor period.

As most current researchers have noted, there is a lack of systematic, extensive, problem-oriented research into coastal Weeden Island period village life. However, there are several long-term projects concerning Weeden Island period culture in Florida being carried out even as this chapter is written. Undoubtedly, the 1980s will see a profound increase in our knowledge of the Weeden Island period peoples of Florida and adjacent areas.

Swift Creek Culture

The Swift Creek culture was first recognized in central Georgia during the late 1930s. Federal relief archaeology programs carried out near Macon at the Swift Creek site uncovered complicated-stamped pottery which was named after that site. Soon researchers in other areas, especially West Florida, were also reporting similar complicated-stamped pottery from village sites and from ceremonial mounds.

Since the 1930s, when Swift Creek Complicated Stamped pottery was first described as a ceramic type, a plethora of complicated-stamped motifs have been included under the rubric of Swift Creek. Little attempt has been made to seriate these motifs to determine if there is any developmental sequence, or to see if certain motifs are geographically restricted. Also, many kinds of complicated-stamped pottery that are not Swift Creek have been mistakenly identified as Swift Creek motifs.

Swift Creek, as used here, refers to that primarily Woodland culture whose primary decorated village ware was Swift Creek Complicated Stamped. Willey has offered stringent definitions for this pottery based on large samples from the Florida Gulf Coast (Willey 1949a:378–383). In Florida the villages of the Swift Creek culture are restricted almost entirely to northern (nonpeninsular) Florida. Eastern distribution of the culture is the western edge of the Atlantic coastal flatlands, whereas the western distribution fades out at about the Escambia River.

Because of nonrandom excavation, most of the Swift Creek sites in Florida that have been investigated are within the Gulf coastal strand, either immediately adjacent to the salt marshes or back from the marshes in the hardwood hammocks. Surveys have shown, however, that the largest number of villages are in the highland forests, especially the Tallahassee Red Hills in the panhandle. Small scattered campsites are found as far south as Alachua County in the peninsula, but these are rare. The period of the culture in Northwest Florida is about A.D. 100–300, although radiocarbon dates obtained by Phelps (1969) would extend it somewhat later. Evidently some late Swift Creek and early Weeden Island sites overlap temporally. This, however, remains to be thoroughly investigated.

Relative to other cultures, few Swift Creek villages have been excavated and reported. The information on village life reported here comes almost entirely from the work of Phelps (1969), Penton (1970), and various archaeologists of the State Division of Archives, History and Records Management (Fryman 1971a:3), all of which was carried out in Northwest Florida.

Penton's excavations at a coastal strand hammock site in Wakulla County provide the most comprehensive view of Swift Creek culture, albeit only one portion of the total Swift Creek subsistence pattern. The reports by Phelps, and those of the Florida Division of Archives, History and Records Management, offer hints on the remaining portions of Swift Creek subsistence although specific published information is lacking at this time. The presence of Swift Creek villages in three types of environments seems to indicate that there were three main types of sites occupied. The first are the inland villages which are found in the river valley forests where game, nuts, and seeds are available. Soils at such locations were suited to horticulture, and gardening may have played a role in the Swift Creek diet. Phelps has identified one squash seed recovered from a coprolite found at the coastal Refuge Fire Tower site. Most likely, evidence of squash and, perhaps, other cultigens will be forthcoming from inland sites. The inland sites usually consist of horseshoe or annular middens which reflect a similar community plan. At such sites, burial mounds are frequently present.

The coastal sites are of two main types. One is very similar to the inland circular or horseshoe-shaped middens. The coastal middens of this type are composed of shellfish, humus, and other living refuse. As with the inland sites, a burial mound is usually present adjacent to the village area. The third type of site is the linear shell midden. Generally, these middens are less extensive than those at the other coastal sites, and they may represent sporadically occupied shellfish-collecting and/or fishing camps. The nature of the larger annular middens suggests planned villages that were occupied on a more sedentary basis. Although it is possible that the villages that were occupied on a seasonal basis — horticultural activities and hunting and collecting taking place in the spring and summer at the inland sites, and hunting, collecting, fishing, and shellfish-collecting taking place at the coastal villages during the winter months—there is not enough evidence available to determine accurately the validity of this model.

Almost all of our information on Swift Creek comes from the coastal strand villages and camps. Those sites directly on the marsh seem to have been occupied by Swift Creek people whose hunting—collecting efforts were centered on the salt marsh and the tidal streams. Phelps has estimated that 95% of their protein diet came from fish and shellfish, although this may be too high. Deer were probably the primary meat source at most other sites. Other animals eaten were turkey, turtle, rabbit, and opossum. Charred hickory nuts have been recovered at one site.

Another possibility concerning settlement patterns is that the seasonal movement may not have been between inland and coastal strand localities. Rather, it may have been between the more permanent villages, both those few adjacent to the coast and those located inland, and the smaller campsites, both those on the marsh proper (for fishing and shellfish-gathering) and those in forest areas (for hunting). The central-base villages, if that is indeed what they are, were located on ecotones; in the one case, the salt marsh and hardwood hammock, and in the other, the inland river valleys and the mixed hardwood forests. Movement to the coast could have added another dimension to the yearly subsistence round.

Little is known about the tools used by the Swift Creek people. Penton's excavations at the Bird Hammock site indicate that bone and stone tools occur in greater numbers than they did during the preceding Deptford period. Although little comparative information from contemporary Weeden Island coastal villages is available, such artifacts also seem to be less frequently found in those sites than at Swift Creek sites.

Bone tools consist of awls, polished pins, flakers, and bone scrapers. Cut and polished carnivore mandibles and drilled carnivore teeth are found in the village middens, and must be objects of personal or ritual adornment. No bone fishhooks have appeared at Swift Creek sites, suggesting that fish were taken by other means—perhaps nets or traps. Shell tools are rare, consisting of a few conch hammers and possible scrapers. Shell discs and pendants occur in small numbers also. None of the bone and shell tools are very diagnostic, and they closely resemble those found at both inland and coastal sites elsewhere in Florida.

More distinctive is the lithic complex, especially the widely occurring stemmed knife or projectile point which Phelps has called the "Swift Creek" point. The tang is only slightly narrower than the width of the blade and expands somewhat. In appearance, the point closely resembles the Columbia point described by Bullen (1975:19) for the Weeden

Island period. These points are probably hafted knives or multipurpose tools, since many exhibit repeated resharpening. Some specimens, due to such repeated sharpening, have blades only slightly longer than their stems.

Another distinctive Swift Creek lithic tool is the bifacial knife which seems to have been manufactured from triangular blades. The width at the shoulders is always shorter than the length of the specimen, giving the finished tool a linear appearance. Bases are either flat or slightly rounded. Other stone tools include spokeshaves, hammerstones made from expended cores, flake scrapers, limestone nutting stones (with one to four indentations), and sandstone abraders used to sharpen the bone awls.

The ceramic inventory from the Bird Hammock site was composed almost entirely of plain and Swift Creek Complicated Stamped pottery (Figure 20); these types constituted 61 and 35% of the total ceramic inventory recovered, respectively. Minority types include check-stamping, simple-stamping, Crooked River Complicated Stamped, St. Andrews Complicated Stamped, and cord-marking (Figure 21a−c). There is evidence from western Georgia Swift Creek sites that check-stamping declines in popularity relative to complicated stamping, with plain pottery always constituting about 50% of the sherds recovered. Such a trend suggests that the Swift Creek sites in inland portions of Georgia are earlier than those in Florida, especially those on the coast. This is to be expected if it is argued, as is done here, that the Swift Creek culture represents a gradual diffusion of ideas or, perhaps, an actual population movement from Georgia into Northwest Florida.

Vessel shapes for both the plain and complicated-stamped pots are of two main types: squat bowls about 25 cm in diameter and 10 cm in height, and deep cylindrical pots with conoidal bottoms 30 to 40 cm in diameter. Several rim treatments were used—crenulating, notching, and scalloping. All of the pottery is sand-tempered.

Although it is generally assumed that Swift Creek complicated stamping was done by pressing a carved wooden paddle into the wet surface of the clay pot, at least one baked-clay stamp has been found. The specimen has a complicated stamp on one side and a negative check stamp impression on the other, pointing out rather dramatically the fact that Swift Creek peoples used both types of decorative techniques. Examination of the complicated-stamp design on many vessels has verified, however, that most paddles were made of wood. Other distinctive Swift Creek artifacts are small rubbing tools made from sherds and used to smooth pottery, and baked clay or steatite equal-arm elbow pipes. A relatively large number of baked-clay figurines have been found within Swift Creek

FIGURE 20. *Swift Creek Complicated Stamped pottery.*

FIGURE 21. *Swift Creek and Weeden Island pottery; a—b, St. Andrews Complicated Stamped; c, New River Complicated Stamped; d—f, Carrabelle Incised; g—i, Carrabelle Punctated.*

village middens. All are bare-breasted females wearing skirts with high, wide bands around the top. These may have been some sort of household fertility cult icon and have been found at a variety of sites within the Hopewell period (Walthall 1975).

The general picture of Swift Creek village life derived from limited excavations and surveys is one of a woodland subsistence pattern with primary emphasis on exploitation of riverine and forest habitats. In the case of the coastal strand villages, the use of marine products added another dimension to this pattern. In general, however, the main population seems to have been located inland, both along the river valleys in Northwest Florida and along those in southwestern and western Georgia, and along the Chattahoochee River in extreme eastern Alabama. A great deal more research is needed to determine the relationships between Swift Creek village life and that of the Deptford and the Weeden Island cultures. However, at this time Swift Creek appears to be a woodland-type culture that did not develop out of the coastal Deptford culture. Most likely, it developed out of the West Georgia check-stamped-pottery-making cultures, such as that represented at Mandeville. Swift Creek represents a movement of new styles of village life into Northwest Florida.

Ceremonialism of the Swift Creek peoples seems to be transitional from the Yent complex into the later Weeden Island ceremonial complex. Sears has organized traits from four Swift Creek burial mounds into the Green Point complex (Sears 1962:5 – 18). Swift Creek ceremonial mounds all appear to have been constructed for burial purposes. They are circular or oval, ranging in size from about 10 m in diameter to 20 m in diameter (for the circular mounds). The oval mounds measure about 50 by 23 m. None of the mounds appear to be higher than 2 m. Oval mounds are probably circular mounds to which later additions were made to cover subsequent burials.

The early Swift Creek mounds appear to have been built in several discrete ceremonies, each involving the deposition of burials and the placement of caches of artifacts in the mound. At times, each subsequent mound layer was capped with a clay layer. Burials are generally flexed, although single skull and bundled burials are known. Possibly the burials were stored in charnel houses before interment. The later Swift Creek mounds seem to have been constructed in a single ceremony. In such cases, a charnel house for storage of bodies must have been in use.

Most of the caches in the mounds are composed of pottery vessels like those in use in the villages—Swift Creek Complicated Stamped, St. Andrews Complicated Stamped, Crooked River Complicated Stamped, and plain vessels. A few are zoned rocker-stamped vessels, probably traded into Northwest Florida from the Gulf or lower Mississippi Valley cultures found farther west. Vessel shapes and decorative techniques of the ceremonial pots are the same as those of the secular ware, unlike the earlier Yent and later Weeden Island ceramic wares. Swift Creek ceremonial vessels do, however, appear to have tetrapods more often than do the vessels in use in the villages. The metal and shell ornaments of the Yent complex are found in the earliest Swift Creek mounds, but these items slowly disappear from the later mounds. The transition from Yent and Swift Creek ceremonialism into Weeden Island ceremonialism is gradual, and perhaps an indication of the merging of Swift Creek culture with indigenous Weeden Island peoples in Northwest Florida.

Other artifacts found in caches in the Swift Creek mounds include the Swift Creek points, the bifacial knives, and sheets of mica. Although the caching of sacred vessels in the mounds was done because the vessels had religious significance, these artifacts probably were simply items cached to accompany the dead. Stone and fired-clay elbow pipes also are occasionally placed with burials.

In several Swift Creek mounds, conch-shell drinking cups occur with pottery caches. The cups are identical to those in use during the later Mississippian period in the Southeast. Such cups were ritual items and served as containers for drinking black drink, the ceremonial tea or medicine made from leaves of the *Ilex vomitoria* plant. When the cups are found in mounds they are generally accompanied by small bowl-size ceremonial vessels. It is quite likely that the caching of the cups and ceramic vessels in the mounds was done as some sort of a discarding ceremony of sacred vessels. Temples or charnel houses containing both dead individuals and ceremonial items might have been periodically cleaned and the items deposited in the ceremonial mound where they did not pose a threat to the well-being of individuals not qualified to deal with such objects. Similar distribution of conch-shell cups with ceremonial vessels in Yent mounds suggests that black drink may have had a long history among the prehistoric peoples of Florida.

Wakulla Weeden Island Culture

The tri-state or Wakulla Weeden Island culture was first recognized by Joseph R. Caldwell from his excavations at Fairchild's Landing on the lower Chattahoochee River. This culture, which dates from the Weeden Island 3—5 periods according to Percy and Brose's chronology, is ceramically characterized by the use of Wakulla Check Stamped pottery as the primary utilitarian ware. For the time being, Wakulla seems to be an appropriate tentative designation for the culture, although it is somewhat misleading since Wakulla County, from which the name for Wakulla Check Stamped pottery was originally derived, is on the coast. Distribution of this culture seems to be along the Flint River in Georgia as far north as Bainbridge, and along the Chattahoochee River as far north as the fall line. The southern extent of the culture seems to be in the Apalachicola River Valley at about Bristol, Florida—the point where the Torreya Ravines highlands region meets the coastal flatlands (Kelley n.d.; Milanich 1974). This region lies within the Weeden Island heartland. The Wakulla culture in Florida is adapted to the highland river valley forests of the coastal plain, especially the forests of the southwestern Dougherty Uplift—a physiographic region that extends diagonally across Georgia from Augusta down into Northwest Florida. Most likely, the Wakulla Weeden Island culture is related to the many check-stamped-pottery-making cultures of the eastern Alabama coastal plain, some of which are associated with Weeden Island ceremonial mounds.

Along with Cades Pond, the Wakulla culture is the other Weeden Island culture for which we have a relatively large amount of descriptive information regarding village life. Unfortunately, nearly all of these data come from a restricted environmental area, the Torreya Ravines region which stretches along the eastern side of the Apalachicola River from Chattahoochee, Florida, south to Bristol. Percy has carried out intensive archaeological surveys of sites in that region and has excavated portions of a large Wakulla village site located in Torreya State Park. Milanich also has excavated sites in the Torreya Ravines. The latter research focused on a very small hunting campsite and one household area adjacent to a much larger and earlier Weeden Island village. Little information is available on village life of the Wakulla peoples occupying environmental zones other than the ravines. It should be stressed that the information presented here, which is based on the research of Percy (1971a, 1971b) and that of Milanich (1974), may reflect only one portion of the Wakulla subsistence and settlement pattern.

Two types of Wakulla settlements are found in the ravines. One is small, sporadically used campsites. These are located along freshwater streams in the foothills of the ravines back from the Apalachicola River. Perhaps these sites were occupied by deer hunters for short periods of time. No floral or faunal remains were excavated at the one such site investigated, and no statements concerning season of occupation can be made. However, the close proximity of these camps to the larger villages—several kilometers—suggests that the two were not occupied at the same times of the year. It seems logical to assume that hunters so close to the base village would not camp out at night but would return to the village. Such reasoning may be incorrect, since it cannot be established at this time that the camps were occupied over the same general periods of time as the larger villages.

The two Torreya villages thus far excavated are quite similar in layout. Both are characterized by "hot spots" of artifacts (concentrations of midden from individual house sites) widely scattered over several hundred meters or more. At the Torreya State Park site, these house sites (at least 13 of them) are strung out in a roughly crescent-shaped line around the springheads of a small creek. Percy noted that this site was occupied during two distinct periods, Weeden Island 3 and 5, and that, although the community pattern was the same in both instances, the two villages were placed in spatially distinct areas. In both cases, the best estimate of houses occupied at any one time is five to seven. Small burial mounds were constructed near the villages, although these have not, as yet, been excavated.

The community pattern at the Weeden Island, Aspalaga site located farther north in the Torreya Ravines and examined by Milanich, is quite similar. Midden concentrations are thinly scattered over a roughly circular area about 900 m in diameter. At the center of this circle are three ceremonial mounds, all of which were excavated by C. B. Moore early in the twentieth century. Close to the mound area there is a dense horseshoe-shaped midden about 95 m long and 75 m wide. However, the dense midden and the mounds probably date earlier in time than the single household area excavated by Milanich. Surface collections from the dense midden and Moore's report (Moore 1903) both indicate a date before Weeden Island 3 times. The later, Wakulla period house sites are spread out like those at the Torreya site. The mounds and central midden might have stood as a landmark around which later (Weeden Island 3–5) houses were built.

Milanich's excavations adjacent to the central midden focused on one household area including the house itself, associated outside pits and work areas, and a freshwater shell midden dump. The area has been given the separate name of Sycamore to differentiate it from the earlier mound—village complex. Subsistence information gathered from the house and dump and the style of the house itself—a wigwam or hothouse of the common Southeast Indian type—suggests that the house was occupied during the fall and winter months. An adjacent eroded area of dense midden may have been the location of a warm weather structure. No subsistence remains were recovered to support this possibility.

The subsistence pattern reconstructed from the household excavations shows a tremendous reliance on deer and acorns. In projected meat weight (ignoring shellfish), venison accounts for 88.2% of the meat diet. Other mammals eaten include black bear, raccoon, rodent, wood rat, squirrel, and opossum. Turtles comprise the second largest meat source. In addition, some freshwater fish, freshwater mussels and clams, and turkeys were taken and used for food. Plants eaten were acorns, walnuts, hickory nuts, and wild plums. Some maize kernels were recovered, indicating that horticulture was practiced, as would be expected. The Wakulla peoples seem to have exploited the river valley hardwood forests and the small streams draining into the Apalachicola. Radiocarbon dates from the house placed its occupation within the latter portion of the ninth century A.D.

The types of foods represented in the Aspalaga house strongly suggest a fall—winter occupation and not the whole year, as noted before. The use of summer houses apart from winter houses is common throughout the Southeast during the early historic period, and seems to be an established household pattern. Additional excavation at either of the Torreya Ravines Wakulla sites may provide the needed information to clarify this point. The heavy reliance on deer during a portion of the year also is common. Deer can be taken year-round with great success. However, during the fall rutting season they tend to be somewhat more inquisitive and may be taken more easily. Hunting, though, remains a fall—winter occupation, since the spring and summer months were spent largely in horticultural activities. After the harvest was completed in the late summer, males could turn toward other subsistence pursuits.

The Aspalaga house structure was an oval wigwam about 5.8 by 8.8 m; wall support-posts were placed about 60—90 cm apart. A description by John Lawson of a tenth century Siouian wigwam from Virginia amply portrays the Sycamore house:

> These savages live in wigwams, or cabins built of bark which are made round, like an oven, to prevent any damage by hard gales of wind. They make the fire in the middle of the house and have a hole at the top of the roof right above the fire, to let out the smoke. These dwellings are as hot as stoves, where the Indians sleep and sweat all night. The floors thereof are never paved or swept, so that they have always a loose earth on them.
>
> The bark they make their cabins withal, is generally cypress or red or white cedar; and sometimes, when they are a great way from any of these woods, they make use of pine bark, which is the worser sort. In building these fabrics, they get very long poles of pine, cedar, hickory, or any other wood that will bend; these are the thickness of the small of a man's leg, at the thickest end, which they generally strip of the bark, and warm them well in the fire, which makes them touch and fit to bend. Afterwards, they stick the thickest end of them in the ground about two yards asunder, in a circular form, the distance they design the cabin to be (which is not always round, but sometimes oval) then they bend the tops and bring them together, and bind their ends with bark of trees, that is proper for that use, as elm is, or sometimes the moss that

grows on the trees, and is a yard or two long, and never rots; then they brace them with other poles to make them strong, afterwards they cover them all over with bark so that they are very warm and tight; and will keep firm against all the weathers that blow . . . [Lawson quoted in Swanton 1946:410−411].

The long axis of the house was oriented north−south. A doorway seems to have been present on the east side leading out to a work area immediately adjacent to the house. On the north end of the house, artifact distribution and posthole placement indicated that perhaps another opening was present. A large irregularly shaped shallow hearth for heating the house, and for cooking, was present in the central portion of the structure. Several circular fire pits with straight sides and basin-shaped bottoms also had been used to cook in; later they were filled in with discarded refuse. One such pit was inside of the house, and two outside on the east side. In addition to cooking, the outside fire pits might have been used to generate smoke for meat preservation. One was centered among several postmolds, indicating, perhaps, the presence of a drying rack.

Several large, deep, circular storage pits (or wells) with straight sides and flat bottoms, were also spaced about the east, north, and south sides of the house. One such pit, containing large amounts of oxidized acorn meats and shells as well as hickory shells, maize kernels, and a plum seed, was inside of the house. The depth of these pits varied from about 76 cm deep to more than 90 cm deep. The depth seems to vary according to the depth of an almost impermeable clay zone which underlay the house; the deeper the clay stratum, the deeper the pit. Thus it is possible that the pits were dug to intersect the ground water table that periodically flowed above the clay.

The size of the house, its structural features, and the associated pits and artifacts all indicate that the structure was occupied during at least a portion of the year by a nuclear family. The quantity of debris suggests that the house was reoccupied over several years, perhaps as many as 10 or more.

About 27 m to the south of the house was a dump containing mostly shellfish but with food bones, potsherds, and other debris, including ash and charcoal present. The dump, accumulated over several years, represents garbage discarded by the occupants of the house. Most likely, the charcoal and ash were cleaned out of the house hearth and the fire pits.

A large assortment of pottery, tools, and other artifacts was recovered from the house. The lithic assemblage is probably typical of inland Weeden Island peoples in Northwest Florida. The pottery types are also typical of the Wakulla Weeden Island peoples, although their exact frequency of occurrence reflects their relative popularity at that time, in this case about A.D. 860. Utilitarian ware includes the following types in the quantities indicated (sample of 8383 sherds): Wakulla Check Stamped, 48%; sand-tempered plain, 21%; sand-tempered plain with burnished surface, 20%; Northwest Florida Cob Marked, 5%; Swift Creek Complicated Stamped, 2%; and linear check-stamped, West Florida Cord-marked, Thomas Simple Stamped, Keith Incised, Carrabelle Incised, Carrabelle Punctated, Tucker Ridge-pinched, together totaling 4% (Figure 21d−i, p. 122; Figure 22).

Nearly all of the lithic tools were made of local flint. About 10% showed evidence of thermal alteration. One flint blade appears to have been manufactured out of material quarried north in the Georgia Piedmont, as did several pieces of stone gorgets and a steatite sherd. None of the tools displayed a high degree of workmanship; all were worked only enough to make them functional. Only the Hernando projectile points showed any pressure retouch; the rest were roughly fashioned by the percussion method. The bow and arrow was used by the Wakulla peoples and may have been an important deer-hunting weapon. The small basally notched Hernando arrowheads (Bullen 1975:24) were used to tip the arrows. Tools included bifacial and unifacial end and side scrapers made from linear flakes and crude blades; turtle-backed scrapers made from expended cores; hafted, stemmed scrapers fashioned out of reworked projectile points or knives; and small flake scrapers. All of these scrapers were probably used to clean and process hides or in working wood or preparing split cane for making baskets. Small triangular knives, flake knives, and stemmed knives (the latter very similar in appearance to stemmed Archaic projectile points) were common tools used for cutting. River cobbles were fashioned into crude choppers and hammers. Foods such as nuts were processed on flat grinding stones, some made of granite, where they were ground with manos made from river cobbles or flint. Fist-size quartz river rocks were dried out to prevent their exploding and then used as boiling stones.

Other artifacts and ornaments used by the Wakulla Weeden Island peoples were hematite paint stones from which red pigment was taken to decorate pottery, and probably to paint other items; flat slate gorgets used as bow-string wrist guards or ornaments; shell pendants, both circular and shoehorn-shaped; and clay pipes. The pipes, made from fired local clay and measuring a little more than 2.5 cm in total diameter, had a small hole cast in them to draw the smoke through. The hole was made by placing a twig in the clay stem. During firing the twig burned out, leaving the hole. Pottery earspools more than 5 cm in diameter were worn by some individuals.

FIGURE 22. *Weeden Island pottery; a − c, Keith Incised; d − g, Weeden Island Plain rims.*

Information emerging from Brose's work in the Apalachicola drainage indicates that by A.D. 1100 the Wakulla Weeden Island culture was evolving into the Fort Walton culture. The latter, a Mississippian culture, is discussed in Chapter 8.

Weeden Island Ceremonialism and Sociopolitical Organization: An Overview

Weeden Island ceremonialism is thought to have evolved out of the earlier Yent and Green Point ceremonial complexes in northern Florida and adjacent regions of Alabama and Georgia. Sears (1956a) has noted similarities between Weeden Island ceramics and Troyville — Coles Creek wares, suggesting that the development of Weeden Island ceremonialism and sociopolitical organization was, perhaps, influenced by the diffusion of ideas eastward from the Lower Mississippi Valley cultures. However, later investigations at the McKeithen site in Columbia County in North Florida produced a series of dates from A.D. 200 — 700 which suggests that Weeden Island village life and ceremonialism in that region developed more independently of the Mississippi River Valley cultures than previously thought. However, contact between the two groups did occur, and ideas undoubtedly passed in both directions. Religion and sociopolitical organization together supported the behavioral patterns necessary for the maintenance of the Weeden Island economic system. Thus, after about A.D. 200 the Weeden Island region began to be characterized by new behavior patterns by which the Weeden Island populations adjusted to their environment and to other cultures.

Weeden Island society was probably organized into lineages and membership, household residence, inheritance patterns, and access to horticultural produce were most likely determined on the basis of female descent (i.e., an individual was a member of the same kinship group as his or her mother). Within Weeden Island society, some kinship groups and individuals were probably regarded as more important and having higher status than others. Early Weeden Island societies were not chiefdoms, but they were beginning to develop the more complex forms of social and political structure that would reach a florescence among the later Mississippian societies.

Data from Kolomoki, a site in Georgia, on differential status of individuals as reflected in burial practices, and ethnographic analogies suggest that the Weeden Island society occupying that site was organized into a chiefdom (Sears 1956a). That political unit was headed by a great chief who resided at the major ceremonial center of Kolomoki and who controlled the lesser chiefs and the villagers within his polity.

The relationship of the Kolomoki Weeden Island chiefdom to other Weeden Island groups is uncertain. Sears has hypothesized that the entire Weeden Island region was one polity with the Kolomoki site functioning as the major center. Status, in the form of certain ceramic wares, and other valued items such as exotic stone, was distributed out from Kolomoki to local and village chiefs. Other archaeologists argue that the Weeden Island region was divided into several separate political units with Kolomoki having greater importance because of its geographical position between the Florida Weeden Island peoples and the more northerly cultures of the Southeast. This location perhaps gave Kolomoki a favored trading position. A great deal more research needs to be completed before we can determine with confidence the nature of the Weeden Island political system(s), although evidence from the McKeithen Weeden Island region seems to clarify much of the uncertainty regarding the function of the early Weeden Island mounds in northern Florida. Data from the McKeithen site in North Florida are presented as archetypical of the northern Florida Weeden Island cultures.

The distribution of early Weeden Island sites in North Florida seems to be from modern-day highway U.S. 90 north and eastward toward the Okeefenokee Swamp. Smaller camps, especially late Weeden Island sites, are found within this region as well as south and west to the Suwannee and Santa Fe rivers. Early villages, ca. A.D. 200/300–700, appear to be nucleated settlements, often with one or more mounds present. A large number of late, post-A.D. 700 sites seem to be present. Like in the Torreya Ravines in Northwest Florida, many of these seem to be composed of scatterings of "hot spots," possible individual homesteads, situated along creeks. A number of small special-use camps extend out from both early and late settlements. Presently, Brenda J. Lavelle is completing analysis of extensive testing and survey of Weeden Island sites recently located in North Florida. At this time, most of our data concerning village and ceremonial life come from the McKeithen site, apparently the largest early period site and the only one with three mounds. Thirty weeks of mapping and excavation have been completed in the village (Kohler 1978) and 30 weeks have been spent in the excavation of all three mounds. Radiocarbon dates for the village bracket the occupation at about A.D. 200–750 (Kohler 1978:224).

The McKeithen site, covering approximately 20 ha, is composed of three sand mounds arranged in an isosceles triangle (Figure 23). The base, from Mound A to Mound C, is 290 m; from both of those mounds to Mound B, the apex of the triangle, is 270 m. The axis of this triangle (a perpendicular bisector drawn from Mound B to the base) points approx-

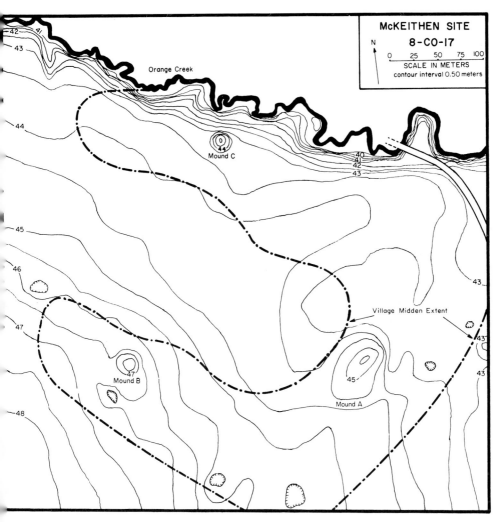

FIGURE 23. *McKeithen site, Columbia County.*

imately 62.5 degrees east of north, or approximately toward the rising sun at the summer solstice. Possible alignments of the site are being further investigated.

A horseshoe-shaped village midden extended around the three mounds (and under Mound B) with the open end toward the northwest. Extensive testing of the midden was carried out by Kohler (1978) and showed that cultural material was absent from an area approximately 60 m wide and 240 m long within the area bounded by the three mounds.

This probable plaza was oriented southeast to northwest approximately along the axis of the horseshoe-shaped village. A person standing in the flat plaza facing east would view mounds A and B to his or her left, both erected on a ridge paralleling the creek to the person's right. This ridge was about 2 m higher than the floor of the plaza and would have made both of the mounds appear higher than they were.

Kohler's sampling of the village was intended to produce evidence of social differences as measured by differential access to certain types of artifacts including types of pottery and trade goods. Kohler (1978:224−229) suggests that during the middle period of occupation, ca. A.D. 350−500, nonrandom distribution of status artifacts reached a peak; he postulates that a certain social group(s), perhaps lineage based, had greater control of certain exotic goods than other such groups. Thus, weak social stratification was present though power was not centralized. The society did not have the same complexity of structure as is known to have been present at later Mississippian sites in Florida. Most likely, the Weeden Island society at the McKeithen site was not organized into a chiefdom.

Excavation of the three mounds supports Kohler's data. The mounds were not tombs for certain elite persons (or chiefs) as was apparently the case at Mounds D and E at Kolomoki in Georgia. The three mounds all were built about A.D. 375 and were associated with mortuary and related activities which were apparently coordinated by a specialist who was awarded some special status and who had other duties. Support of the communal mortuary activities by the occupants of the village and perhaps those from outlying settlements served to promote social unification between lineage groups. Religious beliefs were a strong force in social control. Evidently the main period of village occupation, A.D. 350−500, encompasses the period of occupation of the mortuary center.

Mound B, the apex of the triangle formed by the three mounds, was originally a small rectangular platform mound 10.5 by 14.1 m with a height of less than 50 cm. This platform and the 6.9 by 10.2 m rectangular structure built on it were both oriented parallel to the base of the triangle formed by the mounds (and approximately perpendicular to a line drawn from the structure to the position of the sun at the summer solstice). The structure was built of pine posts placed in individual postholes. Perhaps thatched (no evidence of daub was found) with rounded corners, the structure apparently functioned as the residence of the religious specialist. An entrance to the house and a privacy screen shielding the doorway were on the opposite side of the structure from the plaza. Within the house were several hearths and small charred posts which may have been supports for benches positioned along the end walls. The number of posts suggests that the structure had been rebuilt at some point. Food bone, quartz pebbles, mica flecks, red ochre, pottery, and stone artifacts were found strewn about the floor of the structure, especially against the interior walls and outside of the entrance.

The resident of the house, a male about 30 years of age, died and was buried extended and on his back in a very shallow grave pit dug into the floor of the house; his feet were oriented along the axis of the mounds; arms were bent at the elbows with the palms up. Red ochre, possibly hair coloring, was beneath the skull as was a single piece of the occipital bone from another individual, perhaps part of a hair ornament. A small tomb composed of vertical posts set into the ground (with some sort of covering) surrounded him and was subsequently covered with a low mound of earth. The structure was then burned to the ground and much of the charred remains removed. A Weeden Island Zoned Red ceramic bird's head broken off of a pottery vessel was placed just outside the former wall of the structure closest to the individual's feet and facing the body. This head was along the site's axis. At some point in his life the individual buried in the structure had been shot in the left ilium with an arrow. The small triangular projectile point was still embedded in the bone which had grown around it. Apparently this wound was not the cause of death. A cap of earth was placed over the entire platform and the remains of the structure. This circular secondary mound was 17 m in diameter and originally was about 1.5 m high.

The ceramics recovered from the living floor of the structure included portions of six Weeden Island Zoned Red oblong plates, each decorated with a stylized bird motif; portions of a stylized "column" or carved post may also be present. It is easy to speculate that the raptorial bird represented on the plates and by the bird-head effigy was a symbol associated with the house's occupant, the presumed mortuary "director."

Mound A, the largest mound in extent, was originally a platform 32 by 42 m and averaging 50 cm in height. Its main function seems to have been as an area for the cleaning of human bodies. This process apparently involved interring bodies, allowing them to decompose, and then cleaning the bones for storage and later interment in Mound C. The area where this process took place measured 11 by 14 m and was centered on the back portion of the platform, the long axis of which was perpendicular to the long axis of Mound B.

This restrictive charnel area was characterized by multiple empty burial pits, most of which had been redug. Often as many as 10 pits were placed adjacent to one another, and were exhumed at the same time. Old pits also overlapped with new pits. From the size of the few single pits present, we can guess that the bodies were originally interred in flexed position. Large posts or markers, some more than 60 cm in diameter, were erected within the charnel area in the deep ends of long, narrow, sloping trenches. Perhaps they served as grave monuments or markers. In most cases these were removed at some point and perhaps reused. Numerous small fire pits dotted the floor of the charnel area and all were filled with ash and a combusted material that apparently is not wood. Fire pits which used wood as fuel were also present in one restricted area. Liberal amounts of red ochre were strewn about the activity floor which apparently had seen a great deal of use.

This burial preparation area was centered exactly over a portion of the primary mound that was made up of specially deposited layers of soil and organic material. These strata, composed of five thin layers of alternating grey-tan-grey-tan-grey sand were sandwiched between the layers of organic material. All of these strata overlay the submound humus and were under a layer approximately 20 cm thick of the sand on which the rest of the platform mound was constructed. One fire had been lit in a hearth on top of the specially prepared strata before the rest of the mound had been placed over them.

A pole screen 24 m long in a gently curving trench shielded the mortuary area from a portion of the village nearby. The screen did not block the view of the mortuary area from the plaza. When it became time to abandon the activities on the mound, all of the bones were removed and the pole screen is believed to have been torn down and the poles placed atop the mortuary area. A very large fire ensued which left the soil in the mortuary area scorched and which deposited a thick layer of ash in some places. The platform mound was then covered with a very large oval to rectangular mound cap 45 by 80 m which also extended over the adjacent midden opposite the screen. The cap was probably at least 2 m thick in the center.

The cleaned bones from Mound A are thought to have been stored in a charnel house erected on a small circular platform (Mound C), 19 m in diameter. Probably at the same time that Mound A was closed, the stored burials in the charnel house were removed, the house was burned and the remains were scattered around the edges of the primary mound. The burials, which consisted of bundled individuals, bundles of long bones, single skulls, masses of teeth and lower jaws, and individuals mixed together, were placed evenly at 1.5 m intervals around the edge of the circular platform mound and on and beside the southeast quadrant of the mound. Two individuals, still articulated and in flexed position (not cleaned?) were also interred. Along with the burials at least 18 Weeden Island vessels were placed on and beside the southeast quadrant; one other vessel, a Tucker Ridge-pinched bowl, was found under the mound on the west side. Numerous limestone and coarse sandstone rocks were also placed somewhere on the primary mound, but their exact position has been obliterated by other individuals digging in the mound. The entire platform mound and the deposits were then covered with a mound cap about 2 m thick and just large enough to cover the deposits.

The vessels placed in the mound included pedestaled effigies along with well-made Weeden Island Red, Incised, and Punctated vessels (Figures 24 — 26). Perhaps the latter were used either in the Mound A charnel area or in the Mound C charnel house in ritual purification ceremonies. The pedestaled effigies, nearly all with triangular cut-outs, may have functioned as "spirit guardians" for either place and might have been positioned on posts similar to the wooden carvings around the charnel platform at the Fort Center site in South Florida (see Chapter 7), which also dates from about A.D. 300 — 400.

The mounds at the McKeithen site are evidently not unique. Another very similar multiple mound complex with adjacent horseshoe-shaped village is the Aspalaga site whose mounds were excavated by C. B. Moore (1903:481 — 488). Like McKeithen, the Aspalaga site consists of three sand mounds arranged in a rough triangle about an apparent plaza. A fourth low mound may be a natural feature. The horseshoe-shaped village curves around two sides of this triangle and is characterized by dark soil. One mound, 30 by 33 m and slightly oval, contained at least 55 burials, including flexed, bundled burials, and single skulls, and a cache of pottery vessels was present on the east side. Vessels included Weeden Island Red, Zoned Red, Incised, Plain, Carrabelle Punctated, and Swift Creek Complicated Stamped in addition to an often illustrated Crystal River Incised vessel (e.g., Willey 1949a:390). Large rocks similar to those found at McKeithen were also recovered from the mound next to the pottery cache.

Moore reports that the other two mounds were low and "domicilliary in character," most likely platform mounds for structures later covered with mound caps. The parallels between the three McKeithen mounds and the Aspalaga mounds are obvious. Both must date from within the early Weeden Island period (probably sometime between A.D. 300 and 500), possibly from the same time, although Aspalaga may be slightly earlier. Both sites functioned as mortuary centers. A great deal more research is needed to determine whether or not the McKeithen — Aspalaga pattern is present elsewhere.

The patterned mounds with pottery caches found in North and Northwest Florida during the Weeden Island period do not seem to be found in peninsular Florida. Nor are platform mounds well-documented for the peninsula Gulf Coast for Weeden Island times, although they are

FIGURE 24. *Weeden Island pottery; a – c, e, Weeden Island Punctated; d, bird-head effigy, Mound C, McKeithen site.*

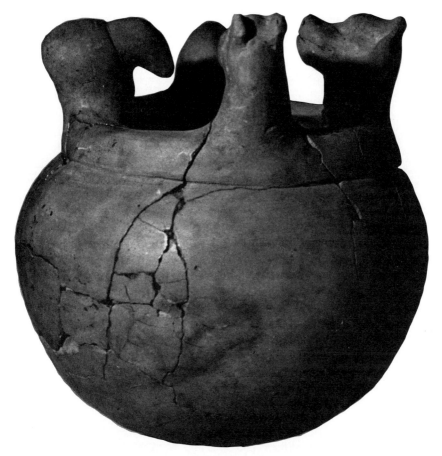

FIGURE 25. *Weeden Island Plain effigy vessel. From Mound C, McKeithen site. Vessel is 14 cm tall at lip.*

present in the interior Cades Pond culture. Along the coast, mounds of the continuous-use type and mounds deposited during one or more discrete construction ceremonies, continued to be used up into the Safety Harbor period. Most of these peninsula mounds contain a very large number of secondary bundle burials, in some cases hundreds of bodies. Age and gender of the individuals in the mound indicate a normal distribution; all individuals were apparently interred in the burial mounds. The mounds were perhaps used over many years.

The mounds excavated on the peninsular coast indicate that individuals, at death, were stored in charnel houses. At some point in time— perhaps at the death of a lineage head, a "priest," or simply when the

FIGURE 26. *Weeden Island Red derived bird-effigy vessel with triangular cut-outs. From Mound C, McKeithen site. Vessel is 22 cm tall at lip.*

structures were full—the accumulated bodies (stored as bundles after the flesh was removed) were placed in the mound. In other instances, bodies were placed in the mound one at a time as an individual died. Bodies were probably placed on the surface of the mound individually and covered with sand.

The use of charnel houses and mound burial appear to be somewhat similar in North and Peninsular Florida. The two subregions also share other traits, especially religious paraphernalia such as ceramic vessels which are well known from the detailed descriptions offered by Willey in his volume on the Florida Gulf Coast. Such pottery types include: Weeden Island Plain (vessel forms include a variety of jars, bowls, multicompartmental vessels, single and double-globed jars, and a variety of effigies; these latter include birds, especially ducks, humans, various quadrupeds, and gourds; some of the later effigies are freestanding forms with cut-out sections); Weeden Island Punctated (vessel forms include jars, a variety of short globular bowls, and some cylindrical vessels; the dot or triangular punctations form scrolls, geometric figures, and highly stylized animals and, perhaps, plants; in some specimens the punctations outline the figure or design); Weeden Island Incised (vessels include a large variety of bowl forms and jars, some of which have effigy adornos; generally the incising sets off the design which is the undecorated area; designs are of the same types as those on punctated vessels; some casuela bowl incised vessels are more than 45 cm in diameter at the mouth); Weeden Island Zoned Red (vessels are often effigies; bowls, plates, and jars also are common; the red design is outlined with a fine incised line; a variety of highly stylized motifs is present on the vessels, including animals and plants); and Weeden Island Red (vessels are most often bowls). In addition to these five types, a variety of other punctated and incised vessels appear in the burial mounds. Although some of these latter motifs are found on secular wares, the ceremonial forms are generally better-made specimens.

These vessels and effigies were probably used in rituals requiring preparation of sacred medicines, as well as in other ceremonial contexts. The cut-out effigy specimens, especially, could not have functioned as containers but seem to be sculptures—perhaps "spirit guardians of the dead" as suggested above. Complicated-stamped vessels also appear in Weeden Island ceremonial mounds. Although some may be late trade items from Georgia, others might well be specimens which had been retained in temples or charnel houses for many generations. Or, indeed, the early Weeden Island cultures overlap temporally with Swift Creek.

A variety of shell and stone ornaments and objects has also been found in Weeden Island burial mounds. Although some seem to be everyday items, such as tools or personal ornaments which accompany burials, others probably had ceremonial use and are found in the mounds in small caches. Such objects made from marine shell include discs, hammers, *Busycon* drinking cups, plummets, pendants, and beads. Greenstone celts and quartz crystals, both items traded into Florida from the piedmont region at least as far away as Atlanta, Georgia, also are found in mounds, although the latter occur only rarely.

As with the Green Point complex, caches of Weeden Island pottery vessels often are accompanied by one or more *Busycon* drinking cups, the latter thought to be for the taking of black drink during various rituals. The drinking of black drink, and perhaps other medicines, as part of an initiatory mound construction ceremony, is indicated from two early Weeden Island mounds. The first, the Davis Field mound in Calhoun County, is a mound which was constructed in two layers, each apparently deposited during separate construction ceremonies (Moore 1903:468–473). On the surface of the primary mound, a small mound (about 45 cm high and 2 m in diameter) had been deposited before the second layer was added. Lying on the top of this small mound were three small bowls; two shell drinking cups were placed on the side of the mound. Immediately adjacent to this cache was a hearth. All had been intentionally covered over with the secondary mound. These objects and their relative positions to one another suggest that some sort of a black drink ritual was held before the second mound construction ceremony took place. The fire may have been for the brewing of the medicine, although fires are known to have religious significance within themselves among Southeast Indians and were an integral part of nearly all Southeast ceremonies.

The second mound indicating black drink usage as part of a mound construction ceremony is the Hope Mound north of Tampa Bay (Smith 1971b:107–134). As at the Davis Mound, shell cups and ceramic vessels were found associated with a hearth on the surface of a primary mound which had been subsequently covered by the construction of a second mound layer. A large, deep vessel was excavated in place on the hearth. Around the hearth were one pan-shaped vessel (possibly for parching leaves), one miniature pot with a killed bottom, three gourd-shaped water jars (one killed), one large killed bowl, and one unkilled bowl. These were accompanied by six *Busycon* drinking cups. No doubt, sacred medicines were brewed and drunk before the second mound layer, with burials and religious paraphernalia placed in it, was deposited. Such a scene is very reminiscent of the burial scene portrayed by the Frenchman, Jacque Le Moyne, for the sixteenth-century Timucua Indians in East Florida (Lorant 1946:73).

The significance of "killing" or cutting holes in the bottoms of sacred vessels placed in mounds is not fully understood. Other items such as celts, shell ornaments, drinking cups, and figurines also were killed by smashing them prior to their deposition in the mound. Many prehistorians feel this practice was done to kill the spirit of the vessel or object so that it would accompany the spirit of the dead person interred in the mound to the next world. This is the same explanation offered for caches of killed goods in Yent mounds (see Chapter 4).

A second explanation for some of the "killed" items, especially sacred vessels, that are found in mound caches is that the objects were accidently broken. Because the items had supernatural power, they could be deposited only in specially prepared repositories away from secular areas. Such objects may have been stored after breaking until such time as a mound was constructed in which they could be placed. Caches of pottery vessels deposited in this manner consist of large sherds which are well mixed as to types, since the broken pots were stored together (and mixed) before being placed in the mound. Mounds, then, were viewed not so much as tombs for the dead, but as sacred, especially prepared repositories for supernaturally powerful materials—both bodies and objects—that had to be kept from harming living individuals.

A third explanation for the caches of destroyed or killed pottery vessels is that the sacred containers were intentionally destroyed, either by shattering them or by cutting holes in their bottoms, and then deposited in the mounds. At the time that the bodies accumulated in charnel houses were to be cleaned out and buried, other ritual items might also have been cleaned out, destroyed, and placed in the mound with the burials. The objects were killed or destroyed to prevent their reuse and/or to keep their "spirits" from harming the living or to signal an end to that particular charnel activity. This cleaning and refurbishing might have been done on a calendrical cycle, or simply at the time that a charnel house was filled and the contents were to be placed in the sacred repositories. Most likely, pottery caches resulted from both of these latter two scenarios.

In summary, our knowledge of Weeden Island ceremonialism is based largely on excavations carried out around the turn of the century by C. B. Moore, on Sears's Kolomoki excavations, and on work at the McKeithen site. There have been few projects in Florida during the modern era.

Our best information, that from Kolomoki and McKeithen, is from the early Weeden Island period, pre-A.D. 800. As yet we do not have definitive data on later mounds from the heartland region.

The Weeden Island ceremonial complex lasted until ca. A.D. 1100 in the Apalachicola Valley in Northwest Florida and possibly as late as A.D. 1200–1400 in portions of North and Peninsular Florida. Weeden Island ends with the development and/or diffusion of new social, political, and religious patterns into Northwest Florida and down the Gulf Coast to the Tampa Bay region. These new developments, part of the Mississippian complex appearing throughout most of the Southeast, are the subject of Chapter 9.

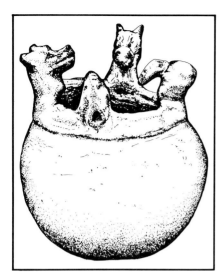

6

People of the Shell Mounds: Cultures of East and Central Florida

The distinctiveness of the aboriginal sites along the St. Johns River and the Atlantic coastal lagoon is best described by two of the early archaeologists who excavated in those sites, Andrew E. Douglass and Jeffries Wyman:

> Throughout the extent of this lagoon, on the one side or the other, appear the shell mounds or ridges left by the Aborigines in consuming shell fish during a vast number of years. Equal in frequency, but vastly inferior in dimensions, the sand mounds keep pace with the shell mounds. . . . It can hardly admit to question that the same people constructed both kinds [Douglass 1885:74−75].

And

> The shell deposits on the [St. Johns] river are entirely different as to their characteristics from the mounds of the sea coast. The last extend around the shores . . . and . . . are of gigantic proportions. They are composed exclusively of marine species. . . . The mounds on the river, on the contrary, consist exclusively of freshwater species.
>
> Anyone who for the first time views the larger ones [shell mounds], sometimes covering several acres . . . rising to the height of fifteen, twenty, or twenty-five feet, might well be excused for doubting that such immense quantities of small shells could have been brought together by human labor [Wyman 1875:9, 11].

Douglass and Wyman were among the first of the nineteenth-century visitors to East Florida who recognized that the "immense quantities of small shells" were piles of refuse left by the aborigines and not natural formations. Wyman, in addition to noting both the differences in composition of the coastal versus freshwater middens and the presence of the numerous sand burial mounds, astutely recognized another type of site which he referred to as "shell fields" (Wyman 1875:9, 11). Today we think that such fields were actually villages or camp locations. These shell fields, largely destroyed by modern construction activities and farming, represent midden refuse discarded within and around houses and other structures which were adjacent to the large distinctive shellfish dumps.

Wyman and other of the early archaeologists established that the shell heaps were deposited in discrete layers or strata, indicating a considerable period of time for their deposition. In addition, they recognized that some of the middens contained no aboriginal pottery in the lowest levels. By 1918 the observations of N. C. Nelson combined with those of the earlier archaeologists (especially Wyman, who actually quantified ceramic differences from arbitrary levels) produced the following sequence of aboriginal pottery in the shell middens of the St. Johns region (from earliest to latest): (1) no pottery; (2) pottery tempered with vegetable fibers; (3) disappearance of fiber tempering and the appearance of chalky ware pottery; and (4) the appearance of chalky ware pottery which was check-stamped on the surface (Goggin 1952:38−39).

During the last half century, archaeologists, most notably Bullen, have confirmed this sequence many times over and, through the use of radiocarbon dating in the last 25 years, they have established absolute dates for the rise and fall in popularity of the various ceramic types. Radiocarbon dating, an important analytical tool, has provided an excellent temporal framework over which we can describe and explain the evolution of the shell-midden peoples of East and Central Florida.

In Chapter 3 we described the shift in subsistence emphasis by Archaic populations from the North-Central Florida highlands to the St. Johns River area. It was hypothesized that this shift was due to a climatic change which affected forest cover and possibly the levels of lakes and other sources of water in the highlands. Most likely, this shift was gradual. From as early as 5000 B.C. the Archaic inhabitants of the highlands, as a part of their yearly round of hunting and gathering, must have camped on the St. Johns occasionally to fish, hunt, gather shellfish, and plant foods. As the shift from oaks to pines occurred in some of the highland forests, especially after ca. 4000 B.C., there was perhaps a decrease in the amount of food available per capita from those habitats. Shortly after 2000 B.C., as evidenced by the appearance of fired-clay pottery and the first utilization of marine resources—fish and shellfish— gathered from the coastal lagoons, year-round occupation of East Florida had occurred. This basic life-style—hunting, fishing, and collecting of wild resources, and occupation of villages and camps on the St. Johns River and on the coastal lagoon—persisted up into the historic period. The introduction or evolution of new traits, such as the change from gardening to more extensive forms of horticulture or the appearance of more complex forms of burial ceremonialism, are, of course, reflected in the archaeological record. However, when viewing the culture sequence of the St. Johns area, one is struck more by the similarities between the early and late cultures than by their differences. Clearly, the basic way of life established by 2000 B.C. or shortly after, was well suited to the occupation of East Florida.

The culture sequence for what is generally referred to by archaeologists as the St. Johns region is shown in Table 2. The applicability of this sequence to the Central Florida lake district in Lake, Orange, and Seminole counties has not been firmly established due to the paucity of archaeological research carried out in that region. However, the few excavations and the collections gathered to date strongly suggest that the prehistoric inhabitants of that district followed the same evolutionary sequence as did the St. Johns populations. No variations in ceramic styles or other artifact types have thus far been established, and the Central Florida lake district is included with East Florida in our discussion of the East Florida aborigines (Figure 27). Environmental similarities exist between the lake district and the middle portion of the St. Johns River. Thus, it is not surprising that the same archaeological cultures occupied both areas.

As noted in Chapter 2, the boundaries of the St. Johns region are hazy. Thus the Melbourne area displays traits of both East Florida and South Florida. Likewise, the south end of the lake district is transitional to the Kissimmee region cultures. The same is true for the west and north boundaries of the St. Johns region. These tangential cultural variations are given only passing notice in the following discussion of East and Central Florida.

Mount Taylor Culture

By 4000 B.C., as evidenced from radiocarbon dates from the Tick Island site (Bullen 1962; A. K. Bullen 1972:166; Jahn and Bullen 1978:22), the Archaic hunters and gatherers of North-Central Florida were spending more of their yearly rounds along the St. Johns River than they were in the highlands. This point in time marks the beginning of the Mount Taylor period in East Florida. The name "Mount Taylor" was derived by

TABLE 2
East Florida Culture Sequence[a]

Period	Dates	Distinguishing ceramics, other traits, and cultural influences
St. Johns IIc	A.D. 1513 – 1565	St. Johns Check Stamped pottery; European artifacts in some mounds. Burial mounds still present. Severe population reductions due to European diseases.
St. Johns IIb	A.D. 1300 – 1513	St. Johns Check Stamped pottery; some Fort Walton and Safety Harbor pottery and Southeastern Ceremonial Complex objects in mounds. Mississippian influences.
St. Johns IIa	A.D. 800 – 1300	Appearance of St. Johns Check Stamped pottery in villages and mounds; increased use of burial mounds; late Weeden Island pottery and copies in some mounds; some pottery caches in mounds.
St. Johns Ib	A.D. 500 – 800	Weeden Island, Dunns Creek Red (early) and St. Johns pottery in mounds; village ceramics almost all plain St. Johns ware; Weeden Island influences.
St. Johns Ia	A.D. 100 – 500	Village pottery nearly all plain St. Johns ware; Hopewellian – Yent complex objects in early mounds; some possible log tombs. Late Deptford and Swift Creek pottery traded and copies locally manufactured; Dunns Creek Red common. Weeden Island influences appear late.
St. Johns I	500 B.C. – A.D. 100	Village pottery all St. Johns ware, both plain and incised; some Deptford pottery or copies present. Burial mounds appear for first time. All pottery coiled.
Transitional	1200 – 500 B.C.	Village pottery both fiber and mixed fiber – sand tempered; some coiled; bowls common. Decorations include incising, pinching, triangular punctuations, side-lugs. Poverty Point influences.
Orange	2000 – 1000 B.C.	First appearance of pottery; hand-molding (some coiling late); fiber-tempered. Early pottery all plain, later forms incised. Shallow, flat-bottomed bowls and rectangular vessels. First occupation of coastal lagoon.
Mount Taylor	4000 – 2000 B.C.	No pottery. Lithic projectile points mostly stemmed Archaic varieties with triangular blades, Newnan points most common. Contact with other Archaic peoples; increased sedentism.

[a] Adapted from Goggin (1952) and Bullen (1972) with revisions.

FIGURE 27. *East Florida (St. Johns) region and sites discussed in text.*

Goggin from the Mount Taylor site in Volusia County excavated by C. B. Moore (1893:12–13, 113–115) in the late nineteenth century. The discussion of the Mount Taylor culture that follows is based on the work of Goggin (1952) and several important excavations carried out by Bullen (1955c, 1962) and by Bullen and Bryant (1965) along the St. Johns River. A paper by Cumbaa (1976) on Mount Taylor diet, especially the relative importance of shellfish within the diet, provided most of the data on food resource utilization.

The Mount Taylor period is that portion of the Archaic previous to the invention of fired-clay pottery, about 4000 B.C. to 2000 B.C. It was during this period that Archaic peoples began to occupy East Florida on a more permanent basis. Certainly, East Florida, especially the St. Johns River Valley, was frequently visited by hunters and shellfish-gatherers previous to this time. The commencement of the Mount Taylor period, however, marks the time when this sporadic occupation became more sedentary and village life in that region began.

It is very doubtful if these first villages established along the St. Johns were occupied year-round. Rather, there seems to have been seasonal shifts in occupation of older highland forest camps. Because shellfish spoil rapidly in the hotter months and because red tide is frequently present in those same months (those without an "r" in their names: May, June, July, and August), the best shellfish-gathering locales were probably not occupied during those months. The summer months were spent at locations better suited for hunting and/or collecting of other wild resources, some of which were in North-Central Florida.

The composition of the shell middens themselves suggest that shifts between gathering locations also occurred on a regular basis. When the shellfish population adjacent to a village was depleted, the villagers moved to another good location, and the cycle was repeated.

Cumbaa and others have noted that the dominant mollusc in the Mount Taylor shell middens is the pond snail *Viviparus georgianus* which composes 98–99% of the middens' volumes. The sizes of the snails in the middens decrease through time, indicating that food demands did not allow the depleted beds of snails to remain "fallow" long enough for smaller individuals to grow to maturity. During the Orange period the nutritive return from the small snails probably was not worth the effort expended to collect them at the time. The aborigines began to collect the shellfish found along the coastal lagoons, both coquina and oysters. By the St. Johns I period, ca. 500 B.C., the coastal sites used as shellfishing locations were of immense size.

It should be emphasized once again that this shift to coastal shellfish occurred after the end of the Mount Taylor period. There are no documented preceramic coastal shell middens.

Cumbaa has estimated that the snails contributed about 24% or less of the caloric intake to the Mount Taylor diet. Thus, despite the fact that shell refuse is so prominent, shellfish were not by any means all that was eaten, although they accounted for a relatively large percentage of the diet. Other food sources and their relative dietary importance include fish, 1.7%; deer, 24.2%; small mammals, 11.0%; birds, .7%; and various wild plants, 30.6%. These percentages probably remained much the same up to the historic period in East and Central Florida with the substitution of oysters for snails and cultigens for some of the wild plants.

Relatively few artifacts have been recovered from the Mount Taylor shell middens and we can only infer many aspects of subsistence technology. The presence of both steatite bannerstones and heavy, stemmed Archaic projectile points suggests use of the atlatl for hunting. No doubt traps and snares were also used. The points appear to be of two main types: well-made Newnans and somewhat cruder-made Florida Archaic Stemmed varieties (Bullen 1975:31−32). Bullen found three burials at Tick Island with stemmed points sticking in the skeletons, indicating that the points were used in warfare (with atlatls?) as well as for hunting.

Bone points are one of the most common tools found in the Mount Taylor shell middens. Their frequency indicates that, perhaps, they were general purpose tools used as tips on hunting and fishing spears as well as for extracting snails from their shells. Such points are very widespread among all Archaic shellfish-gathering cultures in the Southeast.

Other bone tools include splinter awls and awls which are round in cross-section. These also might have been useful in shellfish processing. A very few peg-topped bone pins, some engraved, have also been found.

The snails were probably collected by simply picking them off of the sand bottoms of the rivers or streams by hand and putting them in net carry-bags or in baskets. A few small flint flake scrapers are present in the middens. Their size and wear patterns suggest that they could have been used to scrape basket splints.

Shell tools, like stone and bone artifacts, are also rare. *Busycon* gouges and *Strombus* celts are known; *Busycon* hammers are rarer. Overall, the tool inventories and their relative scarcity closely resemble those of the west coast shellfish collectors as well as those present on the coasts of Georgia and South Carolina. The Florida assemblages, however, stand in marked contrast to the larger amounts of material items found in the shell middens of Archaic peoples living from the fall line inland, as evidenced by such sites as Stalling's Island in Georgia and Carlton Annis and Indian Knoll in Kentucky.

One of the most interesting aspects of the Mount Taylor culture is the presence of two sites of mass burial interments in specially prepared areas within shell middens. The only modern excavation of such a burial area, Bullen's work at Tick Island, revealed 175 flexed burials which had been interred in distinct groups at various times. C. B. Moore (1893:617−623) may have excavated a similar area at the Orange midden, also in the St. Johns River Valley. At Tick Island the burial ceremony appears to have been as follows. A shallow depression was scraped in the top of the shell midden. Groups of bodies, probably previously stored and wrapped in matting in flexed positions, were laid down in the depression and covered with sand. Some of the sand appears to have been impregnated with charcoal. Eventually, after other burial groups were added, later peoples deposited more shell refuse on top of the burial area, thoroughly covering it.

Mass burial of stored bodies is suggestive of the use of a charnel house for storage and preparation of bodies for burial. Bullen's excavations uncovered a row of postholes perhaps associated with such a structure. Although burial ceremonialism is present among other southeastern Archaic shellfish-gathering peoples, the Tick Island site is unique in having mass burials thought to be associated with a charnel house at such an early date. Radiocarbon dates associated with the burials were 3080 B.C., 3370 B.C., and 3500 B.C. (A. K. Bullen 1972:166), which average about 4160 – 4375 B.C. calendar years (Jahn and Bullen 1978:22).

Preliminary analysis of the skeletal population from Tick Island by A. K. Bullen (1972) showed several pathologies, including syphilitic-like osteopathologies (probably an early form of treponemal infection), healed bone fractures, and periostitis. The life of the Mount Taylor peoples was not an easy one.

Orange Culture

The beginning of the Orange period is marked by the appearance of fired-clay pottery which is tempered with vegetable fibers. Fiber-tempered pottery is very distinctive, and recognition of its temporal and geographical distribution has allowed archaeologists to date thoroughly the development and evolution of the Orange culture. Another important event of the Orange period is the occupation, apparently for the first time, of the Atlantic coastal strand. This event seems to have occurred at about 1500 B.C. or slightly later. As the snail beds along the St. Johns River were gradually depleted, the aborigines shifted their shellfish-gathering efforts to the lagoon where coquina shells were collected in huge quantities.

The Orange culture dates from the end of the Mount Taylor period at 2000 B.C. to the beginning of the St. Johns I period at 500 B.C. It is important to note that this 1500-year temporal division is composed of two very distinct periods: (1) the Orange period proper, 2000 B.C. to 1000 B.C., characterized by the exclusive use of fiber-tempered pottery (Figure 28); and, (2) the Florida Transitional period, 1200/1000 B.C. to 500 B.C. characterized by the use of fiber-tempered and sand- and fiber-tempered ceramics (the latter often referred to as semifiber tempered). Throughout the Transitional period, the use of fibers as a tempering agent continued to decline while the use of sand as a tempering agent increased. By 500 B.C. all pottery manufactured was sand tempered. The semifiber-tempered ceramics are also transitional from the hand-molded vessel shapes

FIGURE 28. a — c, *Orange Incised fiber-tempered pottery; and* **d,** *a St. Johns II wood carving of an owl. The owl is 1.91 m tall from bottom of talons to top of horns.*

of the Orange period to the coil-constructed vessels of the St. Johns period.

As is so often true with prehistoric aboriginal cultures in Florida, changes in pottery manufacturing techniques and surface decorations reflect other changes occurring in the cultures. Thus, the Transitional period was the time of a gradual shift from the Orange subsistence economy—based entirely on hunting, collecting, and fishing—to the St. Johns economic system characterized by the addition of some cultigens to the diet—perhaps squash—and the adoption of more settled village life.

The basic life-style of the Orange period was similar to that of the previous Mount Taylor culture—hunting, fishing, and gathering within the St. Johns River Valley with occasional hunting trips into the central hardwood forests farther west. The yearly round, which was somewhat altered by the shift of some winter shellfish-gathering activities from the St. Johns River to the coastal lagoon, was probably as follows. The winter months were spent mainly on the coast gathering coquina and some clams and oysters, and fishing. Hunting of deer, bear, wildcat, otter, and other animals, and collecting of other smaller animals—opossum, rabbit, turtle—and of some plants also occurred within the coastal strand. Domesticated dogs provided still another source of food. Longer hunting trips into the interior forests might also have been necessary in lean times during these months. Two coastal sites have produced remains of the (now extinct) great auk, as well as other birds which winter in Florida, confirming winter occupation of the sites. Birds taken offshore, including loon, common murre, and gannet, suggest use of dugouts for offshore bird-hunting. An occasional porpoise was also taken. Although there is no concrete archaeological evidence from East Florida, by analogy with Georgia coastal shellfish-collectors we can surmise that these winter camps were inhabited by one or more family groups. It is doubtful if more than 25 to 30 people occupied one of the sites at any one time. Due to the eventual depletion of shellfish and other resources, moving of these winter camps often became necessary. However, the same sites were returned to sporadically over many generations and the large shell middens accumulated. They are still visible today.

With the coming of spring, the house structures built for winter use were abandoned and the Orange people moved westward to the St. Johns River Valley. Central bases were established close to freshwater sources. Fishing and collecting of plants took place nearby. Longer trips were made for the purpose of hunting and collecting certain other plant and animal resources. Although most of the subsistence activities took place within several miles of the central camp, canoes were available for excursions up or down the river. In the late Transitional period, when limited horticulture may have been practiced, the late spring marked the time of preparation of fields and sowing of seeds. Horticultural produce, although possibly present, probably accounted for less than 5% of the total diet at this time.

Throughout the summer months hunting, collecting, and fishing activities continued. Berries, fruits, and nuts ripened and were collected in the late summer. Some were dried and stored for use in the fall. Cultigens (squashes and, perhaps, maize) were harvested near the end of the summer, but sufficient amounts were not available for storage for winter use. After the harvest, nut collecting probably increased. The fall was the time of relative plenty. Traders could be sent out to the west and north to barter marine shells and other items for stone tools and steatite vessels. By the late fall or early winter, the stored supplies were gone; the religious ceremonies which had taken place in late summer and early fall, and the fall trading expeditions, were over for another year. It was, once again, time to move into the winter camps.

The material culture of the Orange culture, excepting the presence of fired-clay pottery, is very similar to that of the Mount Taylor culture. And like the Mount Taylor culture, bone, shell, and stone tools are relatively rare in the shell middens. *Busycon* picks or hammers, *Strombus* celts, and bone pins and awls are among the most common artifacts recovered from excavations. The pins of the middle Orange period often are incised with the same designs found on the pottery vessels. Shell picks or hammers seem to increase through time and may reflect the increased coastal use of clam and oyster as food sources late in the Orange period. Other artifacts, all scarce, include Florida Archaic stemmed projectile points (some are very large and possibly were used as knives), drilled and incised turtle carapaces used as decorative items, hollowed antler sockets for tools, and bone fishhooks. Late in the Orange period, as well as in the Transitional period, stone tools (especially at the river valley sites) seem to increase, and knives and scrapers (some hafted) become more common. Baskets and woven-fiber mats were certainly present during the Orange and Transitional periods. Their impressions have been found on a number of clay pot bottoms (Benson 1959). Most commonly associated with the Orange culture are varieties of twilled basketry. Plaiting and twining seem to appear in the Transitional period and are present in later St. Johns sites.

Of all the artifacts found in Orange culture sites, the most common is pottery. Bullen has presented detailed descriptions of changes in fiber-tempered pottery through time (1955c, 1972). Documenting these changes is useful for the purpose of establishing subperiods within the

TABLE 3
Orange Culture Ceramic Sequence[a]

Period	Dates	Surface treatment decoration	Other characteristics or changes noted
Transitional	1200/1000 – 500 B.C.	Incised, pinched, triangular punctated, side-lugged.	Chalky St. Johns ware and mixed sand and fiber used as temper; some coiling; bowls most common.
Orange 4	1250 – 1000 B.C.	Simple incised motifs.	Some mixed sand and fiber tempering; early coiled forms.
Orange 3	1450 – 1250 B.C.	Incised straight lines, some parallel and slanting; some punctations or ticks; no Tick Island types.	Large, straight-sided and round-mouthed vessels with flat bottoms; some square or rectangular vessels, about 10 cm deep. Walls 4 – 13 mm thick; lips simple rounded or flattened; some lugs on sides below rims. Vessels resemble steatite vessels in form.
Orange 2	1650 – 1450 B.C.	Plain; incised concentric vertical diamonds with horizontal line; Tick Island styles—incised spirals with background punctations (rare).	Same as Orange 1.
Orange 1	2000 – 1650 B.C.	Plain.	Pottery hand-molded and fiber-tempered; thin walls 6 – 7 mm; simple rounded lips; shallow, flat-based and straight-sided bowls; rectangular containers (10 by 20 by 10 cm), some with lug-like appendages.

[a] Adapted from Bullen (1955c, 1972).

Orange—Transitional temporal range. A summary of these changes in decorative and manufacturing techniques is presented in Table 3. Such detailed ceramic information can provide the temporal basis for future studies in the St. Johns region documenting the cultural dynamics of the evolution of hunters and gatherers into later farming populations.

St. Johns Culture

The St. Johns culture in East and Central Florida spans two millennia, from 500 B.C. to A.D. 1565. During this period pottery styles and other traits rose and fell in popularity, some gradually and others abruptly. These changes, the appearance of some traits and the disappearance of others, have allowed archaeologists to define six temporal periods within the 2000-year span of the St. Johns culture. It is no coincidence that these periods often are coeval with other periods elsewhere in Florida, especially North and Northwest Florida. This is due to three related factors: (a) ceramic change usually is a reflection of other cultural changes; (b) the major cultural developments in the Southeast reached their zenith in Florida among the northern Florida cultures, diffusing out from that major region into other areas of Florida; and (c) these new ideas led to changes in the St. Johns culture, changes reflected in the pottery of East and Central Florida. Thus the St. Johns IA period is temporarily equivalent to the Florida Yent—Hopewellian period; St. Johns IIA is equivalent to the late Weeden Island period, and so forth. The various St. Johns periods, their approximate dates, external cultural influences, and distinguishing ceramic types can be found in Table 2, p. 148.

It is extremely important to note that different types of cultural influences cause different types of trait changes. Thus, the introduction of Deptford ceramic styles (and possibly maize horticulture) is related to the appearance of certain Deptford ceramic traits on St. Johns village pottery. Later, the influence of Hopewellianism in Florida leads to the use of new ceremonial ceramics for ceremonial—religious use. While some influences are simply inventions adapted for everyday use, others are religious beliefs and practices which bring changes in the sacred aspects of the culture. Because the St. Johns culture is somewhat geographically and culturally marginal to the major Southeast aboriginal developments, it provides an important and useful cultural reflection of the form, sequence, and spread of these ceramic horizons, ceremonial complexes, and other newly appearing traits.

The basic way of life established in East Florida by the end of the Transitional period continued and was elaborated upon during the period of the succeeding St. Johns culture. Inventions and new ideas—the latter most evident in the appearance of new ceramic styles—in combination with larger populations and increased use of domesticated plants, led to the evolution of more and more complex forms of St. Johns culture. The greatest complexity, typified by ceremonial mound centers and chiefdom level of social organization, was reached by the time of contact with European cultures in the early sixteenth century. After that, due to population decline and other changes, the indigenous culture pattern quickly changed. The cultures of this contact period are discussed in Chapter 9.

Few village sites of the St. Johns I—IB periods have been excavated. However, there is no reason to believe that most tools and other artifacts in use at that time differed significantly from those found associated with earlier Transitional villages or later St. Johns II villages. In fact, from the Orange period on, shell tools, bone pins, bone awls, bone points, and pottery are the most common artifacts. Occasionally, stone points, hollow bone sockets, plummets, or net weights are also found but these are rare. Shell picks or gouges do seem to increase during the St. Johns period, perhaps as a result of increased use of oysters and the need for an opening tool.

Sites of the St. Johns culture are located along the St. Johns River and its tributaries and along the coastal lagoon, a pattern like that of the preceding culture. Perhaps due to changed sea levels, and the establishment of present-day ecology in the lagoon region, oysters must have occurred for the first time in huge quantities. It was in the St. Johns period that oysters became the dominant shellfish species utilized for food, and oysters comprise from 60 to more than 90% of the bulk of the shell heaps in the coastal middens. These coastal camps probably still were occupied mainly during the colder months; spring and summer horticultural villages were located in the St. Johns River Valley and around the many lakes in Central Florida.

The increased population of the early St. Johns periods is reflected in the establishment of villages in the northern St. Johns River Valley. Previously, the lower St. Johns above Palatka was only sparsely inhabited; the Orange culture was centered along the central portion of the river. During the St. Johns I—IB periods, however, there seems to have been a population shift into the northern portion of the valley. Most likely, this was due to the need for more land to support the increased populations.

The presence of burial mounds and larger villages on or near the coast, as well as in the valley by St. Johns IB times, suggest that at some locations coastal villages did occur. The Tomoka River locality may have been the scene of such villages. Other populations, however, moved seasonally from river to coast. Such seasonal movements were common along all of the Southeast Atlantic Coast at the time of European contact, and appear to have been the most efficient way for the indigenous populations to carry on horticulture and still be able to exploit the rich resources of the coastal strand. Continual movement between inland and coastal locales must have occurred.

The coastal shell heaps, composed mainly of oysters left by the St. Johns people, constitute the largest middens in the United States. The most extensive of these middens is Turtle Mound near New Smyrna. Before its partial destruction during the late nineteenth and twentieth centuries, various observers estimated its height at as much as 25 m. It served as a landmark for sailors from early in the sixteenth century and was known to the Indians as the mound of Surruque.

Archaeological investigations in these coastal shell heaps indicate that by far the most extensive occupations occurred during the St. Johns IIA and IIB periods, the time of the largest populations. Excavation of sites such as Castle Windy (Bullen and Sleight 1959) and Green Mound (Bullen and Sleight 1960) have determined the nature of these heaps and provided important information on the coastal subsistence pattern. The inland sites are still little-known, however, since few have been excavated. Animals eaten for food at the coastal sites include deer, turkey, raccoons, opossum, rabbits, wildcats, and a variety of fish, especially snook, mullet, shark, and redfish. An occasional porpoise was also caught for food. Birds that were utilized for food constitute an impressive list: loon, gannet, double-crested cormorant, duck, black brant, turkey vulture, razor-bill auk, herring gull, black-back gull, glaucous gull, laughing gull, wood ibis, brown pelican, great blue heron, bald eagle, and great auk—the latter extinct today.

A tantalizing glimpse at inland subsistence patterns is provided by pottery effigies excavated from a ceremonial cache within a mound at the Thursby Mound site (Moore 1894a:69 – 81). These fired-clay, toylike effigies were modeled in the forms of corncobs, squash, gourds, and acorns, as well as several animal species. Corncob-marked pottery from the St. Johns area also verifies the presence of maize horticulture. The same wild plant and animal species were utilized from the Mount Taylor period through the time of the St. Johns culture into the historic period. And the same techniques for collecting, snaring, hunting, and fishing would also have been used over this 5-millennium span. This perhaps explains why few changes in artifact inventories occurred.

St. Johns ceremonialism appears to have been derived from indigenous elements evolved in the St. Johns region in combination with outside influences such as Hopewellianism and Weeden Islandism. As horticulture became more important to the culture, so did political and social organization become more complex. Such changes were, of course, accompanied by changes in ceremonialism. As would be expected, ceremonialism at the end of the St. Johns IIB period was much more complex than the ceremonialism practiced 2 millennia earlier.

Much of our knowledge of St. Johns ceremonialism has been derived from the early excavations of C. B. Moore which have subsequently been interpreted by Goggin (1952). The discussion which follows is based largely on Goggin's synthesis.

The earliest evidence of mound construction in the St. Johns region is from the St. Johns I period and correlates with the presumed incorporation of limited horticulture into the subsistence system. Undoubtedly, as with other southeastern cultures, fertility ceremonialism and calendrically ordered religious activities increased as horticulture became established. Also, as with most other southeastern cultures, our knowledge of ceremonial life is derived almost solely from the excavation of burial and ceremonial mounds and the materials contained in these mounds. Thus, those ceremonial traits associated with mound structures and the religious paraphernalia placed in the mounds are relatively well known compared to those other aspects of ceremonial behavior which cannot be recovered archaeologically.

Goggin (1952) describes the earliest St. Johns I period burial mounds as low rises or truncated cones usually less than 1.2 m in height, although a few are as high as 3.6 m. Deposits of hematite, a mineral continually associated with St. Johns ceremonialism up into the historic period, were often placed in the mound. Use of a charnel house for burial preparation is indicated by the presence of secondary bundled burials in the mounds. Occasionally, primary flexed or extended burials or cremations were placed in the ceremonial mounds, but these are rare. Burials in the mounds number from 2 to 100, although most mounds contain less than 25 individuals.

Few grave goods are present in the St. Johns I mounds, and there is no indication that only high-ranking individuals in the society were afforded mound burial. Everyone may have been placed in mounds. The burial ritual seems to have been a simple one: Bodies were stored and cleaned in a charnel house; later, the stored bodies were placed in a mound en masse. The same mound might be used more than once for the mass deposition. Hematite usage and charnel-house burial preparation are both traits which date back to the Mount Taylor culture.

After A.D. 100, during the St. Johns IA period, new ideas entered East Florida. Exotic items were acquired through the Hopewellian trade network, and these were often placed in caches in the mounds as well as with individuals. Dunns Creek Red and St. Johns Plain vessels, some with Deptford tetrapods, and Deptford vessels acquired through trade were placed in the mounds. Check- and simple-stamped motifs were often copied on St. Johns vessels. As with the late Deptford cultures on the Gulf Coast, Yent complex-related paraphernalia was also placed in the mounds, either with individuals or in caches. Mica and galena, copper-covered animal jaws and wooden effigies, greenstone celts, and quartz plummets all have been found in the St. Johns IA mounds in small quantities. Other known specimens include copper discs, a copper cymbal-shaped earspool, and a bird-effigy elbow pipe. Indigenous items, such as shell columella beads and shell drinking cups, tools, and pendants also were deposited in the mounds. The mounds of this period tend to be larger than those of the St. Johns I period and all are constructed in the shape of truncated cones. In the later mounds of this period, Swift Creek Complicated Stamped vessels and Swift Creek motifs on St. Johns vessels begin to replace the Deptford-related vessels as the exotic ceremonial ware.

The partial excavation of two late St. Johns IA or early IB mounds by Bullen, Bullen, and Bryant (1967) has provided interesting information on mound structure. The mounds, located at the Ross Hammock site on the coastal lagoon in Volusia County, were constructed of dirt scooped up from moatlike borrow pits immediately surrounding the mounds. As is typical of most mounds dating from this time, the copper and other exotic objects previously available, are not found—a reflection of the breakdown of the Hopewellian trade network. Another horizon marker for the early IB period is the increase in Dunns Creek Red Ware for ceremonial and village use, a trait also observable in Cades Pond mounds in North-Central Florida, and in the early Weeden Island mounds on the peninsular Gulf Coast. In the most extensively excavated mound at Ross Hammock, the archaeologists encountered what might have been a covered-over interior structure. Such interior structures, possibly tombs, are known from a large number of Hopewellian-related sites in the Southeast. Exact identification of the Volusia County structure, however, awaits future excavation.

Burials in the outer portion of the Ross Hammock mound were both mass and single interred, flexed burials. Again, charnel houses may have been employed to store bodies before burial, although the burials were evidently not defleshed before deposition in the mound.

Within the St. Johns IB period, the growth and spread of Weeden Islandism is reflected in the types of exotic pottery placed in the mounds. Late varieties of Swift Creek Complicated Stamped, Tucker Ridge-pinched, and Weeden Island ceremonial vessels were utilized and then placed in the mounds along with St. Johns Plain and Dunns Creek Red pots. Stone celts remained in use although other objects previously traded southward, such as copper ornaments, were no longer obtained. Several stone slab grinding stones have been found.

Undoubtedly changes in Weeden Islandism occurring about A.D. 800 were at least partially responsible for several changes in St. Johns IIA village and ceremonial life. Check-stamped pottery, a horizon marker for late Weeden Island cultures in the Southeast, became the primary form of decorated village pottery (Figure 29e−g). The formation and spread of Weeden Islandism was most likely based on more extensive forms of horticulture, and these new subsistence ideas also found their way into East Florida. This accounts for the increase in the number and size of St. Johns IIA villages over those of the earlier St. Johns cultures. Mounds also became larger, and it appears that ceremonial mound burial was restricted to a certain class of individuals, perhaps the members of the ranking family group. Weeden Island vessels and copies of Weeden Island decorative motifs become more common in the mounds in the St. Johns IIA period. East-side pottery deposits and the practice of constructing mounds in one or two discrete ceremonies were also present in East Florida at this time. However, the amounts of grave goods, the nature of the caches, and the size of the mounds all were not as large or elaborate as they were among Weeden Island peoples. Just as the peoples of coastal strand peninsular Florida remained outside of the mainstream of Weeden Island developments, so were the St. Johns II cultures removed from the cultural and political mainstream. No doubt, the specialized nature of their subsistence system did not allow them to evolve quite to the complexity of those peoples living in the inland, highland forests.

One of the few St. Johns IIA mounds investigated in modern times is the Walker Point Mound on Amelia Island (Hemmings and Deagan 1973). Like many of the mounds reported on by C. B. Moore, the Walker Point Mound was a conical mound composed of a lower submound stratum which contained burials and an upper zone of hematite-impregnated sand. This upper red-to-pink layer served to cap the mound. Burials were extended, flexed, and bundled. Fragments of skeletal material, such as teeth, cranial fragments, and phalanges were also found in the pink zone. These may have been "cleanings" left over from burial preparation in a charnel house and transferred to the mound when the other burials were interred.

It seems likely that the St. Johns IIA mounds of this type were constructed in a single ceremony which involved primary burial of a high-ranking individual. The burial was accompanied by (perhaps) family members and other relatives and individuals who had died previously

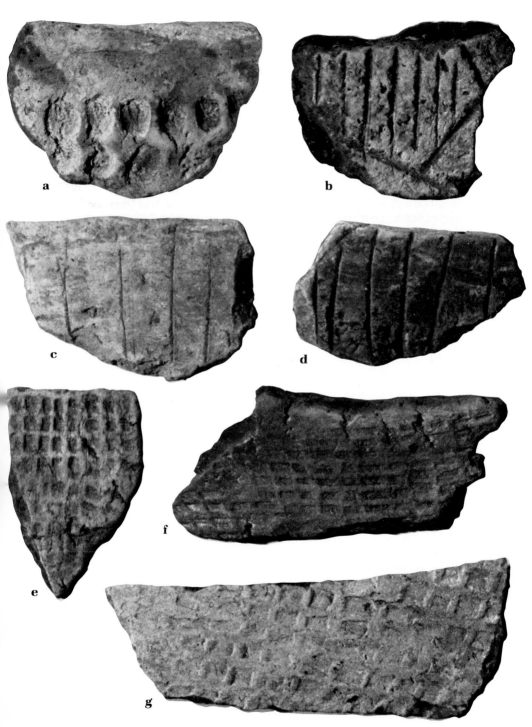

FIGURE 29. *St. Johns pottery; a, St. Johns Pinched; b — d, St. Johns Incised; e — g, St. Johns Check Stamped.*

and been prepared and stored in a charnel house. Such a ceremony is reminiscent of the burial of a chief described by the Frenchman Jacques Le Moyne in the 1560s in the vicinity of Jacksonville (Lorant 1946:115).

Ceremonialism of the St. Johns IIB period, A.D. 1300−1513, is characterized by the adoption of some Mississippian traits. It is after this period, after the time of contact with various European explorers, that the severe population decline which ended the aboriginal patterns of the East Florida Indian took place.

Several large ceremonial mounds, some undoubtedly parts of ceremonial centers similar to those found elsewhere in the Southeast, were excavated by C. B. Moore in the 1890s. The presence of such centers and the materials found in them indicate that the St. Johns region was organized into complex societies, and that some impetus for such organization came from contact with other Southeast Mississippian peoples. Art motifs and objects found by Moore in the Mt. Royal Mound on the St. Johns River in Putnam County are identical to Southern Cult motifs and objects found elsewhere in the eastern United States. The Saturiwa Indians described in the Spanish and French documents of the post-1562 period are the remnants of one such St. Johns Mississippian culture.

The three best known St. Johns IIB ceremonial mounds—all excavated by C. B. Moore in the 1890s (1894a, 1894b)—are the Shields Mound (also called "mound near Mill Cove") in Duval County, Mt. Royal in Putnam County, and the Thursby Mound in Volusia County. All of the mounds are located on the St. Johns River. The Shields Mound is a typical Mississippian truncated pyramidal mound with a ramp leading up one side. The square base measured roughly 60 m on a side (Moore 1894b: 204−205). Evidently built in several stages, the mound must have served as the base for an elevated structure. Moore's excavations revealed about 150 badly decomposed burials, indicating a ceremonial−burial function for the mound. Such truncated pyramidal mounds are common to Florida during the post-A.D. 1000 period. The beginning date of A.D. 1300 for St. Johns IIB probably should be moved back closer to A.D. 1100, based on new data from Mississippian cultures in Northwest Florida (see Chapter 8).

The famous Mt. Royal site, excavated to a large extent by C. B. Moore in two field seasons, contained a copper plate displaying Southern Cult forked eye motifs identical to those found at other Southeast Mississippian sites. Other copper objects (beads and ornaments) were also found, indicating that once again, as during the Hopewellian period, widespread trade networks were operating in the eastern United States.

At the time of Moore, the mound was 4.8 m in height and 53 m in diameter. One of the most intriguing features of the site is a causeway leading 800 m from the mound to a pond which may have been dug by the Indians. The causeway, which varies from 4 to 8 m across, was built by scraping up soil from the ground surface and piling it on both sides of the causeway. These parallel piles or, more correctly, ridges were nearly a meter high and as much as 4 m wide. Similar ridge construction and artificial ponds have both been identified from sites in the Lake Okeechobee Basin (see Chapter 7) where parallel ridges and causeways are quite common. As with other late St. Johns mounds, the Mt. Royal Mound appears to have been capped with a hematite-impregnated sand stratum.

Artifacts in the mound were deposited both in separate small caches and with burials. The distribution of these objects suggests that the mound was constructed during at least several distinct building phases before it was capped, although the deteriorated nature of the burials in the mound makes it difficult to surmise the relationship of burials to one another. Artifacts in the mound included *Busycon* shells (none of which were made into drinking cups, although many seem to have been "killed"), greenstone celts, spatulate greenstone celts, ceramic biconical tubes, and numerous fired-clay vessels. The latter were constructed into a variety of unique shapes and must have had special ceremonial use, such as for the brewing and drinking of black drink or other ceremonial teas. As suggested for other Florida cultures, the taking of medicines must have been an important burial—ceremonial ritual.

The Thursby Mound is a truncated cone 4.2 m high and about 29 m in diameter. A shell causeway was constructed from the mound to the nearby St. Johns River. Such shell causeways are very common in Southwest Florida in the area of the historic Calusa Indians. The specialized ceremonial constructions at the Thursby Mound and at Mt. Royal both suggest that during the St. Johns IIB period, contact with the complex cultures in South Florida was ongoing. The presence in the Thursby Mound of gold and silver ornaments is also indicative of trade with the proto-historic and historic period Calusa Indians.

The Thursby ceremonial mound contained numerous flexed burials, many in deteriorated condition. The exact construction sequence of the mound is not known, although Moore's description of strata indicates that at least a large portion of the mound was originally built in a single phase. Later additional layers were added, or caches of burials and artifacts were placed in the mound. The upper stratum contained some European materials, again giving evidence that such complex sites were occupied up into the early historic period. In addition to a large variety of uniquely shaped vessels, some quite similar to those from Mt. Royal, a cache of effigy figurines of plant products and animals was recovered by Moore. The materials are unique to Florida, although occasionally such small fired-clay figures have been recovered from Mississippian sites elsewhere in the Southeast. Some 48 separate animals were recovered, including 8 fishes and 10 turtles. Other animals represented by the figurines or by effigy vessels were felines (Florida panthers?), bears, squirrels, turkeys, dogs (?), and beavers (?). Some of the figurines are quite easy to identify as to species, while others are very crude. Plant figurines included acorns, gourds, and a corncob. Several of the effigy vessels resemble *Busycon* shells while others may represent sea urchins.

In 1955 a dragline operator pulled a large carved wooden "totem" out of the muck of the St. Johns River near the Thursby site (Bullen 1955b:61). Carved from a single log by burning the wood and then scraping with a shark's tooth tool and, possibly, a stone knife, the "totem" is an owl with "ear" tufts, either a great horned owl or a screech owl (see Figure 28, p. 153). The owl, which measures about 2 m from head to talons, is portrayed perched on a roost. Evidently originally stuck in the ground, the bottom end of the roost is rotted away. A radiocarbon date of A.D. 1300 was obtained from a wood sample from the carving.

It is doubtful if the carved figurine represents a clan totem, like the totem poles found elsewhere in the United States. Since the owl was generally viewed by southeastern aborigines as a symbol of evil or bad luck, the carving may have been placed near a ceremonial area, such as a charnel house, to keep away persons who were not allowed to deal with sacred paraphernalia. Although such carvings must have been reasonably common in Florida among all cultures, the only region where similar large wooden carvings have been recovered is the Lake Okeechobee Basin (see Chapter 7), in South Florida where they were associated with mortuary activities.

The complex ceremonialism, and related social and political systems of the St. Johns IIB period culture, must have been very similar to the systems practiced by the Safety Harbor and Fort Walton cultures, described in Chapter 8. Ethnohistorical reconstructions of the social and political organization of the historic descendents of all of these archaeological cultures—Eastern Timucua, Tocobaga, and Apalachee, respectively—show striking parallels to the historic, post-Mississippian Creek and Cherokee Indians to the north. Clearly, after A.D. 1200 much of the Southeast societies, including the St. Johns peoples, shared many aspects of their ceremonial and political lives while retaining their own specific subsistence adaptations. The St. Johns peoples who retained many of the same subsistence patterns practiced 5000 years ago by their ancestors, achieved at least some of the complexities which other Southeast cultures had evolved previous to the appearance of the Europeans.

Two Regional Adaptations: North-Central Florida and Lake Okeechobee Basin

Florida's varied environment is reflected in the different cultural adaptations present in the state during the prehistoric period. The North-Central highlands and the lowlands surrounding Lake Okeechobee are two such regions inhabited by distinctive cultures (Figure 30). In North-Central Florida this cultural adaptation was the Alachua tradition, a way of life based on the planting of crops and exploitation of the riverine and forest habitats. The Alachua peoples were horticulturalists who moved southward into northern Florida from southern Georgia. They were able physically to displace the indigenous Cades Pond people by more efficient use of the environment, for instance, more energy produced per person as a result of better horticultural techniques.

The replacement of Cades Pond by the Alachua tradition reflects a cultural phenomenon found in many environmental zones throughout the world—the demise of hunting and gathering and the rise of horticulture. Although Cades Pond people probably practiced horticulture on a small scale, the major portion of their subsistence was based on foods gathered and hunted from forest and riverine — swamp habitats. The horticultural Alachua peoples continued to exploit these same habitats, but in different ways. A comparison of the animal species used for food by the two cultures shows that horticulture allowed the Alachua peoples to spend much less time in exploitation of wild animal resources. As a consequence of this decreased emphasis on hunting and gathering, they became much more selective as to when and what they hunted and collected.

FIGURE 30. *Alachua and Lake Okeechobee Basin regions with sites discussed in text.*

In contrast to North-Central Florida and the intrusive Alachua tradition is the Lake Okeechobee Basin, which was probably first inhabited on a year-round basis about 1000 B.C. by Late Archaic peoples. The basin offers a combination of freshwater savannah and hammock habitats not found elsewhere in the state. A very specialized economic system developed in the basin, one based on hunting and gathering of a wide variety of animals, and on maize horticulture. This subsistence system provided the base for the distinctive village and ceremonial life present in the basin for the next 2 millennia.

Alachua Tradition

The Alachua tradition spans the time range from about A.D. 800, or slightly later, up to about A.D. 1700. This beginning date marks the time of the establishment of Alachua peoples in North-Central Florida. By 1700, disease and other factors had decimated the historic Timucuan-speaking descendants of the Alachua tradition. The various Timucuan groups are further discussed in Chapter 9.

The origins of the Alachua tradition seem to lie in southeastern and coastal Georgia. Similarities of projectile point types, and pottery manufacturing and decorating techniques, have been noted between the early Alachua tradition and the Wilmington and Savannah cultures on the Georgia coast. There is, however, a major problem in postulating a movement of Wilmington coastal dwellers, who lived primarily by exploitation of salt marsh and marine resources, into North-Central Florida where we find Alachua-tradition horticulturalists. Some surveys and limited tests (Milanich *et al.* 1976; Snow 1978) in southern Georgia well inland from the coast have clarified the situation by revealing the presence in the river valleys of ceramic complexes similar to Wilmington. These inland Georgia sites lie within the major physiographic region known as the Dougherty Uplift, a highlands zone that cuts diagonally across Georgia from Augusta down to Northwest Florida. This area has soils and river valleys suitable for exploitation by horticultural populations. The region is similar to North-Central Florida, although the latter has a much larger distribution of hardwood forests. It seems likely, then, that the Alachua-tradition peoples were inland Wilmington-related populations who moved into Florida from villages located within the Dougherty Uplift. Such a movement was probably more of a gradual expansion due to increasing populations than it was a rapid migration.

The geographical region occupied by the Alachua tradition corresponds quite well with the prehistoric distribution of hardwood forests in North-Central Florida. This region ranges from the Santa Fe River in the north, southward to about Belleview. The western and eastern boundaries are marked by the beginnings of the coastal scrub flatlands. In the east, these begin west of the St. Johns River; in the west, they begin at about a line drawn through Bronson and Trenton.

Although modern construction has altered the original distribution of the forests inhabited by the Alachua-tradition peoples, modern motorists can still note the changes in topography and flora when they drive out of the region to the east, west, and south. Due to its adaptation to the forested highlands, the Alachua tradition bears many similarities to the Woodland cultures located in other hardwood forest regions of the eastern United States.

Because the University of Florida is located at the approximate geo-graphical center of this region, there have been a number of surveys and excavations of Alachua-tradition sites carried out by archaeologists and students from the university. Goggin first recognized the distinctiveness of the culture in the late 1940s. Since that time a number of village sites spanning the time range of the culture have been excavated and re-ported. The remainder of this section relies heavily on the previously published work of these University of Florida archaeologists (Bullen 1949; Goggin 1949; Milanich 1971, 1972; Symes and Stephens 1965).

During the millennium that the Alachua-tradition peoples occupied North-Central Florida, the popularity of various pottery-decorating tech-niques increased and decreased as culturally defined styles changed. Because a large number of sites from different time periods have been excavated, a seriation table graphing these changes through time can be constructed. Such a table is invaluable in helping to date sites. Based on ceramic changes through time the Alachua tradition has been divided into four temporal periods. These period designations and their dates are Hickory Pond, A.D. 800 (or later) to A.D. 1250; Alachua, A.D. 1250 to A.D. 1600; Potano I, A.D. 1600 to A.D. 1630; Potano II, A.D. 1630 to A.D. 1700. (A seriation table can be found in Milanich 1971:28.)

The Hickory Pond and the Alachua periods are differentiated solely on the basis of changes in ceramic types. During the earlier Hickory Pond period, 45 – 70% of the pots manufactured had their surfaces roughened by malleating the wet clay (before firing) with a wooden paddle wrapped with twisted fiber cord. Through time, this technique at first rose and then fell in popularity. The beginning date of the Alachua period marks the point when a new surface treatment technique, that of malleating and/or scratching the pot surface with a dried corncob, became more popular. The Hickory Pond period is also distinguished by the presence of pots whose surfaces had been roughened, or malleated, with fabric-wrapped paddles, a technique not present during the Alachua period.

The change for the Alachua period into Potano I at A.D. 1600 is marked by the appearance of Spanish artifacts in village sites. Beginning about 1600, Spanish missionaries began visiting the North-Central Florida aborigines on a regular basis. Later, beginning in 1606, missions with resident priests were established. The aboriginal ceramics manufactured during the Potano I period are like those of the Alachua period. In fact, except for changes in the popularity of certain ceramic styles, there seems to be little or no change in Alachua tradition material culture and subsistence patterns from A.D. 800 until during the mission period, A.D. 1630. With the establishment of missions, there was a brief period in which traditional village locations were abandoned, and populations were consolidated into new mission villages. During the Potano II period, A.D. 1630 to 1700, a rapid population decrease occurred due to the introduction of European diseases, warfare, and maltreatment of the aborigines. Indians from Georgia began to move southward into northern Florida at this time, and the Potano II period is characterized both by the appearance of Georgia pottery types and by a decline in the number of lithic artifacts. It appears that after A.D. 1630, acculturation caused by the introduction of Spanish traits, and by traits brought by other Southeast Indians entering Florida, led to the disappearance of the traditional material culture of the historic Alachua tradition Indians. The Indians of North-Central Florida during the post-1600 mission period are discussed in Chapter 9.

Because Alachua tradition culture seems to change very little throughout the Hickory Pond, Alachua, and Potano I periods, a synchronic description of the culture can be offered as representative of the cultures during all of these periods. The information provided in what follows comes from seven sites in Alachua County which span these three periods.

Alachua-tradition villages are always found on high ground close to lakes or ponds. Sinkholes or small streams or other water sources also are often located nearby. These freshwater habitats provided both drinking water and access to a variety of fish, turtles, and a few species of wading birds. Catfish, gar, bowfin, blue gill, sunfish, and bream bones have all been identified from the Alachua-tradition villages, and represent sources of food. Many of the panfish remains recovered indicate that the fish were filleted and perhaps smoked. No fishhooks of any kind have been recovered from Alachua tradition sites, and, thus, it seems likely that the fish were taken in nets. The lack of extremely large bass, gar, and catfish (such as those found during the Cades Pond period), and the lack of bone fish leisters, suggest that fish-spearing was not important.

As with the Cades Pond peoples, a variety of turtles was taken from the water and from dry land. Box, snapping, cooter, softshell, mud, slider, musk, and gopher turtles all were eaten. Occasionally box turtle shells (without the carapace) were used as small cooking vessels. The freshwater habitats also provided mud eels and alligators.

Using snares, traps, and bows and arrows, which were tipped with small triangular projectile points made of whitish flint, the Alachua peoples caught and hunted a variety of animals which inhabited the hardwood forests and swamp forests of North-Central Florida. The white-tailed deer was probably the single most important meat source. Deer were butchered at the kill site and the haunches, hides, lower jaws (perhaps with tongue attached), and antlers (if present) were brought back to the village for distribution. At least some of the haunches were roasted over open fires inside of houses; no doubt, venison was also used in a variety of stews. Other mammals known to have been eaten are opossum, rabbit, raccoon, brown bear, skunk, round-tailed muskrat, and several species of squirrels. Hunting seems to have been for specific species rather than casual collecting of whatever species could be found. For example, hunters must have gone out after squirrels at one time, and deer at another. In refuse pits within living areas, the bones of five or more squirrels of several species have been found where they were dumped all at one time after being cleaned for eating.

Freshwater mussels were occasionally collected and eaten, as were wading birds. Unlike the Cades Pond people, birds were not a very important part of the Alachua diet.

The evidence for usage of wild plants by the prehistoric inhabitants of North-Central Florida is scarce. Palm berries, acorns, and hickory nuts have been found at archaeological sites. No doubt a very wide variety of other plants was also used, though evidence of their usage has not been preserved. The presence of maize horticulture comes from impressions of corncobs (some with kernels) on pot surfaces, descriptions by the early sixteenth-century Spanish explorers of stored maize, and charred kernels and cobs recovered from one Potano I site and one Potano II site. Villages were established where fertile, well-drained soils were readily available. Because the growing season is especially long in northern Florida, the aborigines generally planted two maize crops per year. In some years, large yields produced a surplus that could be stored and used until the next harvest. Early Spanish and French documents from the Alachua-tradition region state that beans, gourds, squash, and tobacco were also cultivated.

The horticultural season lasted from March, when the first planting took place, until August, when the final harvest was in. Although the villages were occupied on a permanent basis, a bad harvest necessitated families moving into hunting territories during the fall and winter months in order to survive. In other years, when a surplus could be stored to last throughout the winter, hunting parties could be sent out from the village while the main population remained year-round at the village.

Some prehistoric villages seem to have had a dispersed pattern with some spread out over many hectares. Perhaps fields were interspersed among the households. Most villages, however, appear to have been consolidated, with houses placed close together in clusters. During the Potano I period, villages are known to have covered an area several hundred meters on a side. House structures were circular, about 7.6 m in diameter, and were placed within the villages every 23 m or so. Drying racks and storage cribs were interspersed among the houses. Horticultural fields must have spread out from these villages in all directions for some distance.

At least some of the circular house structures were built by placing poles in the ground every 60 to 95 cm. The tops were probably bent over and tied together to form a domed roof. Thatch (palmetto) was then placed over this framework. Within the houses were pits for building fires for cooking, and pits which must have been lined with hides, or grass, and used for food storage. Along the inside walls of the cabins, sleeping and sitting platforms were constructed by putting small posts vertically in the ground and then attaching horizontal poles. The tops of these bench-size beds were probably 45 to 60 cm off the ground. As anyone who has ever camped near a lake or sinkhole in North-Central Florida can attest, the aboriginal villages must have been invaded by mosquitoes during the summer months. To avoid the insects, the aborigines built small smudge fires under the beds and slept in the smoke.

The small, triangular Pinellas points (Figure 31f–k) mentioned before are typical throughout the temporal range of the Alachua tradition (Bullen 1975:8). Other lithic tools (Figures 31 and 32) include expanded-base drills, linear drills which are round-to-lenticular in cross section, gravers, spokeshaves, and sandstone hones for sharpening bone tools. Flakes and small blades struck from irregular polyhedral cores were used as knives and scrapers. Some large blades were worked into end scrapers and bifacial knives. Bifacial, ovate knives are also common. A variety of grinding equipment, both mortars and manos, is present at Alachua-tradition sites. Grinding tools were used for processing maize, nuts, and seeds. Cakes made from acorn meal or flour were eaten by the aborigines of Florida in the sixteenth century, and probably for hundreds of years before. Multipurpose "hoes," shaped much like late Acheulian hand-axes from the Old World, were used both as chopping tools to work wood and as digging implements.

The variety and types of lithic tools greatly resemble the lithic complexes associated with other Woodland cultures in the Southeast. Because the tools functioned well, and because there were evidently no changes in Alachua-tradition subsistence patterns or life-style during the period of the tradition, the tools also remained unchanged.

Much less is known about the bone tools of the Alachua tradition. Only a few awls and pins, the latter perhaps used as clothing or hair fasteners, have been recovered. Potsherds, which have grooves worn in them from

FIGURE 31. *Alachua tradition lithic artifacts;* **a − b,** *ovate, bifacial knives;* **c − e,** *linear, bifacial knives;* **f − k,** *Pinellas points;* **l,** *Tampa point;* **m − n,** *Ichetucknee points.*

FIGURE 32. *Alachua tradition lithic artifacts;* **a,** *spokeshave;* **b – d,** *perforators;* **e – f,** *blade knives;* **g,** *hoe.*

the action of sharpening bone tools on them, are common, however, and bone or wooden perforating implements must have been used more frequently than is evident from the archaeological record.

The few items related to personal adornment that have come from Alachua villages indicate that shell ear pins, made from the columella of *Busycon* shells, were worn in the earlobes. Also, red hematite pigment was probably used as body paint. *Busycon* shell drinking cups served as containers for everyday use. The cups were also used for the drinking of the black drink.

The pottery manufactured and used by the Alachua-tradition peoples is quite distinctive from that of the earlier Cades Pond culture. Vessel shapes include both cylindrical pots, smaller than those of the Cades Pond people, and simple, small bowls 25 cm or less in diameter at the mouth. Some of the pots made during the Hickory Pond period had clay lumps and/or sand present in the clay as temper. Later, only sand was used as pottery temper.

In the manufacturing process, probably nearly all of the clay pots had their surfaces roughened prior to being fired. Perhaps this helped to compact the clay coils, adding more strength to the pot. Usually, about half of the vessels were then smoothed over on the surfaces. The resulting vessels appear to be plain. Occasionally, however, the final smoothing process was not thorough and the original surface-roughening can be seen. Alachua Plain pottery reached its greatest popularity during the Potano II period, when vessel shapes began to copy those of the Spanish. Burnishing of the clay surfaces became common at that time. Such burnished pottery is generally referred to as Miller Plain. The types of Alachua pottery (Figures 33 and 34) with roughened surfaces are Prairie Cord Marked, Alachua Cob Marked, Lochloosa Punctated, Prairie Punctated-over-Cord Marked (rare), Prairie Fabric Impressed (plain twined openwork and plain plaited fabric were used—both rarely), and Alachua Net Impressed (rare) (Milanich 1971:29—36). Potsherds were occasionally ground down into discs 12 to 25 mm in diameter (Figure 34f—h). Possibly these were used as game counters.

Very little is known about Alachua-tradition ceremonial life during the prehistoric period. Only two Alachua tradition burial mounds have ever been located and adequately excavated, one reported by Bullen in 1949, and one by Loucks and Fairbanks in 1975. Subsequent excavation of the village adjacent to the Woodward Mound excavated by Bullen has shown that the mound dates from early in the Hickory Pond period. The second mound was isolated; no nearby village was present. This raises the interesting possibility that other isolated, small sand burial mounds in North-Central Florida were built by Alachua peoples. Because of acidic

FIGURE 33. *Alachua tradition pottery; **a**−**b, e,** Prairie Cord Marked, **e** has a mending hole; **c**−**d,** Prairie Fabric Marked (plain twined openwork); **f**−**h,** Lochloosa Punctated.*

FIGURE 34. *Alachua tradition pottery and sherd discs; a – e, Alachua Cob Marked; f – h, sherd discs, g – h are manufactured from Prairie Cord Marked sherds.*

soils which destroy human skeletal materials, and because no grave goods were placed in the mounds, excavation of such mounds cannot ascertain whether or not they are Cades Pond or Alachua. Most likely, they date from the Alachua-tradition period.

The Woodward Mound is described by Bullen (1949) as an annular sand mound about 16.7 m in diameter and measuring about 1 m in height. Excavations revealed that the initial construction of the mound was preceded by digging a circular depression about .45 m deep and 10.9 m in diameter. A mixture of dark gray sand and charcoal was used to fill in the depression, forming a ritually prepared mound base. Two or three initiating burials were then placed in separate pits in the mound base. All were adults, and two were accompanied by a deposit of red ochre powder which was placed under, and beside, portions of the bodies. After the interment of these burials, a mound cap about 1.35 m in height was placed over the central 7.6 m of the base, covering the burial pits.

Later, through time, 26 additional burials were interred in the mound. These individuals were placed on the eastern slope of the mound cap surface, usually in extended position. Each was then covered with a meter or more of dirt. Heads were oriented toward the northwestern edge of the mound, and feet toward the edge. Gradually the mound grew in height and diameter as these subsequent burials were added. Three of the later burials were bundled, with only the skull and long bones buried. Two child burials were accompanied by shell beads, the only items placed with ony of the burials. Analysis of the burial population suggests a normally distributed population of male/female and adult/child ratios. Most likely, all of the individuals within the village who died over an unspecified period of time were interred in the village mound.

The mound reported by Loucks (1976) was similar in size and content to the Woodward Mound, measuring 10.9 m across its long axis, and 1 m in height at the time of excavation. Initially, a mound base about 60 cm thick was deposited on the ground surface. Several trophy skulls, one flexed burial, and five extended burials were placed in, or on, this stratum. Sand was scraped up from around the mound and used to cap the primary structure. Later, through time, other burials were laid out on the surface of the mound and covered with sand. Most of these burials were placed on the eastern slope of the mound; this accretion process gave the mound a slightly oval shape. Of the 41 burials contained in the mound, 24 were extended, 10 were trophy skulls, and 5 were flexed and secondary (2 were too fragmented to ascertain burial form). As with the Woodward Mound, age distribution ratios seemed normal. However, of the 16 individuals analyzed for sexual attributes, 15 were classified as male. Many of the burials were interred with red ochre deposits around

the head, shoulders, and chest. Twelve individuals were in direct association with charcoal, or charred logs, placed on, beside, or under the body.
No burnt sand or bone was apparent, suggesting the wood was charred
before it was placed with the bodies. Perhaps fire was a part of the
burial ritual, used prior to interment. One burial, an adult female, had
several deer phalanges (one split), a bone pin, and freshwater mussel
shells placed under the head.

As with the Woodward Mound, the burials were oriented with their
heads toward the northwestern edge of the mound. Both mounds are
very similar in structure, and the same burial rituals seemed to have been
involved. Not enough is yet known about historic Potano burial patterns
to allow comparisons.

The Potano Indians observed by the de Soto expedition in the early
sixteenth century probably were living much like their prehistoric ancestors had during the Hickory Pond and early Alachua periods. Although
de Soto presents a picture of a lush aboriginal life-style, with cribs of
stored corn, this view was relative to the Gulf coastal cultures that the
Spanish had observed when they landed at Tampa Bay. Also, the de Soto
expedition was passing through North-Central Florida just after the time
of the horticultural harvest when stored food supplies were at a maximum.
Most likely, the Alachua-tradition peoples maintained a tenuous balance
with their environment, one that could be upset by drought or pest
attacking their crops. During the historic period this relationship was
tilted beyond the limits of survival, and the North-Central Florida
aborigines ceased to exist.

South Florida and the Belle Glade Culture

Although at one time South Florida was thought to be a homogenous
culture area (Goggin 1949:14, 28−32), researchers have now begun to
separate the area into several diverse but related areas, basing their divisions on geographical, environmental, and cultural factors (Sears 1971a,
1974; J. W. Griffin 1974). Today we can delineate three areas:
Caloosahatchee, Lake Okeechobee Basin, and Circum-Glades.

The smallest of these three areas is what might best be called the
Caloosahatchee region, ranging along the Southwest Florida Coast from
Charlotte Harbor south to the Ten Thousand Islands. During the historic
period, this portion of the coast was occupied by the Calusa Indians. The
region encompasses the mangrove swamp and piney flatwoods habitats,
both on the mainland and the offshore keys. Inland are the barren pine
flatlands. Perhaps the most important habitats, in terms of aboriginal

food production, were the small freshwater streams which drain into the marine bays, the bays themselves, and the bay-estuarine systems. Fish and shellfish seem to have constituted the largest portions of meat in the coastal aboriginal diet.

The Caloosahatchee River functioned as a canoe highway to tie the Caloosahatchee area to the Lake Okeechobee Basin. It is possible that the impetus for the prehistoric cultural development along the coast came from the basin. When visited by the Spanish, these two areas were linked by trade and political networks. Thorough understanding of the cultural evolution of the region awaits a great deal more research; the region remains one of the most unknown and enigmatic in all of Florida. The Calusa and the archaeology of the Caloosahatchee area are discussed in more detail in Chapter 9.

The second and largest of the South Florida regions is the Circum-Glades area. This includes the southwestern coastal strip from within the Ten Thousand Islands southward to, and including, the Florida Keys, and the southeastern coast from the Keys up to Indian River County. The archaeology of this region is also reviewed in Chapter 9.

When examining the archaeology of South Florida, one cannot help but feel that the most complex prehistoric cultures were centered, not on the coasts but inland in the Lake Okeechobee Basin, the third area. It is there that the early South Florida populations reached their greatest complexity, basing their life-style on a specialized adaptation to the savannahs and hammocks present in the basin, and to the dominant natural feature of the region, Lake Okeechobee. The "flavor" of the other cultures in South Florida was heavily influenced by the events taking place in the basin. Late development of the Caloosahatchee region may have been due in part to the Belle Glade peoples occupying the basin. The coastal dwellers, hindered by an environment largely unsuitable for horticulture, could never duplicate the level of culture achieved in the basin. And, not only was the Belle Glade culture important within South Florida, but the Belle Glade peoples may have provided a link between Mesoamerica and the Southeast United States through which knowledge of maize horticulture came to some of the prehistoric peoples of the East. However, no evidence of direct contact has been discovered.

Such events began to take place shortly after 1000 b.c. These new ideas rapidly spread out of South Florida and, as maize horticulture was adapted to local growing conditions throughout the East, other peoples developed cultures eventually more complex than those found in the basin. The story of the Belle Glade culture and its unique adaptations and adjustments to the Lake Okeechobee savannahs is a remarkable one which, when compared to the Alachua tradition, illustrates the diverse ways in which Florida's aboriginal populations lived and made use of their environments.

The view of the Belle Glade cultures presented here is relatively recent, one derived almost entirely from the research of Sears. For a 6-year period, Sears directed excavations at the Fort Center site, a large complex located along the prehistoric western edge of Lake Okeechobee on Fisheating Creek. The information on the Belle Glade culture presented here is taken from Sears's published accounts (1971a, 1974; Sears and Sears 1976), and from information gathered from him in conversation.

Sears was not the first to recognize that the Belle Glade region contained sites unique in Florida. Early travelers in the region could not help but notice the large mound complexes and, in the 1930s and 1940s, WPA archaeologists and other individuals excavated, or visited, several of the sites. These large complexes include Tony's Mound (Figure 35) in Hendry County (visited and mapped by Allen [1948]); Big Mound City in Palm Beach County (described by the botanist, John Small, in the 1920s, and test-excavated by WPA archaeologists [Willey 1949b]); Ortona Mound in Glades County, and the Belle Glade Mound in Palm Beach County (partially excavated by WPA archaeologists [Willey 1949b]). Other sites have since been located by the use of aerial photographs.

Tony's Mound, Big Mound City, and several other sites are collectively known as Big Circle sites, a name given to them by Allen (1948:17) because of the unique shape of the similar narrow, semicircular or horseshoe-shaped sand embankments present at all of the sites. These embankments average about 150 m across at the opening. Extending outward from each semicircular embankment are 5 to 10 linear enbankments, each terminating with a small round or oval mound. Usually other mounds and embankments, or other types of earthworks, are also present at the sites—including large middens sometimes set across the openings to the horseshoe-shaped mounds. Tony's Mound, a typical Big Circle site, is shown in Figure 35.

In order to test research hypotheses concerning the Belle Glade culture, named for the Belle Glade site excavated in the 1930s, Sears selected the Fort Center site as the focus of a long-term project. The site contained numerous mounds and embankments (including a ceremonial center), middens along Fisheating Creek (which runs through the site), and several circular ditches similar to Adena "sacred circles" found at more northerly sites in the midwestern United States. In all, the site covers roughly 260 ha.

As Sears suspected, the various Fort Center mounds date from very different temporal periods, and different mounds had different functions. The project was able to describe and interpret the evolution of the

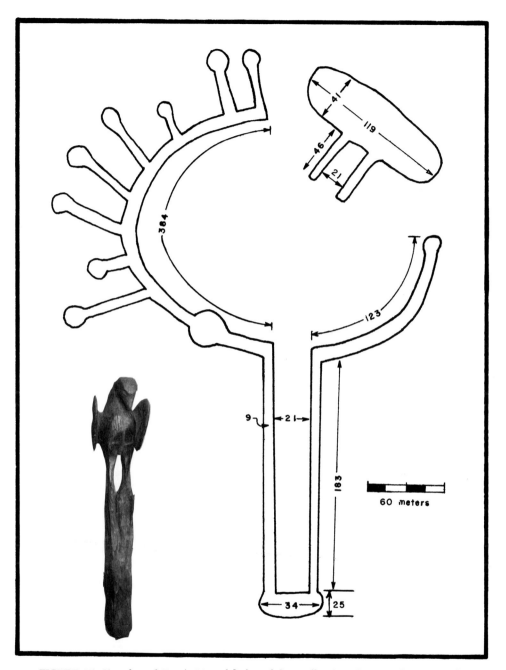

FIGURE 35. *Site plan of Tony's Mound [adapted from Allen (1948)]; inset shows carved wooden eagle recovered from Fort Center site. The head is reconstructed, but it is very similar to a head recovered by William Sears from the same site. Overall the base and eagle are 1.57 m tall; the eagle alone is 67 cm from head to feet.*

Belle Glade culture at Fort Center and in the basin from ca. 500 B.C. to the historic period. The mound and midden components of other sites in the basin can now be dated, using the data gathered by Sears at Fort Center.

The basin was first occupied on a year-round basis between 1000 B.C. and 500 B.C. These earliest Belle Glade peoples were hunters and gatherers who also possessed knowledge of maize horticulture by this early date, certainly by 450 B.C., a date supported by radiocarbon analysis. It is possible that the Belle Glade peoples moved inland into the basin from the southwestern Florida Coast. We know that a portion of that coast was occupied before 1000 B.C., and that the coastal dwellers, like the Orange—Transitional peoples to the north in the St. Johns region, first made fiber-tempered pottery, then later pottery tempered with fiber and sand, and still later, only sand-tempered pottery. The earliest pottery at Fort Center is fiber and sand tempered. Known as semifiber tempered, this type of pottery is the same as that found on the southwestern coast and elsewhere in Florida during the period 1000 B.C. to 500 B.C.

The reason for a population shift inland from the coast may have been horticulture. Sears has noted that the Lake Okeechobee Basin greatly resembles the lowlands of the Gulf Coast of Mexico in terms of vegetation, rainfall, growing season, and daylength. Maize is a crop that requires adaptation to local conditions. If maize were introduced to Southwest Florida via trade expeditions from Mesoamerica or some other means, it could have been grown in the basin. Southwest Florida is accessible from Mexico by boat, either around the Gulf Coast or, more likely, via Yucatan and the Caribbean islands (Sears 1977). Cushing's collection (Cushing 1897:36–38) of wooden objects from Key Marco included a toy catamaran canoe and parts of full-sized rigging, including a possible bark-mat sail, a spar, and blocks. And we know from documents that during the historic period the Calusa were capable of sailing to Cuba. Whatever the means by which maize and the knowledge of cultivation reached the basin, maize cultivation was apparently there by 500 B.C.

Sears (1974) has divided the Fort Center Belle Glade culture sequence into three periods based on radiocarbon dates and changes in mound and midden patterning. During the earliest of these periods, dating from at least 500 B.C. to A.D. 1, the site was first occupied. A population of probably less than 50 persons lived out in the savannah, perhaps in extended family groups, on small house mounds. Some occupation of the higher natural levee on the south bank of Fisheating Creek also occurred.

A variety of animals was collected and hunted; in fact, almost every edible species was utilized. The only exceptions are birds, which were only sparingly eaten, perhaps due to cultural taboos. No single animal species constituted more than 10% of the meat diet (although together, several turtle species accounted for a significant portion), a situation unparalleled outside of South Florida. At all other Florida aboriginal sites, except those in the basin and on the Southwest Florida Coast, deer are the single most important meat source, usually constituting more than 50% of the meat diet. In the basin, animals eaten for food include opossum, mole, fox squirrel, muskrat, cotton rat, raccoon, grey fox, blue goose, green water snake, brown water snake, black vulture, bobcat, deer, turkey, frog, siren, nine species of turtle, mud snake, king snake, cottonmouth, alligator, gar, mudfish, and a variety of other species of fish. This basic life-style, the collecting of plants and a variety of local animal species, especially those inhabiting the lake and wet portions of the savannah, continued up to the historic period. Such a subsistence pattern is unique to Florida, just as the basin environment is unique.

These wild resources were apparently supplemented by maize grown in a unique garden plot south of the occupation living area. The presence of maize has been substantiated by the identification of numerous grains of maize pollen recovered from the midden fill of a portion of the ditch, the interior of the circular ditch and elsewhere at the site (Sears and Sears 1976). Maize does not grow well in damp soil; consequently, a means was needed by which the garden area could be kept partially drained. This end was accomplished by the digging of a large circular ditch 365 m in diameter. The ditch, which averaged about 9 m in width at the top with gently sloping walls, cut through the underlying hardpan stratum which previously prevented rapid percolation of water down into the ground. By cutting through the hardpan, water within and outside of the circle seeped out over the hardpan into the ditch where it dissipated down into the subhardpan strata. The water in the open ditch also evaporated rapidly. At least two "causeways," unditched portions of the circumference of the circle, allowed access to the interior of the circle.

That this drainage system worked is evidenced by the presence of two other ditches at Fort Center which are overlapped by the latest, most complete ditch, and which precede it temporally. Sears (1974:347) has obtained a radiocarbon date of 450 B.C. from the fill of the latest-built ditch, indicating that the earlier two were probably built previous to 500 B.C.

Other circular ditches have been located by using aerial photographs in the basin region. One lies west of Lake Okeechobee on the Caloosahatchee River on the fringe of the basin. Sears believes that the ditches were used up to A.D. 500 and later, when new garden plot forms were put into use.

An excellent sample of material culture items from this and later periods was obtained from the excavations of the middens, ceremonial mounds, and house mounds at the site. The same types of tools were evidently used throughout the various temporal occupations. Probably the same tool kit was used throughout the region of the Belle Glade culture, since the Fort Center specimens are like those recovered from the Belle Glade site located on the southeastern edge of the lake. The latter site appears to be contemporary with at least a portion of the last period at Fort Center—post-A.D. 500/1000 to the sixteenth century.

Analysis by Steinen (1971) of artifacts from Fort Center shows that a variety of tools was used by the Belle Glade people; sharks' teeth, which were hafted either singly or in groups by perforating, notching, or thinning the bases, were used for cutting, carving, and sawing wood. Striations on some of the wooden figures recovered from the Period II charnel pond described in the following show that shark-teeth instruments were used for detailed wood-carving. Bone leisters (probably used for spearing fish and animals), fids (used for weaving or basketry), awls, and points were also common implements.

Lithic tools are more common at the Fort Center site than at the South Florida coastal sites, indicating access (probably through trade) to the cultures in more northerly parts of the state. Trade with the north is also evidenced by a few steatite sherds and by tools made from igneous rocks not found in South Florida. Lithic "points" are of three main types: small to medium triangular projectile points; Hernando-like, basally notched projectile points; and a variety of triangular-blade, stemmed, Archaic-like specimens, most of which appear to have been hafted knives although a few were used as saws. Limestone abradors, hones or sharpening stones, and food grinders also were all utilized by the Belle Glade peoples.

A variety of implements was manufactured from marine shells brought inland from the Gulf Coast. The tool types are like those found throughout South Florida and include celts, adzes, gouges, picks, and hammers. The latter two types, manufactured from conchs or shells, were often hafted by cutting one, two, or three holes in the shell.

Throughout this early period, semifiber-tempered pottery continued to be manufactured at the Fort Center site, although it declined rapidly in popularity, giving way to pottery which was tempered with sand. Most of the sand-tempered ceramics closely resemble the sand-tempered varieties manufactured elsewhere in Florida at the same period although some of the Period I pottery was very crudely made, having a laminated, crumbly paste. Period II at Fort Center, A.D. 1 to A.D. 500/1000, is delineated by changes in the ceramic inventory (i.e., the absence of fiber-tempered pottery and the appearance and subsequent increase in popularity of the ceramic type, Belle Glade Plain). This type, manufactured in the same bowl forms as the earlier secular sand-tempered ware, is differentiated by having a smoothed or "tooled" surface achieved by scraping or cutting the almost dry clay surface with a wooden tool. This process leaves characteristic drag marks caused by grains of sand being moved across the surface. Belle Glade Plain continued to increase in popularity until it was the majority form of secular ware in Period III.

Subsistence during this period seems to have been little changed from that of the preceding period. Maize was still grown in the circular, ditched field, and most of the inhabitants of the site lived on the various middens adjacent to or near the creek.

Period II is also characterized by the construction of several ceremonial structures utilized in the preparation and the disposal of the dead. The ceremonial center consists of two mounds, an artificial, aboriginally dug mound, and a surrounding earthwork (Sears 1971a:326 – 328). A low, flat-topped platform mound was constructed as the base for a charnel-house structure. Bodies of dead individuals were prepared in the house for deposit. Bones were stripped of flesh, and then stored as bundles. Sears's excavation of the charnel house uncovered living refuse mixed with odds and ends—small human bones and teeth—lost during the preparation of the bodies. Evidently, the charnel specialist(s) whose task it was to clean the bones was not a neat housekeeper. A ceremonial deposit was placed on the edge of the mound nearest the pond. The deposit contained an infant skullcap, an adult skull, a worn carnivore mandible, bird-bone tubes, eight shell cups, and a set of nested scallop and clam shells (Sears 1971a:327).

Immediately adjacent to the charnel platform was the pond, measuring about 36.5 m in diameter and dug to a depth of 1.5 m below ground surface. A wooden structure constructed out of tree trunks and unshaped timbers was placed in the pond, forming a platform above the surface of the water on which the bundle burials were placed. Vertical corner and support members were carved into large animals: a life-size cat, a bear, and a larger-than-life bird. Other smaller carvings, many with tenon bases, were placed along the edges of the platform on the tops of mortised poles. The largest number of the carvings are of birds, both raptorial species and waterbirds (Figure 35). Perhaps these were totemic symbols, explaining why birds were only scarcely eaten. The famous eagle totem on display at the Florida State Museum is thought to have been recovered from the Fort Center charnel pond in 1926.

Bundles were periodically removed from storage in the charnel house and placed on the platform in the pond. Eventually the platform, loaded with 300 or so individuals, collapsed into the pond. Many of the burials were salvaged and redeposited on the platform mound after removal of the charnel house. The burials and platform were then covered with a large mound of sand. Those wooden carvings and platform supports left in the pond were preserved by the water and muck for almost 2000 years.

On the opposite side of the pond from the charnel house, another low platform was constructed on which one or more wooden house structures were built. A large quantity of living refuse was deposited on the low rise, including potsherds, bones of animals used for food, and flint and shell tools. Lime, obtained from burning freshwater mussels, was found on and around the living area. Most likely, the lime was used to process the maize, a technique common in Meosamerica.

A circular earthen embankment, with its ends attached to the living area, surrounded the pond and charnel mound, demarcating the entire area. As Sears (1971a:328) has pointed out, this Period II ceremonial center has a great many features similar to those found at Hopewell-period sites elsewhere in Florida and in the eastern United States. These features include the separation of ceremonial activities from secular activities, using earthworks, and the presence of a number of artifacts known to have been traded among Hopewell peoples as valued items intended for ceremonial use and deposition. The latter include clay platform pipes, plummets of quartz crystal, a galena hemisphere, and designs represented on bone tools, as well as the carvings along the charnel platform. This Hopewellian-related complex at Fort Center had as its subsistence base intensive harvesting of a variety of wild foods, mainly animals, coupled with some maize horticulture.

During Period III at Fort Center—A.D. 500/1000 to the historic period—changes took place. The importance of the site as a ceremonial center seems to have ended with the collapse of the charnel platform; no doubt ceremonial activities were transferred to another center in the basin. The ceramic inventory during this period remained rather stable with Belle Glade Plain being the majority secular ware. Sand-tempered plain bowls continued to be manufactured in small quantities, and sherds of the type St. Johns Check Stamped, thought to date after A.D. 800/1000, appeared.

The circular drainage ditches no longer were constructed for horticultural purposes, and a new method was employed to keep the crops relatively dry. Long, linear, earthen embankments were constructed on which to grow crops. Such linear earthworks measure 60 m to more than 180 m in length. Often the linear embankments are terminated with circular house mounds. During this period, occupation of the riverbank middens seems to have continued also. Use of wild resources is little changed over the preceding periods.

In the prehistoric New World, garden plots such as these were not unique to Florida. Similar linear embankments have been described for northern South America (Parsons and Denevan 1967; Denevan 1970) and for Campeche, Mexico (Siemans and Puleston 1972). At the Fort Center site the raised plots were probably utilized into the historic period. A few intrusive burials and historic artifacts were recovered from the top of the mound built over the burials salvaged from the charnel pond.

There are no good historic period descriptions of the culture occupying the basin in the sixteenth century, although one account notes that roots which were grown "inland" were brought to the Gulf Coast Calusa. The exact political and cultural relationships between the coastal Calusa and the historic Belle Glade peoples are poorly understood at this time due to a lack of excavated data from that time period. One trend evident from collections made by local nonprofessional archaeologists and collectors is that more historic artifacts, such as goods salvaged from Spanish ships wrecked on the Florida coasts, found their way to inland villages than to coastal villages. If such European items were, indeed, valued by the aboriginal populations, this would indicate that the inland peoples controlled the networks along which such goods were traded.

The populations of the basin, as the other South Florida Indians, rapidly declined in numbers following contact with Europeans. By the first quarter of the eighteenth century, the cultures were destroyed.

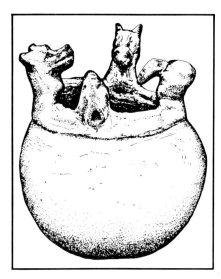

8

Fort Walton, Pensacola, and Safety Harbor: The Mississippian Peoples

Driving southward from the Midwest or from New England, some modern day visitors to Florida are compelled by a strong interest in their country's Indian heritage to stop along their route and visit well-known archaeological museums and sites. At centers such as Moundville near Tuscaloosa, Alabama, and Etowah near Cartersville, Georgia, they learn about the Mississippian peoples of the Southeast who, after A.D. 1000, built and occupied those and other large mound-and-village complexes. They learn about Mississippian towns with populations numbering in the thousands, ruled by Indian chiefs and their families. These chiefs were treated by their subjects like European royalty, both in life and in death.

If the tourists study the museum displays with an eye to visiting more Mississippian "centers" while in Florida, they will usually note two dots denoting Florida Mississippian sites. One dot is at Mount Royal at the lower St. Johns River and the other at Key Marco on the southwest Gulf Coast.

However, if our tourists head for either of these two locations, they will learn that one cannot get to Mount Royal (and most people do not know what or where it is), and that Key Marco no longer exists, having been destroyed by modern construction activities. Further inquiry may lead our visitors to conclude that Florida had no Mississippian populations, since the reason Mount Royal and Key Marco are noted on Mississippian maps is simply that, in the nineteenth century, artifacts were found at those two sites which were either obtained by trade from more northerly

Mississippian towns or which were similar to Mississippian artifacts found elsewhere in the Southeast.

But parts of Florida were indeed inhabited by Mississippian peoples. Mississippian cultures appeared first in Northwest Florida and later along the central peninsular Gulf Coast, centered around Tampa Bay (Figure 36). Research presently underway indicates that in Northwest Florida the development of the Fort Walton culture was as early as similar Mississippian developments in the eastern United States. Excavations near Tallahassee have now revealed many examples of the ornate Missis-

FIGURE 36. *Regions of the Florida Mississippian cultures and sites discussed in text.*

sippian copper and shell artifacts identical to those found at Etowah and Moundville. Such artifacts are known to have been religious paraphernalia associated with high ranking Mississippian chiefs and their families who resided and died at those two sites. At the time of the writing of this chapter, ongoing research is continually adding to our knowledge of Florida's Mississippian cultures.

Fort Walton and Pensacola

The two Northwest Florida Mississippian cultures, Fort Walton and Pensacola, bear many resemblances to other southeastern Mississippian cultures. Artifact assemblages, mound and community patterns, and the behavioral patterns inferred from these archaeological data leave no doubt that these were Mississippian peoples with social and political systems that were more complex than those that had previously evolved in Florida.

At the present time, Fort Walton and Pensacola are distinguished from one another on the basis of differences in geographical distribution and in ceramic types; however, there is considerable overlap of ceramic decorative motifs and it is difficult to place an exact dividing line between their two geographical regions. Most researchers agree that the Fort Walton culture characterized by sand- and/or grit-tempered pottery, extends from the Apalachicola River drainage east to the Aucilla River. Fort Walton sites are located from the Gulf Coast inland through the hill region of Northwest Florida and up the Chattahoochee drainage into the Georgia—Alabama coastal plain. The Pensacola culture, characterized by shell-tempered pottery but with some sand-tempered pottery, is found west of the Apalachicola drainage, extending as far as Mobile Bay in the west and into Alabama on the north. As one moves west from the Fort Walton region, the relative percentage of sand-tempered ceramics at Pensacola sites decreases (Lazarus 1971:42).

There is no doubt that the Apalachee Indians encountered by the Narváez and de Soto expeditions in Northwest Florida in the second quarter of the sixteenth century correspond to the late Fort Walton archaeological culture (see Chapter 9). European materials have been found at a number of Fort Walton sites. The large Lake Jackson site, a mound village complex north of Tallahassee, was probably the main town of Apalachee visited by de Soto.

Spanish colonial-period items have also been found at Pensacola sites. The Pensacola archaeological culture was represented in the historic period by the various tribes located west of the Apalachicola River within the coastal plain. These probably included the Chatot and the

Pensacola tribes. Differences in the Fort Walton and Pensacola archaeological complexes thus seem to reflect the same ethnic differences as those present in the historic period. At this time, however, we do not have sufficient archaeological data to differentiate between Fort Walton and Pensacola behavioral patterns, such as political or social systems. Presumably, they were much the same, as evidenced by similar archaeological traits. However, this remains to be thoroughly proven.

Until the mid-1970s, most researchers argued that the Fort Walton and Pensacola cultures represented intrusions of Mississippian peoples into the Florida panhandle after A.D. 1350. Because of similarities in types of ceremonial pottery vessels, the lower Mississippi River Valley was viewed as the probable origin of these populations. Similarities in pottery found at Moundville in Alabama and at Pensacola and Fort Walton sites also pointed toward the Alabama Mississippian peoples as a major source of influence in the formation of the Florida cultures.

Today, largely through the work of David Brose and his students of Case Western Reserve University, a very different picture of Fort Walton origins and evolution emerges. Data gleaned from excavations at two large Fort Walton mound complexes (Yon and Cason sites) on the Apalachicola River near Bristol indicate that the Fort Walton culture evolved out of the earlier Wakulla Weeden Island culture (see Chapter 5) as early as A.D. 1000. More than 25 years ago, John Griffin espoused the same idea, based on observations made at the Lake Jackson site. Quite likely contact down the Chattahoochee River with other emerging Mississippian peoples in the Southeast brought new ideas to the late Weeden Island people, ideas for organizing increasingly larger societies and ideas for more intensive and efficient agriculture. Fort Walton therefore represents the "Mississippianization" of Weeden Island society.

Fort Walton sites are found in Northwest Florida within two broad environmental zones. Many sites are located along the coast adjacent to bays and especially estuaries. At all of these coastal strand sites, significant amounts of shell refuse are present. Other sites are found well inland in the Tallahassee Red Hills region, north of an east—west line drawn approximately through Tallahassee and Blountstown. This region is characterized by mixed hardwood and pine forests and by loamy, clayey soils which are excellent for farming. Inland sites tend to be found along major waterways, such as the Apalachicola River, or adjacent to lakes, swamps, or ponds. Large sites are found in Leon County around Lake Jackson, Lake Iamonia, and Lake Miccosukee (Leon County is the most thoroughly researched panhandle county in Florida).

Fort Walton sites are also found west of the Apalachicola River in northern Jackson County, where floral and soil conditions similar to the

Red Hills are found. Few surveys have been carried out at inland locations farther west in what is presumably the inland Pensacola culture
region. However, it is probable that such inland sites will eventually be
found in the western panhandle in the areas of mixed hardwood and
pine forests (i.e., north of Interstate Highway 10 which approximates the
boundary between coastal flatlands and inland forests).

To date, most of the Pensacola sites located and investigated have been
along the Gulf Coast. Fort Walton and Pensacola coastal sites occur in
similar settings. In both regions a few sites occur in the coastal flatlands
along the rivers which provided communication routes between inland
and coastal settlements.

Limited excavations in coastal shell middens indicate that the Pensacola and Fort Walton peoples living in such localities drew upon much
the same wild food sources as their Weeden Island predecessors. The
bones of deer, turkeys, various birds, and a variety of fish and turtles have
been identified from coastal sites along with many species of shellfish
(Percy 1974:83). At the present time there is no direct evidence of farming
at the coastal middens, but cultivation of maize and probably other crops
must have occurred. Often small Fort Walton and Pensacola sites are
found on top of the black dirt, fertile middens of earlier cultures, suggesting a conscious selection for such locations as fields for crops.

Mississippian coastal middens in the panhandle are of several types.
Some are small, presumably the refuse from one individual household.
Others are much larger and appear either as linear piles of shell and
other refuse as much as 200 m in length or as many small individual piles,
possibly from multiple household villages. At still others, overlapping
piles have accumulated to form large circular heaps as much as 100 m in
diameter.

At Fort Walton Beach a very large temple mound and an adjacent
village midden probably represent the "capital town" for a single Pensacola polity. A number of other outlying villages and homesteads represented by shell middens around Choctahatchee Bay most likely had
religious and political ties to the center where the chief resided. We can
guess that this chief's dwelling was on top of the mound. Burials in the
eastern side of the mound may represent the interment of important
individuals (from the chief's kin group?) or individuals sacrificed to accompany a deceased chief to the afterlife. Such interments are common
at Southeast Mississippian sites and presumably reflect the nonegalitar-
ian nature of the chiefdom-level societies who inhabited those towns.

The little information available from the coastal shell middens suggests
that the shell, bone, and stone artifacts present are not significantly different from those found during the earlier Weeden Island times. One

difference is the presence of small triangular flint and chert arrow points like those found at other Mississippian sites throughout the Southeast.

At a surprisingly large number of coastal Fort Walton and Pensacola sites Spanish materials have been found. Some coins and beads have been documented to the sixteenth century, and it is probable that other of the European artifacts also date from this time. European materials include glass finger rings, looking glass fragments, various objects manufactured from silver, gold, or brass. Iron tools and hardware (axes, knife blades, chisels, spikes, fish spears, adzes, boxes, pointed rods, hoes, and horseshoes) occur most frequently (Smith and Gottlob 1978:12−13). Quite likely, these goods were obtained from the early Spanish expeditions in Florida as well as from wrecked Spanish ships. The quantity of Spanish goods is much larger at the coastal sites than it is at inland locations. This may be a reflection of the source of these artifacts (coastal contact versus inland contact), or it may reflect skewed sampling (more coastal sites have been located and collected than inland sites).

The presence of large Fort Walton mound and village sites at inland locations has been recognized for many years. Sites with multiple mounds and extensive middens such as those on Lake Jackson and the central Apalachicola River were observed by early visitors to those regions in the nineteenth century. Modern archaeological surveys, especially in the general Tallahassee region, have also documented a high density of smaller Fort Walton sites in the hill region of the Florida panhandle from the Apalachicola River eastward. (As previously noted, the inland region west of Apalachicola River Valley is little known, and it is likely that a similar high density of sites will be found there where good soils and mixed pine and hardwood forests are found.)

In addition to the large mound and village complexes, these additional inland sites include villages with single mounds and small middens with no associated mounds. In discussing the distribution of these latter sites, Fairbanks (1971) notes "almost anywhere where there is either red clay soil (which is Eocene residual soil) or where there are sandy well-drained clay loams, we will find Fort Walton sites. . . . The largest of them is considerably less than an acre and a good many of them would be only the size of [a large] room [p. 39]."

A thorough survey of six selected Leon County regions cross-cutting different environmental habitats was carried out by Tesar (1976) whose findings echo those of Fairbanks. Of a total of 174 site components encompassing all archaeological cultures from Paleo-Indian times into the historic period (at a total of 150 sites), 97 (or 56%) were Fort Walton. An additional 18% were from the mission period (Apalachee sites) while the remaining 26% were from periods earlier than Fort Walton. These data would seem to suggest a large population increase during the Fort Walton period and a conscious selection for site locations in the Red Hills, most likely for agriculture.

Charred maize kernels or cobs have been found at at least six Fort Walton sites in the Apalachicola and Chattahoochee drainage region and in Leon County (Bullen 1958; Neuman 1961; Jones and Penman 1973:72, 88; Peebles 1974:640; Tesar 1976). Relative to earlier Weeden Island sites in those same areas, this is an extremely large amount of charred maize to be recovered archaeologically and it reflects the increased importance of maize within the aboriginal diet. The inland Fort Walton peoples, like other inland Mississippian peoples, must have been successful horticulturalists who supplemented their diet with other cultigens (presumably beans and cucurbits) and with wild foods that were hunted and collected. The difference in farming techniques between the Fort Walton populations and the earlier Weeden Island peoples might have been one of row agriculture versus hillock and slash-and-burn cultivation (Fryman 1971b).

The patterns of inland Fort Walton communities seem to reflect the same political and social hierarchy present among other Mississippian cultures. At the top of the hierarchy was a single, large, multiple mound and village site. Certainly the Lake Jackson site in Leon County with six mounds (which served as the bases for structures), a plaza, and an extensive village midden was such a site. It probably functioned for a long period of time as the major Fort Walton center, a "capital" city. The largest mound at Lake Jackson, Mound 4, measures 48 by 65 m along its rectangular base and is 8 m high. It is built in typical truncated pyramid shape and had a ramp (of earth and logs) constructed up one side, providing access to the "temple" or residence that must have been erected on the top.

At this capital resided members of the ruling family or kin group including the major chief. Society was stratified with some kin groups and individuals ranking above or below others. As was true among other Mississippian peoples, the chief commanded life and death obedience from his subjects who included residents of the capital city, residents and village chiefs of the outlying villages (characterized archaeologically by village middens with single mounds), and the inhabitants, probably single families, of the small households that were scattered among the various villages. The villagers and homesteaders who made up the bulk of the population were at the bottom of the political hierarchy. They were subject to the chief of the nearby village who was in turn vassal to the major chief at the capital city. Together, these individuals formed a single polity.

Status within this political unit was reinforced and symbolized in various behavioral patterns and in dress or costume and other paraphernalia. The head chief, his family, and perhaps certain "associate" chiefs (other individuals responsible for conducting certain rituals or ceremonies or who had other important civic or religious duties) dressed in "costumes" symbolic of their office. As at Etowah or Moundville, such paraphernalia included copper and shell ornaments. The objects and the various distinctive motifs that decorate them have been grouped together into what is called the Southeastern Ceremonial Complex.

Salvage excavations at one of the Lake Jackson Fort Walton temple mounds revealed a number of such Southeastern Ceremonial Complex items placed with burials interred in graves dug down from superimposed clay layers. Calvin Jones of the Division of Archives, History and Records Management, who directed the excavations, has interpreted the clay layers as the floors of successive structures built on the temple mound. After the death and burial of a priest-chief, the structure (temple?) which he used or inhabited on the mound was removed, the mound enlarged, and another structure erected for the next chief. Through time, the clay floors, each with their respective burial tomb, were deposited on top of another. Family members, other high status individuals, and sacrificial victims, trophy skulls, and/or the bones of ancestors were also buried in the mounds especially on the flanks outside the main structure. This pattern of burial, rebuilding, and enlarging is common at Mississippian sites in the Southeast.

Jones's excavations revealed that the individuals buried in the tombs had been interred wearing their costumes and with other paraphernalia symbolic of their high rank. Repoussé copper breast plates were found on several individuals. Fabric, preserved by the copper and adhering to backs of some plates, evidently supported the plates while worn. All of the plates recovered by Jones were made from copper nuggets that had been cold-hammered into thin sheets, riveted together, and then embossed with a dancing human figure identical to those on plates from the Etowah site. Each figure is wearing a falcon mask, an elaborate headdress with a bilobed arrow motif, and a pointed pouch hung from the waist. Each figure is also adorned with a feather cape and is holding a mace or baton club in the right hand and a human head or mask in the left (Hudson 1976:399—400). The garters and waist sashes depicted on the figures were probably beaded and finger-woven like specimens known for nineteenth- and twentieth-century Seminole peoples.

The figures on the plates may represent a deity symbolized by the chiefs themselves. Several pounds of columella beads and a shell gorget incised with a dancing figure accompanied one Lake Jackson burial.

Copper celts found in different burials were probably hafted in wooden handles carved in the form of woodpecker heads like the clubs found at Spiro, a Mississippian site in Oklahoma (Hudson 1976:248).

Near the head of another chief in the Lake Jackson mound were several copper bird-figures embossed on copper plates. Hudson (1976:129 – 130) suggests that these are peregrine falcons. Each has a forked eye (one of the Southeastern Ceremonial Complex motifs) which is derived from the natural eye markings of falcons.

Use of the falcon and other motifs and symbols of the Southeastern Ceremonial Complex were restricted to only a few upper echelon individuals within a tightly stratified social system. Fort Walton and other Mississippian peoples were concerned with expansion of their territory and hegemony and needed such a society in which one or a few individuals could organize and control expansionistic activities.

Whether or not the entire Fort Walton population at any one point in time was united into a single chiefdom under a single chief is uncertain. However, the Apalachee of the early sixteenth century seem to have been a single polity, one so important that it was known throughout Florida. Its wealth and power were spoken of in awe by the Tampa Bay-area Indians when the early Spanish expeditions came ashore in the 1520s and 1530s. So it is likely that by 1500 a large part of the Fort Walton region eastward from the Apalachicola River was unified into a single political unit.

Although some Fort Walton individuals of high status were awarded special burial in mounds, most people were interred in cemeteries (Willey 1949a:456). Two such cemeteries have been excavated and both contained about 100 persons buried either individually in flexed or extended position or buried in mass graves. Secondary burials, perhaps skeletons which had first been cleaned and retained in a charnel house, also were interred. Such cemeteries are unique in Florida to the panhandle Mississippian Fort Walton and Pensacola cultures.

At the Winewood site near Tallahassee (Jones and Penman 1973), burials were also found in abandoned trash or fire pits. These were placed next to a possible cemetery area containing extended burials in separate graves. However, there is also evidence from site 8-Ja-5 (Bullen 1958) that Fort Walton burials were indeed placed in village areas. Perhaps at least some dead individuals were interred within their houses, in pits originally dug for other purposes.

Burial mounds (as opposed to temple mounds with burials) are also known for the Pensacola and Fort Walton cultures, but are less common than cemeteries. Burials in the mounds are both flexed and secondary. It may be that mound burial was a practice held over from Weeden Island times which gave way to cemetery burial. A number of Fort Walton and Pensacola burials that have been found in mounds containing Weeden Island burials are perhaps also an indication of continuity in burial ritual.

Like the earlier Weeden Island peoples, Fort Walton and Pensacola people manufactured some pottery vessels that appear archaeologically in special contexts, including caches in mounds and cemeteries (where they usually have been intentionally broken) or with individual mound or cemetery burials as grave furniture. In some instances, a single bowl was placed inverted over the skull of a burial. "Urn" burials have also been recorded. Special vessels are frequently in the shape of cazuela bowls or bottles. Most often such vessels are incised with curvilinear motifs, although some rectilinear motifs are found. Curvilinear designs include volutes, scrolls, loops and circles (many multiple lined) and are generally interlocking and repeated around the entire vessel. Designs are often restricted to a band around the upper portions of the cazuela bowls. Punctations may occur in zones defined by the incised designs. Other vessel shapes include shallow bowls with lateral extensions (generally forming four or six extensions), gourd effigies (dipper-shaped), collared globular bowls and flattened globular bowls (Willey 1949a:460 — 462). Some incised specimens may have red or white pigment rubbed into the incisions and occasionally red-slipped vessels have been found.

These special vessels often have animal head adornos (especially on bowls). Animals include: eagle, woodpecker, duck, goose, quail, heron, owl, turkey, buzzard, snake, lizard, alligator, frog, fox, otter, opossum, squirrel or dog, bear, and cat (Lazarus 1971:46; Jones and Penman 1973). This is a greater variety than the animals shown on earlier Weeden Island effigy vessels. In addition Southeastern Ceremonial Cult symbols or motifs are occasionally incised on special vessels, especially on the bottle forms.

The bottle-shaped vessels found in Pensacola and Fort Walton sites are ubiquitous among Southeast Mississippian sites. Also many of the Fort Walton and Pensacola incised design motifs are very similar if not identical to those of other Mississippian peoples. Vessel shapes and design elements, like the Southeastern Ceremonial Complex, cross-cut Mississippian cultures. These objects and motifs are symbols closely associated with the social, political, economic, and settlement patterns that were an integral part of the Fort Walton and Pensacola polities as well as other Mississippian chiefdoms.

Much less is known about the village life of Fort Walton and Pensacola peoples than about the activities reflected in mounds; few research projects of any duration have focused on inland village or household middens. The available evidence suggests that the life-style of these peoples was very similar to that of the Indians living in the Moundville or Etowah regions. A village, whether a "capital" town with multiple mounds placed around a plaza or a village with a single mound fronting on a plaza, was made up of a number of individual households. Most likely the households were placed around the mound(s) and plaza complex where ceremonial life was centered. There is evidence from one Fort Walton site in Leon County for a circular structure 15 m in diameter (Tesar 1976), perhaps a council house if it was not a house for a single (extended?) family. A council house would probably also front the plaza area.

Individual families, both those in the villages and those on outlying farming homesteads, inhabited small, rectangular houses. Griffin's (1950) excavations at the Lake Jackson site revealed some evidence for such a house measuring 3 by 5 m. Later work by Fryman (1971b) at the same site uncovered a portion of a wall trench believed associated with a house structure. Wall trenches are a common building technique of Mississippian peoples.

Possibly several structures, both summer and winter houses and storage structures, constituted a single household. Some of the village house structures, perhaps the winter houses, may have been made of wattle and daub; other structures were probably thatched. Daub has been found at the Winewood site (Jones and Penman 1973) as well as at historic Apalachee sites (e.g., Jones 1973). However, wattle and daub, also a European technique, may have become more widespread after the establishment of the missions in the seventeenth century.

Evidence for fire pits and cooling or smoking racks within living areas is provided by the Winewood site, but more evidence on specific household activities is lacking. It is probable that many of the same household activities practiced by the inland Weeden Island peoples in Northwest Florida continued into Mississippian times.

Evidence for village ceramic and tool industries is provided by the excavations at sites 8-Ja-5 (Bullen 1958), Winewood (Jones and Penman 1973), and Lake Jackson (Griffin 1950). Like the earlier Weeden Island ceramic inventory, Fort Walton village pottery is largely plain, undecorated ware. Generally 85–90% of the total sherds recovered from sites are plain while only 6–11% are incised (the types Fort Walton Incised, Safety Harbor Incised, Pensacola Incised, Marsh Island Incised, and Point Washington Incised: see Willey 1949a:460–466). Often the incisions are not executed with as great care as the same designs when they are on vessels made for special use (Figure 37).

The most popular village vessel shapes, unlike the earlier Weeden Island period, are open bowls and collared, globular bowls. A small percentage of the plain pottery (2–6% of the total sherds) represents lips

FIGURE 37. *Fort Walton pottery;* **a−b, e,** *Lake Jackson Plain,* **b** *has a handle;* **c−d, f−h,** *Fort Walton Incised.*

which are notched or which have small lugs or loop or strap handles (placed vertically) added as appendages (Figure 37b).

At Pensacola village sites the amount of plain village ware is less, generally totaling 70—80%. Incised pottery is more popular, constituting 15—20% of site totals. At later sites, some of the nonincised pottery of the Pensacola series has a brushed surface; this may be a smoothing technique. At one site reported by Lazarus (1961:58), more than half the undecorated pottery had been brushed.

Other than the typical small, triangular arrow points, the stone tool complex of the Pensacola and Fort Walton cultures seems to resemble that of the earlier Weeden Island peoples. Spokeshaves, side scrapers, polishing stones, and grinding stones have all been found. Limestone hones were used to sharpen bone tools, but the acidic nature of the soils in Northwest Florida has destroyed the bone tools that were deposited in inland middens. Stemmed "points," similar to but smaller than Archaic points found at Fort Walton sites are probably hafted knives.

Other village artifacts found inland include pottery and limestone discs, perhaps gaming stones; drilled discs; greenstone celts, probably used to cut wood; and equal-arm clay pipes. It is likely that most of the Apalachee artifacts for which we have historic descriptions (see Chapter 9) were also used by the Fort Walton peoples, but as yet we do not have a good archaeologically recovered sample of inland village material. However, charred pieces of basketry or matting have been identified from Lake Jackson.

Trade between inland Fort Walton dwellers and coastal peoples must have occurred since marine objects, shell tools and ornaments and sharks' teeth (from tools?), occur at inland sites. We know from descriptions of chiefdoms like those of the Mississippian peoples that redistribution of resources was an important function of the chief. Tribute, probably cultigens, other foods, hides, and other materials, was paid to head chiefs by the chiefs of outlying villages. In return these chiefs were conferred status by the head chiefs and possibly received certain objects (Southeastern Ceremonial Complex objects) to signify that status. Village chiefs (and their people) also received aegis and other benevolence from the head chief. The support and allegiance of the Fort Walton people to their leaders provided the foundation for the complex political and social hierarchy that existed. Villagers and the people from the homesteads probably served as agricultural labor for fields controlled by the chiefs as well as labor to erect and maintain civic and religious structures. Also, warfare was conducted with warriors obtained from the people.

Beliefs concerning themselves, their origins, and their world around them rationalized this system for the villagers. Just as we today believe in and support our way of life, so did the Northwest Florida Mississippian peoples maintain their societies through their beliefs and actions.

Into this well-ordered world the Spanish in the early sixteenth century brought their diseases, leading to a rapid decrease in aboriginal populations. By the time of the establishment of the Spanish missions in the Fort Walton region in 1633 (then known as the territory of the Apalachee Indians), the most complex of the aboriginal cultures in Florida and the most dense aboriginal society had been decimated. The Indian cultures of the historic period are only a reflection of those which had evolved prior to the "discovery" of the New World by Europeans.

Safety Harbor

In Chapter 5 we said that the central Gulf Coast of peninsular Florida, that region from Pasco County to Charlotte Harbor, was occupied until about A.D. 1400 or earlier by a variant of the Weeden Island culture. By that date—perhaps made possible by a combination of factors, including ideas brought southward from the Fort Walton region, growing populations requiring more social controls, and the relatively propitious marine environment of Tampa Bay—the Indians in a portion of the central coast developed a more complex culture. Known as Safety Harbor after the type-site on Tampa Bay, the region of this culture ranged from Tarpon Springs south to Sarasota; the densest distribution of sites is around Tampa Bay.

The Safety Harbor archaeological complex was originally defined by Willey (1949a). Later Griffin and Bullen (1950) excavated at the Safety Harbor site itself, and Bullen reported on a number of excavations at other mound—village complexes and provided several overviews of aspects of the Safety Harbor culture (Bullen 1951, 1952b, 1955a). Sears (1967) has also carried out archaeological research on the Safety Harbor culture.

Safety Harbor was undoubtedly the archaeological culture associated with the Tocobaga Indians and their relatives among whom the Panfilo de Narváez and Hernandez de Soto expeditions landed in the sixteenth century (see Chapter 9). Bullen has discussed geographical correlations between Safety Harbor archaeological sites and the actual villages visited by de Soto (Bullen 1952a, 1978).

The date of A.D. 1400 for the beginning of the Safety Harbor period is somewhat arbitrary, and is not backed up by radiocarbon analyses. Bullen and other researchers based their estimate on the then accepted date of 1400 given as the beginning of the Fort Walton period; this date, we know now, is not early enough. It may be that future research will also show that the Safety Harbor culture was present prior to A.D. 1400, although there is at present no indication that such a date would be as early as dates presently being derived for early Fort Walton.

Safety Harbor culture is relatively well known, although excavations have for the most part focused on mounds rather than on village middens. Thirteen mound—village complexes have been located (Bullen 1955a:51). The community plan of these towns is much the same: truncated pyramidal mounds adjacent to plazas with surrounding village middens. Several of the towns have burial mounds in addition to the temple mounds. Only one mound—village complex, the Parrish site, has been found inland.

Typically, such towns each had a single, large temple mound measuring 6.5 m or less in height with the base 45 m or less on a side. Excavations have shown that this temple mound was periodically rebuilt, increasing in size as new layers were added. A ramp extended down from one side of the flat-topped, mound platform toward the plaza. The mound platform measured about 6 by 12 m (Bullen 1955a:50) and served as a base for a wooden, thatched structure. This structure probably served as the chief's residence, even though Spanish accounts refer to it as a temple. Between the mound and the villagers' residences was a plaza devoid of occupational debris. The village living area usually appears as a linear shell midden which lies parallel to the nearest portion of the Gulf of Mexico or Tampa Bay. However, village excavations have not been extensive enough to determine the exact position of house patterns within the town.

At the Safety Harbor-type site excavated by Griffin and Bullen (1950) the temple mound was placed on a point of land extending out into the bay with the ramp pointing inland toward the plaza. Shell middens extended down both sides of the point, enclosing most of the plaza. A burial mound at the site was about 385 m away from the temple mound and well beyond the village midden. At other sites where burial mounds are known to be present, they are always placed off to one side of the town away from the temple mound and plaza.

The archaeological evidence for the typical Safety Harbor town correlates closely with a description provided by a member of the de Soto expedition in 1539 (Smith 1968:23—24): "The town was of seven or eight houses, built of timber and covered with palm leaves. The chief's house stood near the beach, upon a very high mount made by hand for defense; at the other end of the town was a temple, on the top of which perched a wooden fowl with gilded eyes."

The villagers' houses might well have been quite large, housing several related families, perhaps a lineage or other kin group. However we do not have any archaeological confirmation for this.

The temple described in the 1539 account was most likely a charnel house in which bodies, cleaned of flesh, were stored prior to interment.

Juan Ortiz, a Spaniard from the Narváez expedition who lived among the Tocobaga until rescued by de Soto, told his rescuers that he had been made to guard a temple which contained bodies of the dead. A Spanish account of the de Soto expedition, that of Garcilaso de la Vega (Varner and Varner 1951:65 — 66), described one such temple as containing wooden boxes placed above the ground and covered with rocks or boards and which served as tombs for the dead.

Archaeological evidence for a charnel house is provided by Reichard's 1934 excavation of Parrish Mound 2 (Willey 1949a:146 — 152). On the surface of a platform mound he uncovered a rectangular structure composed of four adjacent rows of posts, each placed about 15 cm apart. One corner of the structure had been strengthened with additional posts and contained evidence of cremations. Possibly the thick wall was to prevent animals from raiding the bones stored there. European articles recovered from the mound indicate that the charnel house had been utilized during at least a portion of the historic period. Evidence for charnel house usage is also provided by Sears's excavations at the Tierra Verde burial mound (Sears 1967).

From the first-hand European accounts and the archaeological data, we can reconstruct the burial process associated with these Safety Harbor "temples." Bodies were partially or entirely stripped of flesh and stored in the charnel house or temple as bundles of bones or as articulated skeletons wrapped in flexed positions. Or the latter may simply have been bodies which had not deteriorated sufficiently for the bones to be disarticulated and transferred to bundles. After certain periods of time, perhaps simply when the storage area was full, the bundled and wrapped, defleshed bodies were placed in separate pits or one large pit dug into the floor of the charnel house. Some bodies may have been cremated.

When this subfloor burial area became full, or for another reason, the charnel house was removed and a layer of sand was placed over the old burial area. Sometimes the burials stored in the charnel house at the time that it was to be moved were placed in the mound cap. The new charnel house was then erected on top of the mound cap, and the process repeated, or it was placed in another location.

These mound—village complexes probably functioned as separate, small chiefdoms. From the Spanish accounts we know that at certain times two or more of these town-chiefdoms were allied, and one chief held the others as vassals, receiving tribute from their villages. Shell midden sites without mound or burial areas may represent outlying villages affiliated with one of the town centers, or they may have functioned as specialized camps periodically reused for fishing or shellfish gathering.

Away from the coast within the Safety Harbor region, small sites have been found (Hemmings 1975a; Padgett 1976). Lithic debris and tools generally comprise the bulk of the artifacts at the sites, although occasionally ceramics are also present. Such sites may have served as specialized camps, perhaps for hunting or for seasonal foraging when the coastal resources were for some reason inadequate to feed a town population. They might also have been camps for the collecting of a resource not available on the coast.

Like their Weeden Island ancestors and their Mississippian relatives, the Safety Harbor villages made and used different ceramic vessels than those vessels used for special, presumably ceremonial, activities. These latter vessels, believed to have been used by the chiefs or priests and found in caches or with burials in mounds, are Middle Mississippian forms and are most closely related to Fort Walton vessels. Although both Safety Harbor and Fort Walton vessels are grit or sand tempered and are sometimes difficult to distinguish from each other, it seems likely that some of the well-made, fine-paste vessels in Tampa Bay sites are actually items brought southward from Northwest Florida.

Occasionally Weeden Island ceremonial vessels are found in Safety Harbor mounds. The best explanation is that these were heirlooms, retained for several or more generations before finding their way into mounds. The mound ceramic caches, both those containing only Safety Harbor vessels and those with both Safety Harbor and Weeden Island vessels, were placed on the eastern side of the burial mounds, either just within the edge or just outside of the mound. Most likely these ceremonial vessels were "cleared out" of the temple charnel house or the chief's residence and placed in the mound at the time the mound cap was placed over the burial area, after the charnel house was emptied of bones.

The Safety Harbor ceremonial vessel forms, like those of other Mississippian peoples, include open, cazuela, and globular bowls; beakers; jars; and bottles. Some jars and bowls have two or four loop or strap handles or rim lugs. A few vessels have adornos placed on the rim, usually crude or stylized animal effigies. Decorative motifs are very similar to Fort Walton designs and include parallel lines incised in various curvilinear and rectilinear motifs and incised and punctated scrolls and guilloches (Figure 38a,b,f). Sears (1967:31 – 55, 65 – 70) has described in detail the form

a

b 2924

c

d

e 2958

f 2919

and decorative relationships between the Safety Harbor ceremonial ceramic complex and those of the Fort Walton and certain other Mississippian cultures.

Because of the dearth of excavations in Safety Harbor villages, we know relatively little about everyday village life. Shell, bone, and stone artifacts are found infrequently in the shell middens. This suggests that the shell middens are heaps of garbage discarded adjacent to the actual house and living areas. Types of artifacts recovered are much the same as those from the earlier Weeden Island cultures who inhabited the Tampa Bay region. Although changes in social and political organization may have occurred between the late Weeden Island period and the Safety Harbor period, the basic pattern of subsistence and the concomitant technology remained much the same.

This similarity is borne out by the meager analyses of faunal remains taken from the shell middens. There is no indication that there was a dramatic shift to more intensive agriculture and a decline in use of non-domesticated food sources. Safety Harbor peoples were largely hunters, gatherers, and fishermen who practiced agriculture much like their coastal-dwelling ancestors.

One new artifact present in Safety Harbor middens is the Pinellas point, a small triangular arrow point very similar to the triangular points found throughout the Southeast at Mississippian sites. Its presence may indicate the first use of the bow and arrow within the central Gulf Coast region.

Safety Harbor village pottery was poorly made, and more than 95% was undecorated and tempered with sand or grit. This continues the long Weeden Island tradition along the peninsular coast (Figure 38c—e). The most common vessel shape is the bowl, a few of which have strap handles like Fort Walton vessels. Sherds of Northwest Florida Fort Walton vessels are occasionally found in the middens, indicating trade or other contact. The Tocobaga Indians of the historic period were certainly aware of the Apalachee, descendants of the Fort Walton peoples, and members of the Narváez expedition were shown European items which were said to have been brought from Apalachee.

The quantity of European items recovered by archaeologists from Safety Harbor sites, relative to the large amounts of supplies left by the Narváez and de Soto expeditions in the sixteenth century and materials acquired later from Spanish fishermen and traders and from shipwrecks,

---

FIGURE 38. *Safety Harbor pottery; **a,** Pinellas Incised; **b, f,** Safety Harbor Incised; **c—e,** Pinellas Plain (**b** has a handle). Note similarities to Fort Walton Pottery in Figure 37.*

is surprisingly small (Bullen 1978). However, there is still a great deal of archaeology to be carried out in the Tampa Bay region.

The Safety Harbor culture represents a Fort Walton-influenced elaboration of the basic Weeden Island coastal life-style. Mississippian ideas concerning social and political organization may have provided the late Weeden Island culture with a means of coping with the pressures of larger populations, a result of normal rates of population growth. The Tampa Bay region is not as well suited to the type of intensive, swidden agriculture possible elsewhere and associated with Mississippian cultures. Thus, the late Weeden Island culture adapted certain Mississippian traits to its life-style, but rejected others, such as those associated with intensive agriculture. The resulting Safety Harbor culture can be characterized as a Mississippian adaptation to a specialized, coastal environment.

Both the Fort Walton and the Safety Harbor cultures were flourishing in the sixteenth century when the first Europeans entered Florida. The next chapter depicts the Florida Indians during the historic period and describes the devastating effects of European contact.

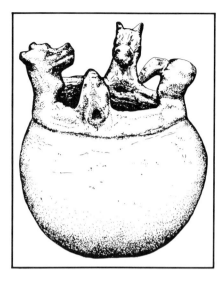

9

Peoples of the Historic Period

At the time of the first European explorations in Florida during the first half of the sixteenth century more than 100,000 Indians inhabited the state. These people, the descendants of the populations described in the preceding chapters, were divided into many different political units and occupied a great variety of environments. Although many aspects of social and political organization were shared by the Indians, some of their basic techniques for obtaining a livelihood were as varied as the natural areas they utilized.

The northern half of the state, above a line drawn from the lower edge of Tampa Bay across to about Cape Canaveral but dipping down to include the Central Lake District, was the home of the agriculturalists. South of this boundary were the people whose diet was based entirely on the hunting and collecting of wild resources (although maize agriculture was present in the Lake Okeechobee Basin in prehistoric times; see Chapter 7).

The major northern agricultural groups were the various Timucuan tribes, descendants of the St. Johns, Alachua, and other archaeologically known societies; the Apalachee, who were descended from Fort Walton populations; and the Tocobaga, known archaeologically as the Safety Harbor culture. Major southern groups were the Calusa and the Tequesta. Smaller South Florida tribes were the Keys Indians, Jeaga, and the Ais (Figure 39).

A very large number of other tribes also lived in Florida. For some we have little or no information about them other than an occasional men-

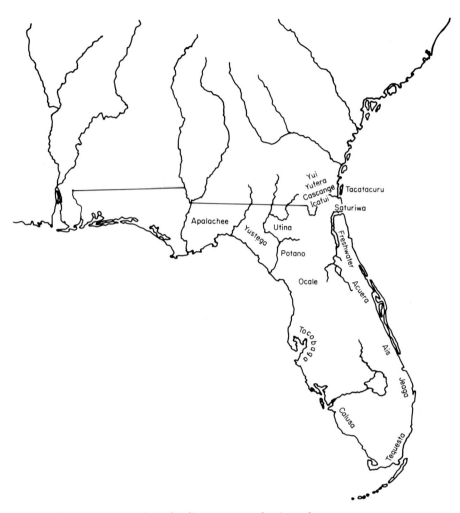

FIGURE 39. *Location of Indian groups at the time of European contact.*

tion in a document, while others are not noted at all. For instance, although we can describe some aspects of the Indian cultures living along the peninsular Gulf Coast north of the Tocobaga and south of the Apalachee basing our observations on archeologically derived data, we cannot provide descriptions based on firsthand accounts or even give the name of the tribe(s). Because the indigenous Indian population of Florida was destroyed as early as the beginning of the eighteenth century, we may never know who these and other aboriginal groups were. Unless more information is eventually uncovered in as yet unstudied documents, we will know them only from archaeological investigations.

The story of the Florida Indians during the historic period is the story of peoples and cultures forced to alter life-styles in an attempt to accommodate the European presence. Explorers and missionaries brought new crops, new ideas, and new diseases for which there were no immunities. As elsewhere in the New World, population size plummeted rapidly as diseases were introduced and then spread outward among the Indians like ripples in a pond, causing vast epidemics. Political systems collapsed under the shrinking populations and subsistence systems faltered, leading to more cultural changes, many of which are obvious in the archaeological record. In two centuries the Indians were devastated, leaving Florida open for settlement by the Indians who were to become known as the Seminole.

In this chapter we will briefly summarize the nature and temporal framework of the European exploration, settlement, and missionary efforts in Florida before describing the important Indian groups. Our knowledge of these historic tribes comes from the narratives and accounts left by these Europeans and from limited archaeological excavations.

Europeans in Florida

The first *recorded* European venture into Florida was the expedition of Juan Ponce de Leon in 1513. Juan Ponce's first voyage probably reached the Calusa somewhere on the Gulf Coast south of Fort Myers before moving up the east coast (Davis 1935). But his was not the first voyage to Florida; one of the Indians he encountered already understood Spanish.

During the period 1513 — 1528 other Spanish explorers sailed along the Florida coasts, including Lucas Vasquez de Ayllon who reached the eastern Timucuan tribes before sailing northward, possibly to the Carolinas. These voyages, some of which were for the purpose of enslaving the Florida Indians for work in the Caribbean, served to introduce diseases and to make the Indians wary of future contact with Europeans.

The first major overland expedition into Florida was that of the Spaniard Panfilo de Narváez who landed at Tampa Bay with several hundred men and their supplies in 1528. Moving northward to the Apalachee region near Tallahassee, the expedition traveled through the swampy flatlands paralleling the coast where they encountered few Indians. The expedition was beset by one misfortune after another and only a handful of survivors eventually reached New Spain (Mexico) almost 10 years later. One survivor, Nuñez Cabeza de Vaca (Smith 1871), recorded the observations and trials and tribulations of the ill-fated expedition.

Perhaps the most famous sixteenth-century Spanish intrusion into the United States was that of Hernando de Soto. De Soto, with about 600 men, livestock, and provisions, landed at the south end of Tampa Bay in 1539 and moved northward toward Apalachee through the regions of the To-cobaga in Tampa Bay and the Timucuan tribes in North-Central and North Florida. Eventually, after wintering among the Apalachee in 1539—1540, the de Soto entrada continued northward into Georgia, then westward eventually reaching the Mississippi River (Swanton, ed. 1939).

The effects of this expedition on the Florida and other Southeast Indians is poorly understood. But it may be no coincidence that at about the time of de Soto's journey, there were apparently rapid changes in the ceramic inventories of some of the Timucuan tribes and the Apalachee. These may reflect other cultural changes which are not clear at this time, but which may be related to the effects of de Soto's expedition.

Despite the failure of these early expeditions to find gold or other wealth among the Florida Indians, the Spanish crown still wished to control the Florida coasts in order to protect her shipping lanes, so important to supplying the circum-Caribbean colonies and for the safe passage of the Plate Fleet from the New World to Spain. In June 1559, Tristán de Luna y Arellano set sail from Vera Cruz with more than 1500 soldiers and settlers to establish a permanent Spanish settlement at Pensacola Bay. Although the exact landing place of the expeditionary force is not known (it is thought to be somewhere from Mobile Bay east and south to Choctawatchee Bay), it is probable that de Luna eventually reached Pensacola Bay.

The de Luna expedition ended in total failure; a hurricane destroyed a part of the fleet before they even landed, and starvation and discontent beset the group after landing. In a little more than a year the remnants of the Spanish withdrew and for a short time the Spanish crown closed Florida to further exploration (Smith and Gottlob 1978:4—5).

However, a Spanish adventurer was able to convince the crown to underwrite another attempt at settlement. Plans for the expedition of Pedro Menéndez de Avilés were speeded up when it was learned that the French, under Jean Ribault and René de Laudonnière, had established Fort Caroline at the mouth of the St. Johns River in 1564. Ribault had previously explored the coast from Florida north to Virginia in 1562. The accounts of these Frenchmen provide valuable information on the Indians of the entire coastal region.

Menéndez was able to destroy Fort Caroline and oust the French from Florida, establishing St. Augustine in 1565 as a permanent Spanish garrison and frontier town. The story of Menéndez's adventures and misadventures in the New World is an interesting one which has been the subject of scholarly study by Eugene Lyon (1976). Lyon notes that St. Augustine was just one of a group of garrisons established by Menéndez in Florida. Others, which included soldiers as well as Jesuit missionaries charged with administering to the Indians, were among the Tequesta (in modern Miami), the Calusa (near Fort Myers), the Ais (on the southeast Florida coast), and the Tocobaga (Tampa Bay). All of these latter garrisons lasted only a short time and were soon abandoned. However, the accounts of the Jesuit priests are particularly informative and many have been published (see Zubillaga 1946).

The Jesuit missionaries began the establishment of missions along the Georgia Coast, but met with little success and they were withdrawn from Spanish Florida in 1572. Later, in 1584, Franciscan missionaries came to St. Augustine and founded a series of permanent missions along the Atlantic Coast among the Timucuans and the Georgia and South Carolina coastal tribes. Traveling priests went inland from these permanent missions to administer to other of the Indians, including those in North Florida.

Missionary efforts were expanded as more Franciscans came. Beginning in 1606, a string of missions was established inland from the Potano Indians near Gainesville westward to the Aucilla River among other Timucuan tribes. Missions, none successful, were also placed inland among the Timucuans below Palatka on the St. Johns River. After 1633 missions were also established among the Apalachee, and by the mid-seventeenth century the Spanish road from St. Augustine to Tallahassee was dotted with missions.

During the last quarter of the seventeenth century, Georgia Indians were moving southward into Florida, pushed out of their traditional grounds by the raids of the English and their Indian allies who used the Carolinian colonies as their base. These raids eventually reached down into Florida, and the Spanish attempted to establish missions among the Indians in the Apalachicola — Flint — Chattahoochee region in order to form a protective buffer.

The Spanish efforts were unsuccessful, and in 1702 the English entered Florida, destroying some missions and laying seige to St. Augustine. In late 1703 and early 1704, Colonel James Moore with a force of 50 soldiers and as many as 1000 Indians completely destroyed the Apalachee missions and a large number of the Timucuan missions, effectively ending Spain's hold on northern Florida and signaling the final death knell for the North Florida Indians.

The surviving Timucuans and Apalachee moved out of their homelands, some west and some east to the vicinity of St. Augustine where a number of small villages, some of Georgia Indians, lasted into the 1730s. After that time, the few remaining Indians seem to have become incorporated into St. Augustine, most within a growing mestizo population.

When Spain withdrew from Florida in 1763, leaving it in the control of Great Britain, 83 Indians are listed among the people taken to Cuba.

The fate of the South Florida Indians is not as well documented as that of the Timucuans and the Apalachee. Spanish traders, fishermen, and victims of shipwrecks continued to have intermittent contact with the various tribes, and the populations continued to diminish throughout the seventeenth century. In the 1740s Jesuits attempted to establish a mission in the Miami area to serve Indians who were living there, remnants of the once numerous Calusa, Tequesta, and other groups. By the early eighteenth century the Florida aborigines had been destroyed.

Timucuans

In the early sixteenth century Timucuan Indians occupied most of the northern third of peninsular Florida, extending into southeastern Georgia about to Brunswick. This area encompassed North, North-Central, and East Florida including the Central Lake District. Although some individuals have also labeled the Tampa Bay Tocobaga and the coastal tribes immediately to the north as Timucuans, there is at present no documentary evidence confirming their linguistic affiliation as Timucuan (although some of the Sarasota area place-names do appear to be Timucuan).

The Timucuan tribes spoke dialects of the same language, but they constituted distinct political units and practiced several different, although related, subsistence systems, a result of living in quite different environments. Researchers have not yet satisfactorily determined the relationships of Timucuan to other New World languages, but it is certain that it is not a Muskogean language like that of the Apalachee and various Creek groups (see Crawford 1975). Timucuan may have been a widespread language in the Southeast which was replaced by Muskogean as a result of the growth of Mississippian cultures.

Generally the Timucuans are divided into two divisions, eastern and western (Deagan 1978; Milanich 1978b). The eastern tribes were the Saturiwa, Freshwater (or Agua Dulce), and Acuera who, like their St. Johns ancestors, lived spaced along the St. Johns River and also used the resources of the Atlantic coastal lagoon; the Cascange, Icafui, Yufera, and Yui (Ibi)—related tribes who inhabited mainland southeastern Georgia; and the Tacatacuru who were on Cumberland Island. The Tucururu and the Oconi were Timucuan-speaking groups who also inhabited Georgia north of the other groups. In the early eighteenth century a group of Timucuans known as Tawasa were in South-Central Alabama (Swanton 1929).

The western Timucua included the Potano and Ocale, historic representatives of the Alachua tradition in Alachua and western Marion counties, respectively; the Utina in Suwannee and Columbia counties; and the Yustega to the west between the Suwannee and Aucilla Rivers.

The various Timucuan tribes are associated with several different archaeological complexes. In East Florida the Saturiwa and the groups along the St. Johns River manufactured St. Johns pottery and continued the cultural traditions of their St. Johns ancestors (see Chapter 6). The mainland southeastern Georgia tribes are little known archaeologically, although some evidence exists that their archaeological complexes are related to the Savannah culture of the Georgia Coast. On Cumberland Island the Tacatacuru apparently are represented by Savannah-derived cord-marked ceramics as well as by pottery brushed and malleated with dried corn cobs.

Better known archaeologically are the Potano and Ocale, both of whom are represented at the time of historic contact by the Alachua archaeological tradition. As related in Chapter 7, several seventeenth-century Potano villages have been excavated. One late sixteenth—early seventeenth century Utina mission village has been located and tested. The ceramic assemblage present is the Leon—Jefferson complex characterized by Jefferson Ware complicated-stamped pottery and some Leon Check Stamped pottery (Figures 40, 41, 42). This ceramic complex is also present at Yustega sites and is characteristic of Apalachee mission villages (Boyd, Smith, and Griffin 1951:161—174).

Reports and documents of the Spanish priests, the accounts of the French, and, to a lesser extent, the narratives of the de Soto expedition provide most of the documentary information on the Timucuans. The Saturiwa, being closest to Fort Caroline and St. Augustine are the best known tribe. The famous Le Moyne drawings are based largely on observations of that group (Lorant 1946). Archaeological teams directed by Kathleen Deagan from Florida State University have begun investigation of the sixteenth-century Saturiwa in St. Augustine. These new data promise to correct and supplement the documentary sources.

Although the various groups of Timucuans living in different regions utilized their environments in different ways, all of the tribes were agriculturalists who grew corn, beans, tobacco, and other cultigens and who also relied heavily on hunting, fishing, and gathering wild foods whether those foods were marine fish, acorns, or shellfish. Contact between the tribes had occurred for hundreds of years and many social, political, and religious traits were shared. The following sketch is a composite picture of the Timucuans as they appeared at the time of first European contact.

Timucuan subsistence was centered on fishing, hunting, and collect-

a

b

c

ing in the forests and swamps, and planting maize, beans, and squash. Deer was the single most important meat source, although a number of types of animals were eaten. Tobacco was also planted. In some riverine areas, such as on the St. Johns River, shellfish were collected for food. Many of the eastern Timucuans also collected oysters and other marine shellfish from the Atlantic coastal lagoons.

Charred corn cobs have been found at historic Timucuan sites, although other cultigens have not been reported yet. The earliest maize ears, probably the same type grown at the time of contact, were about 6 — 8 cm long and featured eight rows of kernels; rows were paired. Later ears were larger and had 10 — 12 rows of kernels, perhaps a result of hybridization.

Hunting and fishing techniques included deerskin disguises, fish spears, fish traps and weirs, deer fire-drives, and the use of bows and arrows with quivers, spears, and snares for birds and deer. Arrows were tipped with small triangular Pinellas points. Extensive seasonal collection of palm berries, acorns, and other nuts, all recovered archaeologically, also provided a portion of the diet.

Basketry and cordage were both manufactured and clay vessels were fired in a variety of forms, especially bowls. Often, surfaces of pots were roughened with dried corn cobs (Potano) or malleated with carved wooden paddles (Saturiwa and Utina). Gourd and wooden containers were used also. Food preparation techniques included cooking or smoking meat on barbecue frames, boiling fish and other meat in water, grinding of corn flour, the making of corn fritters, and the boiling-down of meats and possibly nuts for broths.

Villages, sometimes palisaded (although none have been located archaeologically) were built near freshwater streams or next to lakes. Dugout canoes were available for transportation on the water as well as for fishing. Individual houses were inhabited by nuclear families (there is some evidence for polygyny, but whether or not joint families lived in the same structure is unknown). Houses were circular with palm-thatched walls and roofs. Those partially excavated at the Richardson site were about 7.5 m in diameter. The roofs apparently were dome-shaped with the upper "attic" being used for storage.

Other structures found in the villages were public granaries, separate family storage houses built up off the ground, and round council houses. Villages also had open ceremonial squares or plazas lined with wooden

FIGURE 40. *Mission period artifacts from Suwannee County; a, Jefferson Ware sherd with a complicated stamped cross motif; b — c, Spanish majolica plate sherds.*

FIGURE 41. *Mission period artifacts; **a—c,** Jefferson Ware complicated stamp sherds from a Spanish-Utina mission in Suwannee County; **d—e,** both sides of a carved wooden club recovered by William Jones from mission San Juan del Puerto in Duval County. The club is 59 cm long.*

FIGURE 42. *Mission period pottery from northern Florida;* **a, e,** *Ocmulgee Fields Incised;* **b, d,** *Leon Check Stamped;* **c,** *Aucilla Incised;* **f,** *characteristic Jefferson Ware rim.*

benches. Similar benches were used in the houses as beds. As yet only individual houses have been excavated.

Social, religious, and political systems of the Timucua were quite similar to those of other southeastern Indians. Ranked clans (matrilineal and exogamous) were present and had names such as Panther, Bear, Fish, Earth, Buzzard, and Quail. Both wealth and title were inherited within the clan from one's mother's brother. Village chiefs and other civil officials came from specific clans with the head chief or *ano paracusi holata ico* (or *olato aco*, or *utinama*) coming from the White Deer or Great Deer clan. Clan membership was also important in the selection of some of the lesser officials, such as the *inihama* and the village councilors. The *inihama* assisted the chief and led him by the hand during formal occasions. The name *inihama* was probably borrowed from the Creek word *heniha*. Evidently many aspects of culture diffused among the Southeast peoples during the Mississippian period.

Chiefs and other prestigious persons often had more than one wife, and husbands had sexual rights to their wife's sisters, and males had sexual rights to their brother's wives. Sexual relationships between wives and fathers-in-law and between husbands and mothers-in-law also seem to have been accepted practices, much to the dismay of Spanish friars. Homosexual relationships (both male and female) are also indicated from Spanish descriptions.

Chiefs extracted tribute from their villagers in the form of produce which was stored in a central storehouse. During the seventeenth century, cassina leaves were paid as tribute, according to one document. Individuals were required to perform services for the chiefs, such as working in their fields. Documents also indicate that chiefs kept black slaves as consorts. Black slaves were brought very early to Florida by the de Soto (in 1539) and by the Don Tristan de Luna (in 1559) expeditions.

Spanish descriptions and the French narratives document the presence of transvestites or berdaches among the Timucua. These individuals were used to perform specialized tasks such as carrying the dead and wounded.

The attire of the Timucua is well known from the drawings of the Frenchman Jacques Le Moyne (Lorant 1946) and other descriptions. Young children appear in the drawings naked and adults and children went barefoot. The women dressed in Spanish moss skirts (at times with a sash over one shoulder attached to the opposite hip) and wore their hair long and unbound. Chiefs' wives are shown tattooed and decorated with beads worn on the neck, wrists, and ankles. Shell and glass beads (the latter blue beads were traded by the Europeans) have been found at sites. Fingernails were long and served both as decoration and as weapons. Double fish-bladder ear plugs were common for both Timucuan men and women, and frequently these were dyed. Shell ear pins as much as 10 cm long also were worn by some individuals. During special dances the women wore a breechclout-like girdle with metal objects hung from the bottom. Berdaches also wore moss skirts and long hair.

Men wore breechclouts and had their hair tied up. Headdresses of feathers, or a single feather stuck in the topknot, were worn as war paraphernalia. Skins and stuffed animals (birds, cats, and various other mammals) were also worn on the head or attached to the back of the breechclout. One Le Moyne drawing shows a feather-adorned basketry hat.

Chiefs and subchiefs were tattooed over almost the entire body, and they wore beaded baldrics, metal (probably copper) discs, and beaded anklets, armbands, legbands, and bracelets. Turkey spurs were used occasionally as earplugs. Nobility, both male and female, were transported in litters.

Several types of musical instruments were played by the Timucuans; flutes or trumpets, gourd rattles, and stones struck with a stick. The flute or trumpet players accompanied the chief to announce his presence. Sports activities included footraces, on which wagers were often placed, and the Southeastern stickball game.

Warfare was accompanied by many rituals and usually took place between Timucuan tribes. Bows and arrows, spears, and clubs were used as weapons. Before entering the field of battle, a tea brewed from the leaves of the Cassina plant *Ilex vomitoria* (the black drink) was taken. The caffeine in the tea helped to stimulate the warriors and had medicinal as well as ritual qualities. Priests or shamans were consulted to predict the outcome of the battle, and the decision to fight or withdraw leaned heavily on their advice. At times fire arrows were used to attack enemy villages without open warfare taking place.

Both scalping and body mutilation of the enemy was practiced by the Timucuans. Scalps were dried over fires and kept as trophies. Often the legs and arms which were cut off of the dead enemies were taken back to the home village. There they were mounted on poles, and the victory was celebrated in ceremonies conducted by the village Indian priests.

Many of the beliefs and ritual practices of the Timucua can be extracted from Spanish documents along with information on the roles of the various medical practitioners and Indian priests who one Franciscan priest noted were separated into *medicos* (curers), *herbolarios* (herbalists), *parteras* (midwives), and *hechizeros* (priest – shamans) (Milanich and Sturtevant 1972). Techniques of the curers involved praying, administering certain herbs, and use of ritual fires in conjunction with curing ceremonies. Ritual "taking out" (perhaps sucking) of the evil spirits thought to cause illness was also practiced. The herbalists and midwives (possibly specialized shamans) also cured with prayers and herbs, and they delivered babies and administered to the mother-to-be during labor. Herbs were employed to retard or speed up delivery. Tobacco, a revered plant, was often used in praying, especially by men before hunting. Both special persons who performed prayers and a ceremonial place at which to pray are mentioned by the Spanish.

Certain animals' body-movements or certain other happenings were taken by the Timucuans as omens, and were heeded, lest something bad would happen. These omens included crying fawns, owl hoots, snakes, woodpeckers, lightning, the popping of the fire in the hearth, and the twitching of eyes, eyebrows, or mouth.

Burial mounds, prevalent prehistorically and during the early historic period, disappeared in the seventeenth century when Mission Indians adopted Christian burial practices. When a chief died, he was buried with his shell cup from which he had drunk cassina. Shell cups and elaborate burials, presumably chiefs, have been observed in late prehistoric mounds. Relatives of a dead person cut their hair, bathed, and fasted after attending the funeral. The cleaned bodies of other individuals were apparently stored in charnel houses and buried en masse in mounds. After the adoption of Christian burial form, the Spanish priests found that the Saturiwa still tried to place grave goods as offerings inside burial shrouds.

Two studies of changes occurring among the eastern (Deagan 1978) and western (Milanich 1978b) Timucuans during the historic period have provided the following picture of Spanish—Timucuan relations, which is probably typical of the Spanish—Apalachee contact situation also.

Changes in social and political organization occurred early in the historic period as a result of declining populations and conscious attempts by the Spanish military and missionaries to alter traditional patterns of rank and property inheritance and to reduce centralized, inter-village governmental organization. Early documents, both French and Spanish, refer to tribal chiefs among the Yustega, Potano, and Utina who were "above" village chiefs in rank and to whom village chiefs were vassal. Evidently these three groups, if not all of the other Timucuans, were organized into chiefdoms. The Utina chief was said by the French to have 40 villages under his control, while a Spanish document 4 decades later (1602) still noted 20 vassal villages. But by the mid-seventeenth century such centralized authority, tied in closely with social organization and clan ranking, no longer existed, although two or three villages might recognize a single figure as chief.

Priests and, to a lesser extent, military officials, chose to work through village chiefs and did not wish those individuals to be subject to higher authority. Priests quickly learned that if a village chief converted to Christianity, he could order his entire village to do likewise. Priests also learned that they could achieve quicker results by appointing as chief someone who had already converted. Deagan (1978) has documented several instances of the latter among eastern Timucuan groups.

The Spanish also sought in some instances to encourage inheritance of property and title from father to son rather than from uncle to nephew, the traditional pattern which kept property and rank in the same matrilineal clan. Another aboriginal practice, that of polygyny, was prohibited by the priests. These prohibitions must have been disruptive factors in clan organization and ranking and prevented the Indians from maintaining centralized authority.

Priests actively tried to prevent those religious and secular beliefs and practices which they thought pagan. Father Francisco Pareja, priest of the mission San Juan del Puerto on Fort George Island near Jacksonville, authored a confessional in 1613 listing questions to ask the Indians (Milanich and Sturtevant 1972). The types of questions illustrate those beliefs and practices that the Spanish wanted stopped.

Burial in mounds also ceased at the time of the missions, and Christian-style cemetery burials have been found at a number of both Timucuan and Apalachee missions. Bodies were interred in an extended position, usually with arms crossed on chest. Decentralization of authority might also have been a contributing factor to the decline in mound burial, since large work forces could not have been easy to raise.

Some material items of Spanish manufacture were introduced to the Indians, especially at the missions closest to St. Augustine. However, because these goods came ultimately from Spain, they were relatively few in quantity. They included some metal tools and nails or spikes, some ceramic vessels, and such things as flour and clothing. The most common Spanish ceramics found at historic Indian sites are sherds from olive jars. These wheel-thrown vessels were used as "packaging" to transport oil, grain, and even soap. They inevitably found their way to Indian villages. Majolica plates, cups, and other dishware also have been excavated at historic Timucuan sites. Majolica, a tin-glazed ware often featuring painted floral or other designs on a white background, provides a useful chronological tool at historic sites since certain types had a restricted period of manufacture. Indians often copied majolica vessel forms. The resulting Miller Plain ceramics are shaped like plates, saucers, small bowls with ringed bases, ane even pitchers. A small percentage of the ceramics was red-slipped (Mission Red Filmed).

Stone tools are very rare at the post-1630 sites thus far investigated. Certainly such traditional tools were not replaced by European-manufactured goods, since the latter are also rare. The decline of stone tool technology remains to be investigated.

Changes in subsistence and settlement patterns are harder to detect in the archaeological record than changes in material goods, but a great deal of information is available in documents. The practice of the Indians to disperse into small groups in the fall and winter to hunt and gather specific resources such as acorns or shellfish was discouraged by the priests who needed the Indians to remain year-round in their agricultural villages in order to effectively Christianize them. Mission villages were often established in areas convenient for the Spanish, such as along the Spanish road, resulting in abandonment of older villages. Unfortunately, in the case of some Timucuans such as the Utina, such missions were not necessarily located where the best soils for Indian agriculture were found.

Subsistence changes also involved alterations in the crops grown and in the methods of cultivation. Although metal hoes and machetes might have merely increased efficiency of production, the introduction of new crops must have had more of an effect on the aboriginal cultures. Watermelons, peaches, oranges, and wheat all began to be grown by the Indians. Charred peach pits have been found at several sites. Wheat was often cultivated on Spanish ranches among the western Timucua and was used, along with cattle also raised on the ranches, to help feed the population of St. Augustine. Indians, often having the status of impressed labor, provided the work force for the ranches. Wheat, planted in the fall and harvested at a different time of the year than the traditional Indian crops, must have further disrupted the aboriginal subsistence pattern. Other animals introduced through the missions and farms included pigs, horses, oxen, and chickens, although little evidence of these has been found at Timucuan sites outside of St. Augustine.

Because the ranches and farms had value to the Spanish, individual Spaniards sought to "buy" land from the Indians, especially from the chiefs. But the Indians had no concept of individual land ownership, leading to further harrassment of the Indians and misunderstanding. This harrassment, the use of Indian labor to run the ranches, and the use of Indians to transport produce and cattle overland to St. Augustine were partially responsible for several rebellions by the Indians.

During the seventeenth century, especially after 1680 when the English founded Charles Towne (Charleston) and agitated Creeks and Cherokees against the Georgia coastal missions, many of the Georgia Guale Indians as well as some Florida Indians, moved to the Timucuan mission villages.

The cultures of these newcomers, who may have outnumbered the Timucuans at some of the missions, were merged with that of the Timucuans. In some instances, such as with pottery design motifs, new traits were adopted wholesale by the Timucuans. At the later Potano sites San Marcos pottery and Jefferson Ware are both present. This intrusion of new cultural elements resulted in further changes among the North Florida Indians.

Thus, by 1700 much of the Timucuans' original cultural pattern had been altered. The population was decimated and the Indians' aboriginal way of life had been partially replaced by an intermixture of Timucuan, Spanish, and other Indian traits. These changes are reflected in the archaeological record, and future research should provide more interpretations of the processes of change.

The population of the Timucuans at the time of first contact is difficult to determine, but must have been at least 40,000, not a large amount considering the size of the region occupied by the various groups. Agricultural lands in northern Florida certainly could have easily supported this relatively low population density.

Apalachee

Descendants of the Fort Walton peoples, the Apalachee Indians in the seventeenth century occupied that portion of the Florida panhandle from the Aucilla River west to the Apalachicola River Valley. Although Fort Walton sites are found throughout this region, including on the coast, their villages, like those of the Apalachee of the mission period, were centered in the Tallahassee Red Hills region. The greatest density of historic Apalachee sites seems to have been in Jefferson and Leon counties, where the Spanish missions were established. The population of the mission Apalachee seems to have been greatly reduced from that of the Fort Walton peoples, a result, no doubt, of European-introduced diseases.

Because some late Fort Walton sites contain Spanish artifacts, it seems likely that the Apalachee visited by the Narváez and de Soto expeditions still maintained a Fort Walton material culture. But by the mission period, which began in 1633—1635 in Northwest Florida, the Apalachee archaeological culture was the Leon—Jefferson complex characterized by complicated-stamped ceramics, burial in cemeteries rather than mounds, and habitation in villages without temple mounds. At least 15 different Spanish missions were built among the Apalachee; the most in use at any one time was apparently 13.

By the time of the missions the Apalachee had already undergone a great deal of change as a result of population decline and contact with Europeans. The chiefdom(s) with centralized authority of the Fort Walton period had been replaced by more independent villages, as had occurred among the Timucuans. And the Fort Walton archaeological complex was almost totally replaced by the Leon—Jefferson complex which was further altered during the post-1633 mission period.

The Apalachee were important to the Spanish since their territory was the westernmost region under true Spanish control and fronted the Gulf shipping lanes. Also ranches were maintained among the Apalachee. In order to help protect her holdings, Spain established one garrison, San Luis, near Tallahassee and one, San Marcos, on the coast. But the San Luis garrison was quite small and was not capable of protecting the missions from the English raids on the area in 1702—1704 which totally destroyed the Apalachee. After those raids, in which captives were taken to South Carolina, the surviving Apalachee fled, some to Pensacola and then Mobile and some to St. Augustine. A few Indians returned to their old territory early in the eighteenth century, and at least some merged with the various Creeks who began moving into Northwest Florida, later to be known as Seminole. Like the Creeks, and unlike the Timucuans, the Apalachee spoke a Muskogean language; most researchers agree that their language was a dialect of Hitchiti, which today is the language of some of the Seminole.

Despite having been missionized for almost 70 years, the amount of documentary detail on the Apalachee is not great. The best single source is a long letter by the Bishop of Cuba (Wenhold 1936) who visited the area in 1675. Documents relative to the destruction of the missions, compiled by Mark Boyd (Boyd, Smith, and Griffin 1951) also contain pertinent information. Our archaeological knowledge of the Apalachee is also limited since excavations have largely been confined to Spanish structures at missions. No extensive portions of Apalachee villages have been investigated and reported.

Like the Timucuans, the Apalachee were horticulturalists, growing maize, beans, and cucurbits along with European-introduced crops. And like the other northern Florida Indians, the Apalachee also relied on fishing, collecting of wild foods, and hunting. Deer, bear, fox, raccoon, and opossum were all taken along with many other animals. Pig, horse, and cow or oxen bones have all been identified from Spanish—Apalachee sites. Pinellas projectile points were used to tip arrows and a variety of traps and snares were also used. Many subsistence techniques were shared with the Timucuans.

Although towns of the Fort Walton people may have had as many as

250 dwellings, those of the mission period were smaller. Houses were evidently round and thatched with palmetto, like those of other North Florida Indians. Mission villages contained a church, convent (to house the missionaries), and one or more other structures utilized by the missionaries and their charges. All were of wattle and daub or had vertical plank walls. The dried daub could be plastered over. Several of these multiroomed structures have been excavated by archaeologists, including the mission of San Juan de Aspalaga whose church-related structures were excavated almost in their entirety and have provided a detailed picture of an Apalachee mission (Morrell and Jones 1970). A number of mission cemeteries have also been excavated. Like the Timucua, the Apalachee were interred Christian-style in shallow, long graves with arms folded on the chest. Children were often separated from adults.

Excavations at the garrison of San Luis and the mission of San Francisco de Oconee (Boyd, Smith, and Griffin 1951) have produced a variety of European items probably used and discarded by the Spaniards. These include weaponry (portions of muskets, pistols, cannon, grenades, band chain mail, lance head), tools (axe, hoe, chisel, anvil), hardware (nails, hinges, keys and locks, pins), and religious items (crucifix, rosary beads, copper ornaments).

Relative to the materials of the Fort Walton period, the shell, stone, bone, and ceramic artifacts of the mission Apalachee were less well made and are fewer in number and variety. Some granite pounders and grinders were apparently imported by the Spaniards to Apalachee. And there is no evidence for the fine metal work, especially of copper, present in Fort Walton times. Gunflints were made by the Apalachee, and at times glass from Spanish bottles was knapped like flint (Smith 1956:66). Jefferson Ware bowls, (see Figures 40–41, pp. 218, 220) with outflaring rims are most common. Miller Plain vessels were also made. Strangely, the Apalachee ceramic complex appears to have closer affinities to late prehistoric Lamar ceramics in Georgia than to Fort Walton ceramics.

To the relatively short Spaniards, the Apalachee, like most Florida Indians appeared tall. Little clothing was worn, to the consternation of the Spanish priests. Women often wore skirts of Spanish moss. Cloth was also manufactured from bark and animal hides; mantles or cloaks, some probably woven out of feathers, were occasionally worn. Feather headdresses and body paint were also present.

A few Spanish documents hint that the Apalachee had matrilineal clans named after such animals as deer, bear, fox, panther, raccoon, and wolf. There is no reason to believe that Apalachee social organization differed much from the clan system of their Creek cousins.

A lengthy Spanish manuscript of 1676 describes the southeastern Indian stickball game and its associated myths and legends among the Apalachee. Games were played between two villages with 40 – 50 players participating. A small ball was parried back and forth, the object to strike a post, the goal, with the ball. Eleven such strikes constituted a win (Paina cited in Deagan n.d.).

The ball game itself was one part of an elaborate ceremony that included many separate rituals common to the Southeast. A sacred fire was prepared and tobacco was taken along with black drink, the latter evidently brewed from specially grown *Ilex vomitoria* plants. Fasting, abstention from sleep, and dancing also accompanied the game. Players, who were awarded high status, could be severely crippled or even killed during the melee of the game's action.

Another game known to have been played by the Apalachee was chunkey. A stone disc was rolled and players threw javelins at it, trying to come the closest.

The Apalachee are remarkably similar to the Creeks. In language, apparently in social organization, and even in having evolved out of a prehistoric Mississippian culture, the Apalachee were like the Creek cultural pattern of the historic period.

At the time of the Narváez and de Soto expeditions, the Fort Walton population inhabiting the Apalachee region no doubt numbered at least 25,000 persons, if not more. By the height of the mission period, about 1675, this number had declined to about 5000. Population steadily declined throughout the seventeenth century, although the actual number of mission villages increased after 1659 due to the incorporation of other Indian groups into the Apalachee missions. These Indians included Yamassee (from the Georgia coast), and Tamathli, Caparaz, Chines, Amacanos, and Oconees, all from the Florida—Georgis—Alabama region (Fairbanks 1957:77 – 80).

Tocobaga

The Tocobaga Indians of the sixteenth and seventeenth centuries represent the historic period population of the Safety Harbor culture, and readers are referred to the previous chapter for information on that archaeological culture. Bullen (1978) has summarized Tocobaga culture and demonstrated the correlations of geography, material culture, and political organization with the Safety Harbor archaeological culture.

Although the Tocobaga, a generic name for the several small chiefdoms (such as the Ucita, Pohoy, and Mococo) which constituted the Safety Harbor culture in the Pasco County to Sarasota County region, were observers of the landings of the Narváez and de Soto expeditions, they were never missionized. Menéndez established a garrison at the town of Tocobaga in the 1560s, but it was short-lived. Spanish contact with the Tocobaga was thus much more limited during the late sixteenth and seventeenth centuries than it was for the Timucuans or Apalachee. However, the results of contact were the same. Diseases continued to decimate the Tocobaga and by the time of the destruction of the North Florida missions, the Tocobaga had also been effectively destroyed as an ethnic group.

The early Spanish explorers described the Tocobaga as inhabiting a series of autonomous villages. Occasionally several such village-chiefdoms were allied, with one village chief recognized as supreme, the others being vassal to him. Villages consisted of a small number of thatch-roofed houses built of posts. Special buildings, such as the chief's house and temples (which were also perhaps charnel houses) were constructed on flat-topped mounds. Wooden bird carvings adorned the roof of the temple.

Each charnel house was evidently for the storage of cleaned bones which were saved until they were deposited en masse in a burial mound. One of the men from the Narváez expedition lived among the Tocobaga until rescued by de Soto. The individual, Juan Ortiz, related how he was made to guard the bones stored on shelves in a charnel house from hungry animals.

When Narváez landed among the Tocobaga he was shown wooden boxes in which corpses (bones?) were stored, wrapped in painted deer hides. Apparently, the boxes had originally been filled with goods being transported to or from New Spain and had been salvaged from wrecked Spanish ships. Other items—linen, cloth, feather headdresses, and gold—had also evidently been salvaged from ships destined for Spain. Despite this practice of obtaining salvaged goods and despite the many Spanish items left among the Tocobaga by Narváez and de Soto, relatively few items of Spanish manufacture have been recovered archaeologically from Safety Harbor sites.

Descriptions of everyday Tocobaga life by the Spanish are not very informative; our archaeological information of the Safety Harbor culture, all of which is applicable to the Tocobaga, is more complete (see Chapter 8). We do know that the Tocobaga utilized fish and shellfish as food and that they planted maize, pumpkins, and beans, although no evidence for agriculture has been recovered by archaeologists.

Whether or not the Tocobaga had a clan system is not known. However, the Spanish noted three ranks of individuals: chiefs and their families, common people, and slaves. The latter were often shipwrecked Spaniards.

The language of the Tocobaga Indians is also unknown; no written examples (actually Spanish transcriptions) have been located in archival materials, and it is quite possible that none ever will. Deriving population figures for the Tocobaga is difficult without better documentary or archaeological data. However, it seems reasonable that at the time of the first contact the Indians living within the Tocobaga region, including the relatively propitious Tampa Bay environs, would have numbered 5000−8000. It is possible that even by the time of Narváez, the Tocobaga population had been reduced by diseases transmitted by Spanish sailors.

Tequesta and Their Prehistoric and Historic Relatives

The Tequesta Indians of the Dade County area have been the subject of ethnographic summaries by Goggin (1940) and McNicoll (1941). Juan Ponce de Leon's 1513 expedition, which visited the Tequesta, provides some information on the tribe at that time. Like the Tocobaga, the Tequesta were subject to a short period of intense contact with the Spanish when Menéndez established a garrison among them in 1568, probably within present-day Miami. The garrison, which included Jesuit priests, was withdrawn after a brief time, and the Tequesta had only occasional contact with Spanish military officials, traders, and fishermen thereafter for almost two centuries. In 1743 there was a short-lived attempt by the Jesuits to establish a mission and garrison among the survivors of the Tequesta and several other South Florida groups residing in the area around the mouth of the Miami River (Sturtevant 1978).

The Tequesta were one of a number of small, similar groups which extended from Broward County south and west into Collier County as far as the Ten Thousand Islands area. A variety of names was later used by the Spanish when referring to these very similar groups of which the Tequesta were the most important.

The archaeological sequence of this region, not covered elsewhere in this volume, is reasonably well known. Goggin, writing from the late 1930s into the 1950s, and, more recently, members of the Broward County chapter of the Florida Anthropological Society have written a number of papers on excavations in that region.

These data and additional information gathered by Goggin and John Griffin from the Ten Thousand Island area and the Everglades National Park indicate that the coastal strip of South Florida from the Ten Thousand Islands around through the Tequesta territory and up the southeastern coast to Indian River County constitutes a distinct subregion within the South Florida archaeological province. Because the distribution of sites is *around* the Everglades (with only a few sites actually *in* the Everglades proper), Griffin (1974) has recently suggested the name Circum-Glades region to distinguish this area from the Caloosahatchee region north of the Ten Thousand Islands and from the Belle Glade (or Lake Okeechobee Basin) region (see Chapter 7).

The pottery sequence of this Circum-Glades region (usually referred to as the Glades area) is the primary basis for its separation from the less well known Caloosahatchee area. A great many differences in subsistence, settlement patterning, and occupational history distinguish the cultures of the Tequesta and related prehistoric and historic cultures from the Belle Glade culture of the Okeechobee Basin.

The Glades was evidently first settled shortly after 1000 B.C., and fiber-tempered pottery has been found at the bottom of several sites. By 500 B.C. the Glades cultural tradition, which dominated the region until late historic times, was formulated. Changes in pottery styles through time have enabled archaeologists to divide the temporal range of this Glades tradition into a number of periods (see Table 4). However, the basic patterns of subsistence and settlement—villages at the mouths of rivers or on the coastal lagoon; seasonal occupation of smaller sites farther inland; hunting, fishing, and gathering with no agriculture—persisted relatively unchanged into the eighteenth century. Although the environment of the Everglades region proper changed a great deal during the period of the Glades tradition, we do not yet understand what effect these changes had on the coastal strand cultures, if any.

Glades pottery is nearly all sand tempered and fashioned in the shape of large bowls with incurving rims. Some of the clays used in the pottery naturally contain fossil sponge spicules which give the finished vessel the chalky feel of St. Johns pottery. Although some of these pots may have been brought from East Florida, it is suspected that most were made locally. A very few potsherds of Weeden Island origin have turned up at Glades sites as have a few locally made sherds bearing copies of Weeden Island designs.

A variety of wooden implements, all similar to types found at the Key Marco site on the Southwest Florida coast (Gilliland 1975), have been recovered in the Glades region as a result of modern construction activities, such as digging boat slips or dredge-and-fill operations. Stone tools are very rare, since chert is not native to the region. Those stemmed knives and points used by the Glades people came from farther north in Florida.

Marine shells were used for picks, hammers, chisels, celts, and other tools. Celts manufactured from the lips of the *Strombus gigas* shell must

TABLE 4
Circum-Glades Culture Sequence[a]

Period	Dates	Distinguishing ceramics
Glades IIIc	A.D. 1513—1700	Same as period IIIb; appearance of European artifacts.
Glades IIIb	A.D. 1400—1513	Almost no decorated ceramics; Glades Tooled rims.
Glades IIIa	A.D. 1200—1400	Appearance of Surfside Incised (parallel incised lines below rim); some lip-grooving.
Glades IIc	A.D. 1000—1200	Almost no decorated ceramics; some grooved lips; Plantation Pinched (single line of finger-pinched identations below rim).
Glades IIb	A.D. 900—1000	Key Largo Incised still majority decorated type; some incision on rims and some lip-grooving; Matecumbe Incised appears (cross-hatchured incisions below rim).
Glades IIa	A.D. 750—900	Appearance of Key Largo Incised (loops or arches incised below rim); Sanibel Incised (ticking to form running lines of inverted V's below rim); Opa Locka Incised (half-circles or arches incised in vertical rows with open sides down below rim); Miami Incised (diagonal parallel incised rims below rim).
Glades I late	A.D. 500—750	Appearance of decorated pottery (less than 10% of ceramics at sites); Cane Patch Incised (incised looping line with stab-and-drag type punctations, below rim); Fort Drum Incised (vertical or diagonal ticking on lip or rim); Fort Drum Punctated (punctations around vessel below rim).
Glades I	500 B.C.—A.D. 500	First appearance of sand-tempered pottery (Glades Plain or undecorated Glades Gritty Ware—both types subsumed under plain, sand tempered, not separated as to type); no decoration.

[a] Based on Goggin (1947, 1949) and on unpublished data from the Bear Lake site provided by John W. Griffin.

have been trade items sent northward where they occasionally are found. Shell was also used for beads and other ornaments. Bone tools are relatively common and include points, pins, and other tools, some manufactured from stingray spines.

The nearby lagoons and ocean presented the Glades people with a variety of marine resources, and they apparently drew heavily upon them. Marine turtles, a large variety of fishes, including sharks, sailfish, and stingrays, and sea mammals, both porpoises and manatee, were eaten. One colorful account from Ponce de Leon's voyage describes how sea cows, or manatees, were taken:

> In winter all the Indians go to sea in their canoes to hunt for sea cows. One of their number carries three stakes fashioned to his girdle and a rope on his arm. When he discovers a sea cow he throws a rope around its neck, and as the animal sinks under the waves the Indian drives a stake through one of its nostrils and no matter how much it may dive, the Indian never loses it because he goes on its back [A. K. Bullen 1965:332].

A variety of nonmarine animals were also utilized for food by the Tequesta and their prehistoric ancestors, including deer and turtles. No doubt plants also provided an important part of the diet. From information referring to other nearby Indian groups, we can surmise that the Glades peoples ate the fruits of coco plum, sea grape, and prickly pear along with the root of the zamia plant which could be processed into a starchy flour.

In the historic period the Tequesta used the bow and arrow. The latter were sharpened sticks or were tipped with fish bones. Technology of the Tequesta must have been well adapted to their environment, since tools used to hunt and fish seem to have changed little over 2 millennia.

When contacted by Menéndez the Miami Tequesta had a chief or headman and were residing in villages along the coast and on the Miami River. Other separate groups living to the north and south were apparently at various times under the political domination of the Tequesta.

During part of the year, or several times within the year, the Tequesta gathered in large groups on the coast and jointly utilized the marine resources. Probably at other times of the year they divided up into smaller groups, perhaps families or lineages, and moved farther inland to utilize the animal and plant resources of the adjacent swamp and wetlands. Canoe trails connecting small sites on hammocks within the edge of the interior wetlands have been noted on infra-red aerial photos by members of the Broward County Archaeological Society. Most likely, such small sites were utilized occasionally over many generations; such occupations added to the heights of the hammocks, making small "islands" on which other people camped in the future. These hammock sites, formed by the accumulation of Indian middens, are found throughout the Circum-Glades region.

In some coastal and inland Glades tradition sites, burials have been found placed in villages or camp middens. Another method of treatment of the dead, described in documents from the historic periods, involved the cleaning of bodies and the storage of the bones by the deceased's relatives. Both chiefs and common people were treated in this fashion.

Sturtevant's (1978) analysis of Spanish documents dealing with the short-lived Jesuit mission village of Santa Maria de Loreto established near the mouth of the Miami River in 1743 provides a glimpse of the culture of several remnants of South Florida Indian groups in the eighteenth century. The mission was established to serve 180 aborigines from three groups; the Calusa, the Cayos (or Keys Indians), and the Boca Ratons. The latter evidently were one of the small groups related to the Tequesta who inhabited South Florida. None of the Indians were identified as Tequesta; that name had evidently fallen into disuse late in the seventeenth century, perhaps reflecting the extinction of the group known as the Tequesta.

The Key Indians, according to the Jesuit priest, had been reduced to only a few families due to "drunkenness" and war with the Yuchi Indians, allies of the English who raided the length of Florida in the eighteenth century. All of the Indians at the settlement lived by fishing and by gathering wild fruits. They remained at Miami only a portion of the year, and at the end of September they were taken by Spanish fishermen to one of the islands of the Keys and to the northwest coast, probably meaning the Calusa region near Fort Myers. Later, evidently for another season in the yearly subsistence round, they were moved to Vaca Key. At no time did they practice agriculture.

Most of the adult males spoke Spanish, learned from Cuban fishermen for whom they occasionally worked. Rum was obtained from this work and by trade as well as from salvaging it from wrecks.

Each separate settlement had a chief and an Indian priest or shaman. At the death of a chief or one of his children, one or more children of the village were sacrificed. Among the South Florida Indians in general, children had high value.

The priest described several ceremonies of the Indians. At the initiation of a new shaman (called *obispo* or bishop, a word taken from the Spanish by the Indians), the novitiate ran about for 3 days drinking and probably fasting. This caused him to lose consciousness, symbolic of dying and being reborn as a sanctified figure. The obispo had the power to call the wind by whistling and to divert storms with other cries. Still another type of diviner or shaman could foretell the future and cure the sick.

Among the Indians there was great fear of the dead. Names of the deceased could not be said and daily offerings of tobacco, herbs, and food were made to dead individuals who were buried in special cemeteries away from the villages. In the cemetery was a temple containing two idols. One, called a *Sipi*, was a figure drawn on a board of a barracuda crossed by a spear or harpoon with tonguelike figures surrounding it. A pole, often decorated with flowers and feathers during ceremonies and with silver salvaged from wrecks buried at its base, was placed nearby. The second idol, according to an eyewitness account, was a "horribly good representation" of a bird's head carved in pine (Sturtevant 1978:148). Barracudas drawn on plaques were found at the Key Marco site; carved, wooden birds' heads associated with a burial area were found at the Fort Center site (see Chapter 7). Quite likely the South Florida Indians shared many beliefs and rituals.

The temple in the graveyard also contained masks used in rituals held to honor the fish idol. Graves within the cemetery had offerings of animals (such as turtles and barracudas) tobacco, and other items placed on them to pacify the dead.

Population in the Circum-Glades region Indians in the early sixteenth century probably numbered 5000−7500. By the eighteenth century, the number had declined to several hundred.

Keys Indians

Goggin (1950; Goggin and Sommer 1949), utilizing both Spanish documents and modern archaeology, has described the Keys Indians during the prehistoric and historic period prior to the time they were severely reduced in population and had moved to the Miami area. Goggin's studies have focused on the Matecumbe group who inhabited Upper and Lower Matecumbe keys and several nearby islands. The Florida Keys evidently were first occupied about A.D. 800 by people moving southward out of peninsular Florida. Archaeology of the Keys Indians has shown that their material culture was a variant of the Glades tradition found throughout the Circum-Glades region.

During the historic period Indians moved back and forth between the Keys and Cuba, both of their own volition and by intervention of the Spanish. Sturtevant (1978:143−144) has reviewed documents noting that remnants of the Calusa, Miami, and other South Florida Indians were resettled in the Keys by the Spanish in 1716 or 1718. These Indians had earlier (1710) been taken to Cuba where most had died of sickness. Thus, 30 years before the Jesuit attempt to establish the Santa Maria de Loreto settlement, the South Florida Indians had been severely reduced in population and remnants of former groups were living out of their traditional territories. In addition to the Calusa, Keys Indians, Boca Ratons, and Maimies (also Miamis or Maymis), these remnants included the Tancha, Muspa, Rio Seco, Santa Luce, Mayaca, and Jove (or Hoe-Bay or Hobe).

The diet of the Keys Indians, according to Goggin (1950; Goggin and

Sommer 1949), consisted largely of fish, turtle, molluscs, and sea mammals, especially the whale. Deer and bear were also eaten, as were raccoons. No doubt a variety of plant foods was also used for food and as raw materials for cordage and basketry.

Bone and shark-tooth tools and both stone and shell tools and ornaments have been recovered archaeologically from sites along with sand-tempered potsherds. The subsistence technology of the Keys Indians was well-suited for exploitation of the immense marine environment surrounding them. Canoes, some with sails, provided transportation between the keys and gave access to some off-shore hunting of sea mammals. Goggin cites documents describing the Indian's use of the bow and arrow and dart-throwers, probably atlatls like those found by Cushing at Key Marco.

Early in the historic period the Keys Indians were observed wearing ornaments made from gold and silver. Discs and other shaped ornaments were evidently cold-hammered out of salvaged European metals.

Like the Indians in the Miami area in the early 1740s, the Keys Indians feared the dead. Bodies of the deceased were exposed along the beach, probably so that scavengers could pick the bones clean. This practice caused early observers wrongly to accuse the Indians of cannibalism. Most likely the cleaned bones were later deposited in burial mounds which were built away from the villages.

Little else is known about the Keys Indians, who probably formed a number of separate tribes. Throughout the colonial period various Spanish documents indicate that the Keys groups were vassal to either the Tequesta or the Calusa, a situation which seems to have fluctuated with the political currents.

Nothing is known about the language of the Keys Indians; most likely their language was related to that of the other South Florida Indians, but we can only guess at this. It is probable that the Keys supported a population of about 500 – 1000 Indians.

Jeaga and Ais

Both the Jeaga and the Ais were small groups living along the Atlantic coastal lagoons and inlets and utilizing the coastal strand and the flatlands inland from the coast 16 – 32 km or farther. The Jeaga, the smaller group, probably were a northern Circum-Glades people who lived in the modern St. Lucie County area. They are known almost entirely from the narrative of Jonathan Dickinson, a Quaker who was shipwrecked in 1696 among the Hoe-Bay or Jove, a subgroup (Andrews and Andrews 1975). To the north were the Ais, also described by Dickinson, who were in turn bordered on their north by Timucuans. The archaeology of the Ais region bears affinities both to the St. Johns tradition to the north and the Glades tradition to the south (Rouse 1951).

Both the Jeaga and Ais were hunters and gatherers, relying heavily on marine resources and without agriculture. Together, both probably numbered about 2000 persons at the beginning of the historic period. Like all of the other South Florida tribes, including the Tequesta and Calusa, nothing is known of their languages.

Juan Ponce de Leon may have contacted one or both of these groups in 1513 and Menéndez tried to establish a garrison among the Ais in order to recover shipwrecked sailors, but the garrison was not successful. In the seventeenth century, several Franciscan missions were established in the general Ais—Jeaga region, but their exact location is unknown. Contact with the Spanish in the seventeenth century also involved visits by military groups seeking to trade goods for the return of Spanish sailors. Probably the Jeaga and Ais were among the Indians to whom the Spanish often referred as Costa (coastal) Indians.

From the narrative of Dickinson we know that these coastal dwellers ate a great deal of fish which was taken with spears. Coco plums and sea grapes were harvested, and palm berries, which could be stored, also were important to the diet. Little is known about their material culture; they did use Spanish knives and hatchets along with other items salvaged from wrecked ships. Water travel was by canoe. Catamarans, two canoes lashed together with poles, were used and probably permitted travel even in the ocean.

The Indian men dressed in breechclouts made of woven vegetable fiber. Both men and women at times wore clothing taken from the wrecks, but as a dress-up "game."

A council house (possibly the chief's residence) described for the Ais measured 8 by 12 m and was covered with palmetto fronds. Low benches formed seating platforms along two sides of the interior. Houses of the everyday Jeaga were small wigwams built by covering a framework of bent poles with palmetto fronds. These wigwams may have been quickly constructed, short-term dwellings. We have no archaeological confirmation for either type of structure.

Among both groups the chief received favored treatment from the other villagers. The Ais chief also received tribute in the form of baskets of palm berries from outlying villages. Most likely, some sort of redistributing system was controlled by the chiefs. The environment of the Ais and Jeaga was not the best in Florida, and methods may have been needed to assure that foods were shared when necessary.

Like the Indians at the Santa Maria de Loreto settlement, the youth of the Ais were esteemed at the expense of the elders. The high value of children seems to have been ubiquitous in South Florida.

Dickinson describes several ceremonies of the Indians. One similar one, involving dancing and "chanting," was practiced by both groups. Among the Ais:

> This day being a time of the moon's entering of the first quarter, the Indians have a continuous dance, which they begin about eight o'clock in the morning. In the first place comes an old man and takes a staff about eight foot long, having a broad arrow on the head thereof, and thence half way painted red and white unto an barber's pole; in the middle of this staff is fixed a piece of wood shaped like unto thigh, leg and foot of a man, and the lower part thereof is painted black, and this staff being carried out of the Caseekey's [cacique, a word brought to Florida from the Caribbean by the Spanish, meaning chief] house, is set fast in the ground standing upright. This done [staff set in the ground], he also brings out a basket containing six rattles, which are taken out of the basket and placed at the foot of his staff; then another old man comes and sets up a howling like unto a mighty dog, but beyond him for length of breath; withal making a proclamation. This being done, the most of them having painted themselves, some red, some black, some with black and red; with their belly girt up as tight as well they can girt themselves with ropes, having their sheaves of arrows at their backs and their bows in their hands, being gathered together about this staff; six of the chiefest men in esteem amongst them, especially one who is their doctor, and much esteemed, taking up the rattles begins a hideous noise, standing round this staff, taking their rattles, and bowing, without ceasing, unto the staff for about half an hour; whilst these six are thus employed, all the rest are staring and scratching, pointing upwards and downwards on this and the other side every way; looking like men frighted, or more like Furies; thus behaving themselves until the six have done shaking their rattles. Then they all begin a dance, violently stamping on the ground for the space of an hour or more without ceasing. In which time they will sweat in a most excessive manner, that by the time the dance is over, what by their sweat and the violent stamping of their feet, the ground is trodden into furrows; and by the morning, the place where they danced was covered with maggots. Thus often repeating the manner they continue till about three or four o'clock in the afternoon by which time many were sick and fainty. And then being gathered into the Casseekey's house, they sit down, having some hot casseena ready, which they drink plentifully; and give greater quantities thereof to the sick and fainty than to others; then they eat berries. On these days they eat not any food till night.
>
> The next day about the same time, they begin their dance as the day before. Also the third day they begin their dance at the usual time; at which time came many Indians from other towns, and fell to dancing without taking any notice one of the other.
>
> This day they were stricter than the other two days, for no woman must look upon them; but if any of their women go out of their houses, they go veiled with a mat [Andrews and Andrews 1975:37 − 39].

The similar ceremony described in briefer terms by Dickinson for the Jeaga:

> In the evening . . . the Indians made a drum of a skin, covering therewith the deep bowl in which they brewed their drink, beating thereon with a stick, and having a couple of rattles made of a small gourd put on a stick with small stones in it, shaking it, they began to set up a most hideous howling, . . . and some time after came some of their young women, some singing, some dancing. This was continued till midnight, after which they went to sleep [Andrews and Andrews 1975:25].

During his stay among the Jeaga, Dickinson also witnessed the brewing and taking of black drink. *Ilex vomitoria*, the plant from which the leaves for the tea are gathered, grows wild along the Florida coasts north of the more tropical areas:

> In one part of this house where the fire was kept, was an Indian man, having a pot on the fire wherein he was making a drink of the leaves of a shrub (which we understood afterwards . . . is called casseena), boiling the said leaves, after they had parched them in a pot; then with a gourd having a long neck and at the top of it a small hole which the top of one's finger could cover, and at the side of it a round hole of two inches diameter, they take the liquor out of the pot and put it into a deep round bowl, which being almost filled containeth nigh three gallons. With this gourd they brew the liquor and make it froth very much. [This may explain the appearance of "frothing at the mouth" mentioned by Dickinson when he first saw the Indians.] It looketh of a deep brown color. In the brewing of this liquor was this noise made which we thought strange; for the pressing of this gourd gently down into the liquor, and the air which it contained being forced out of the little hole at top occasioned a sound; and according to the time and motion given would be various. This drink was made, and cooled to sup, was in a conch-shell first carried to the Casseekey, who threw part of it on the ground, and the rest he drank up, and then would make a loud He-m; and afterwards the cup passed to the rest of the Casseekey's associates, as aforesaid, but no other man, woman nor child must touch or taste of this sort of drink; of which they sat sipping, chatting and smoking tobacco or some other herb instead thereof, for the most part of the day [Andrews and Andrews 1975:24−25].

Calusa and the Prehistoric Cultures of Southwest Florida

Certainly the most important aboriginal group in South Florida in terms of population size, political importance, and influence on neighboring tribes was the Calusa. In the early sixteenth century the Calusa inhabited the coastal strand of southwestern Florida from Charlotte Harbor south to the Ten Thousand Islands, a region that correlates with the

Caloosahatchee archaeological region. Inland, the Calusa inhabited and/or controlled the land along the Caloosahatchee River into and including the vast area of the Okeechobee Basin.

The Basin and the Kissimmee River drainage to the north constitute the Belle Glade archaeological region (see Chapter 7). Pottery within the Caloosahatchee and Belle Glade regions is much the same, indicating close contact between the two regions. Excavations at Belle Glade sites, such as Fort Center, have recovered marine items, suggesting trade between the two diverse ecological zones. Most likely, this "close contact" is in the historic period a reflection of the Calusa's political domination of the Basin and its people.

North of Charlotte Harbor several Belle Glade or Caloosahatchee sites have been located, perhaps evidence of attempts by the ancestors of the Calusa to extend their territory into the little occupied lands south of the main Safety Harbor territory. Warfare between the Tocobaga and Calusa over control of villages was occurring in the 1560s.

At various times other of the South Florida tribes, including the Tequesta, formed alliances with the Calusa. Often such political ties were maintained through marriages; for instance, at one point the chief of the Tequesta was a relative of Carlos, the Calusa chief. An allied chief would often give a sister as wife to the Calusa chief. As a consequence of these political dealings, which were on a plane rivaling those of contemporary Europe at the time, Calusa hegemony was extended over much of South Florida. We can guess that much of the complex political organization found among the South Florida hunters and gatherers arose at least partly as a result of contact with the Calusa, which at times may have taken the form of direct intervention.

This vast Calusa domain was ruled by a single chief or king who resided with his family and advisors in the capital city of Calos located on Mound Key in Estero Bay near Fort Myers Beach. Mound Key is a small, roughly circular island cross-cut by Indian-built canals and with huge artificial mounds built of earth and shell serving as platforms for the civic and ceremonial structures of the Calusa. Middens, some more than 7 m thick, also cover portions of the island which must have been occupied over a long period of time. Two scholarly studies of the documents pertinent to the Calusa identify this key as the site of Calos (Goggin and Sturtevant 1964; Lewis 1978).

In 1566 Pedro Menéndez established a garrison and settlement at Calos. Included in the settlement, which consisted of a fort and 36 cabins, were several Jesuit priests whose published correspondence (Zubilaga 1946) for the period 1566–1569 consists of more than 600 pages, much of which deals with the Calusa. In addition we have accounts pertinent to the Calusa by Solís de Merás (1894) and Barrientos (1965), both of whom gleaned first-hand accounts for their descriptions. We also have the narrative of Fontaneda (1945), a Spaniard held captive by the Calusa for several decades prior to the Menéndez settlement. During his captivity Fontaneda traveled through much of South Florida, including the Lake Okeechobee Basin area (the lake was then known as Sarrope). These chronicles and documents have provided a quantity of data on the sixteenth century Calusa, much of which has been summarized by Goggin and Sturtevant (1964) and Lewis (1978). No historic period Calusa sites have ever been excavated and reported. (In 1931 Matthew Stirling dug in an apparent historic Calusa mound on the Collier County coast, but no report was ever written.)

After the abandonment of the Spanish garrison in 1570 there were no further attempts by the Spanish to establish settlements or missions among the Calusa until the Franciscans tried unsuccessfully in the seventeenth century. However, following 1570, contact with Spanish sailors, fishermen, and traders was probably occurring regularly. By about 1720 the Calusa had been severely reduced in population and by the time of the Santa Maria de Loreto settlement only remnants of the population existed. Whether or not any Calusa merged with the Creeks who were raiding South Florida by the 1740s is not known with any certainty.

The complexity of the Calusa political system seems to be tied to the subsistence potential of both the Southwest Florida coastal waters and the savannahs and wetlands of the Okeechobee Basin and to the need to maintain exchange routes through which food could be rapidly redistributed. For instance, should fishing be bad one week at Calos, dried palm berries and smilax or zamia flour (or unprocessed roots) could be already on hand or brought by canoe from a village on Lake Okeechobee via the Caloosahatchee River to Calos. Or smoked fish brought by canoe from a village elsewhere on the coast could feed the Calos villagers. Food surpluses could be moved from one place to another via waterways along established political and economic channels.

The key to such a system is the potential of the environment to produce food surpluses which were relatively easily obtainable and which were storable. Fish, both marine and freshwater, dried meats (especially reptiles from the basin), and starchy roots which could be processed into flour were such foods.

The subsistence potential of the basin is indicated by the variety of foods identified from the middens at Fort Center listed in Chapter 7. An equally long list has been identified from the Caloosahatchee region prehistoric coastal middens including: opossum, rabbit, dog, bobcat, raccoon, gray fox, white-tailed deer, whale, grey seal, loon, gannet, cormorant, great blue heron, American egret, snowy egret, white ibis, greater scaup duck, lesser scaup duck, hooded merganser, red-breasted merganser, turkey vulture, black vulture, long-billed curlew, herring gull, ring-billed gull, Royal tern, alligator, mud turtle, box turtle, diamond-back terrapin, chicken-turtle, gopher tortoise, green turtle, soft-shelled turtle, watersnake, racer, rat snake, cottonmouth moccasin, eastern diamond-backed rattlesnake, 3 species of sharks, 2 species of rays, and 17 species of fish (Wing 1965; Fradkin 1976).

In the latter region, marine fish, which flourish in the Southwest Florida coastal waters (see Goggin and Sturtevant 1964:183 – 186), and shellfish, especially oysters and *Busycon*, formed the basis of the diet. Menéndez was served such a meal of boiled and roasted fish and raw, boiled, and roasted oysters upon his arrival at Calos. Along the coast, fish could have been taken in very large quantities with the types of nets recovered by Cushing (1897:361 – 367; Gilliland 1975) at the Key Marco site. In the shallow coastal region around Fort Myers, busycons occur on the sandy gulf bottom in their largest known density. Some of the platform and temple mounds of the prehistoric Calusa are constructed almost entirely of millions of busycons, all of which have small holes placed in the end through which the muscle attaching the meat to the shell was cut. This meat may weigh as much as 1 kg in adult specimens.

Fontaneda (1945:67 – 68) notes that in the Lake Okeechobee area the Indians ate bread of roots (smilax or zamia), other roots like "truffles," fish, deer, birds, alligators, snakes, opossums, and turtles. Other documents record that roots which could be made into bread were brought to the coast from the interior of the Calusa region. As a consequence of these resources and the political network of the Calusa, the South Florida aborigines, especially the Calusa, displayed much greater social and political complexity and a larger population density than is usually the case with hunters and gatherers.

Within the Caloosahatchee region, subsistence, population density, and political complexity are all reflected in the patterns of settlements along the coast. Although excavations in these coastal sites have been extremely limited (Griffin 1949; Fradkin 1976), the information gleaned from these investigations can be combined with data gathered from site surveys to begin to produce an understanding of the development of the Calusa.

Coastal sites are of two types: shell middens found on the mainland, especially around inlets, and the offshore keys or islands; and larger sites which combine shell middens with various mounds, platforms, causeways, smaller walkways, and embankments, all generally constructed of shell although a few are constructed of shell and earth. As revealed by Fradkin's (1976) study of one such "shellworks" site on Sanibel Island, the mounds were built on top of a much earlier shell midden which provided a convenient rise. At times these mound builders used the shell from the earlier middens as building material, although most of the shellworks were formed by piling up conch shells, mostly *Busycon*. As Cushing noted at several sites he visited in the area, some walkways, causeways, mounds, and other shell constructions were actually "faced" with busycons by sticking the pointed ends of the shells into the shell mound, forming evenly spaced rows of the spiral ends of the shells.

The density and size of some of these mound complexes is staggering. In the vicinity of Sanibel Island, the region with which we are most familiar, mound — midden complexes are found on almost every key from Pine Island to Sanibel. Numerous sites have been found on both of those islands and on Cabbage Key, Useppa, Captiva, North Captiva, Demere Key, Joccelyn, La Costa, and Buck Key among others. The total distribution seems to be from Charlotte Harbor down at least to the Marco Island vicinity, with the greatest distribution north of Mound Key.

A few of the smaller keys like Demere, Mound Key, and Joccelyn consist almost entirely of shellworks and shell middens with enclosed plazas. At some sites, platform mounds as much as 125 m long and 5 m high have other, smaller mounds built on the top. Steep sides are still present on many of the mounds and several have portions of their shell facing intact. At many of the sites, long, linear middens snake through the adjacent mangroves for several hundred meters.

Sites are generally immediately adjacent to the bay side of the island on which they were constructed and the mounds slope down to the water. Artificial canals cutting into the sites are now choked with mangroves although they once undoubtedly provided canoe access into the complexes.

Unfortunately, we do not have good chronological controls for these extraordinary sites and we do not know which were occupied at the same time or for how long they were occupied. From their density and from the size of the shell middens, however, it is quite possible that most of them were occupied together over several or more centuries. The site on Sanibel Island reported by Fradkin was first occupied by fishermen about 500 B.C. shortly after the first portion of the island had been naturally deposited. These people had moved a large amount of beachridge sand to form a flat surface on which to live and deposit their shell and other refuse in a circular, ring-shaped midden. The mounds, constructed in two distinct periods, were begun after A.D. 700. Goggin reported pottery from the site of a type known to date after A.D. 1300 and local residents had collected metal (perhaps of Spanish origin) materials from the mound. The implication is that the mound complex was utilized (and added to?) over several centuries, and was still occupied in the early historic period.

At several sites the shell middens or the shell mounds have been cut by mosquito control ditches or by dredges mining shell for commercial use. The profiles of these cuts clearly show that the bottoms of the shells lie up to 1 m below the present low-tide water line. This mystery, an apparent 1 m or more rise in sea level relative to the land during the last 2000 years, remains to be explained. It does seem probable that the build-up of the shell sites may have actually formed a noneroding base for the continual natural deposition which gives the keys the shape they have today. Obviously, our understanding of these interesting sites is only in its infancy.

These coastal sites and the Big Circle sites of the Belle Glade region provide some basis for population estimates. Goggin and Sturtevant (1964:186−187) have reviewed the estimates from documentary sources and give as probable a population of 1000 for Calos itself and 4000−7000 for the total Calusa. In view of the density and nature of the coastal sites, this figure might conservatively be raised to 10,000−15,000 for the coastal Calusa region with another 5,000− 10,000 for the inland areas under their control, especially the Okeechobee Basin and Kissimmee Drainage. Thus a total of about 20,000 were probably present prior to the population reductions that must have begun early in the sixteenth century, perhaps beginning with Juan Ponce de Leon's voyages.

Our knowledge of the material culture and the arts and crafts of the Calusa comes from the small amount of archaeology carried out, from documentary accounts, and from the magnificent collection of wood, bone, and fiber artifacts which Cushing found preserved in the muck at Key Marco and for which Gilliland (1975) has provided an illustrated catalogue. Fired-clay pottery of the Calusa region is largely undecorated and has sand as temper, very much like that of the Belle Glade region. Vessels are generally the same bowl shapes as are found throughout South Florida. Archaeologically recovered shell and bone tools are like those described for the Tequesta; stone tools are rare. Bows and arrows are described by Fontaneda, although throwing sticks (atlatls) with darts were recovered at Key Marco.

The houses of the Calusa were thatched with palmetto. There is evidence from Marco Island, both from modern archaeology and Cushing's excavation, that at least some houses were built on pilings. This is consistent with the nature and shape of some of the middens observed on Sanibel.

This list of items used by the Calusa would stop here if it were not for the extraordinary finds from Key Marco, evidently a very late, prehistoric Calusa site. The Key Marco collection contains a host of everyday wooden items, preserved in the same condition in which they had been when deposited in the muck (by a hurricane which wrecked the village?). Such wooden items include: bowls; mortars and pestles; pounding tools which look like dumbbells; boxes; trays; and hafts or handles for a variety of adzes, knives, and other cutting tools, many with the shell, bone, or shark's tooth working edges still affixed. Bone pins and tools were also common as were stone plummets. Most of these items were expertly carved and some had intricate designs or adornos. A toy catamaran canoe, a canoe paddle, atlatl handles and darts, and other tools, all of wood, were also found. Most of the wood is pine or cypress and, where woodcarving is evident, was carved with hafted shark's tooth tools. Varieties of bone and shell tools, some also decorated, were apparently also household items. Large portions of fishing nets, some with wooden peg floats and shell or stone weights still attached, attest to the importance of fishing to the Calusa.

Among the Cushing collection are a number of items probably not used in everyday household activities, but which were contained in the houses and apparently reserved for special use. Some of these beautifully carved (some painted) specimens may have come from the house of a priest or other religious functionary, since many were recovered in the same area of the site. All of the items display great artistic skill. Carved wooden masks, some with shell-inset eyes and others painted, may have been used in ceremonies like those described by the Spaniards for Calos or Santa Maria de Loreto. Wooden animal masks, one a composite type of an alligator head, were also used.

A variety of wooden plaques or "standards" deserves special mention, as does one small (about 5 cm²) turtle plastron plaque incised with two very realistic dolphins placed tail to nose. The wooden plaques include both flat "planks" and carved specimens. Perhaps the most famous of the former types is the rectangular, flat plank (about 42 cm long) with a woodpecker painted on it. One type of carved plaque is two-sectioned with a tenon on one end. Specimens were carved with a stylized animal motif, probably feline (although some researchers have called it a spider). This motif is well known as the logo of the Florida Anthropological Society. Other examples similar to this standard, but made from wood, metal, or stone, have been found at sites in South Florida. The metal appears to have been taken from Spanish wrecks and reworked. All of the sites from which specimens have come are believed to be either of the late prehistoric or historic period.

Plain, carved two-part standards and one standard with a carved dolphin also came from Key Marco. Some of the standards measure more than 50 cm in length; their exact use is unknown.

Two truly magnificent wooden objects are a painted deer head and a kneeling feline figurine. The deer head is beautifully painted and the ears were made with pegs to fit them into the head. Measuring 9 cm in height, the feline may be a person with a feline mask or head. Both are exquisite works of art and attest to the Calusa's skill in working with wood, bone, and shell.

According to Fontaneda, who was among the Calusa in the middle portion of the sixteenth century, the chief of the Calusa ruled over 50 villages. At the time of Menéndez's visit, this vast domain was ruled over by the chief called Calos to whom the Spanish frequently referred as *el rey*, the king. It was clear to the Spanish from the trappings of Calos's office and the respect and tribute afforded him that he was indeed a powerful leader, a true Indian king.

Goggin and Sturtevant (1964) have provided an excellent analysis of Calusa political structure, including a reconstruction of the complicated system of succession within the royal family. Their analysis also examines the relatively rare practice of sibling marriage which was practiced by the Calusa chief to assure succession within the family. Polygyny was also practiced by the chief.

Calusa society was divided into two classes with a third group of slaves also present; the latter may have increased during the historic period with the availability of Spanish sailors. Forming the higher class were the king or chief and royal family and the nobles and captains, often referred to by the Spanish as the principal men. These principal men included a war chief or captain general (generally a relative of the chief); a chief priest who was in charge of the idols and who, with the chief, controlled religious knowledge; and sorcerers who cured the sick. Vassals and the common people constituted the second class of people.

The king or chief wore special ornaments symbolic of his office, controlled "treasure" (which most likely included gold and silver taken from Spanish wrecks and paid as tribute by Indians as far away as the Keys), and sat on a special stool, possibly a low four-legged stool like the one recovered from Key Marco. In addition the chief was always greeted in a prescribed manner.

Upon the death of a chief or his wife, servants and perhaps slaves were sacrificed. When other members of the royal family died, children were sacrificed. We know nothing about the burial patterns of the Calusa. However, because the behavioral patterns surrounding the chief and his family and principal men seem to have been similar to patterns reconstructed for Mississippian chiefdoms in the Southeast (see Chapter 8), we would suspect that high ranking individuals within the society were afforded special burial. Most likely this would have been in tombs, perhaps placed in or around temples. And we would expect that the paraphernalia of their respective offices would accompany them in their graves. In burial the same high status would be afforded these individuals as when they were alive.

Our knowledge of Calusa religious beliefs comes almost entirely from the letters of Jesuit priests who lived at Calos in the 1560s and who viewed many of the Calusa beliefs and practices as pagan. We know that the Calusa had full-time religious practicioners and temples, as would be expected in such a complex society. The priests controlled special religious paraphernalia such as the idols and, perhaps, the masks that were used in ceremonies. Standards and plaques might also have had religious significance, but were placed in homes. Numerous documentary references refer to human sacrifices to one idol or god who ate human eyes. During the historic period such sacrifices were nearly all Spaniards. While in Calos, Menéndez's men observed more than 50 human heads, the remains of sacrifices.

Father Juan Rogel, a Jesuit priest among the Calusa who provides the largest amount of data on them, made the following observations about religion:

> They claimed that each man has three souls; one is the pupil of the eye, another one the shadow that each one makes, and the other one is the image one sees in a mirror or in clear water, and when a man dies, they say that two of the souls leave the body, and the third one, which is the pupil of the eye, always remains in the body; and thus they go to speak with the dead of the cemetery, and to ask them advice about things that have to be done, as if they were alive; and I believe that there they get answers from the Devil; because many things that happen in other places or that come up afterwards, they know by what they hear there.

> . . . when someone gets sick, they say that one of his souls has left and the witch-doctors go look for it in the woods, and they say they bring it back making the same movements that people go through when they try to put an unwilling wild goat or sheep in a pen. Later they put fire at the door of the house and the windows, so that it would not dare to go out again, and they report that they put it back in the man through the top of the head by conducting some ceremonies over it.

> They also have another error; when a man dies, his soul enters some animal or fish; and when they kill that animal, it enters another smaller one, until little by little it comes to vanish [Zubillaga 1946:278–281; translated in Lewis 1978:35].

The Calusa and other Florida Indians were reduced to only remnants of their former populations by the early eighteenth century. More than 100,000 people were reduced to several thousand. These remnants were further harrassed and decimated by various Muskogean-speaking tribes, mainly Creeks, who raided and hunted throughout Florida after the early 1700s, eventually reaching even into the Florida Keys by the 1740s. These Creeks soon began to establish permanent settlements in northern Florida, at first living much like their relatives in Georgia and Alabama. The story of the repopulation of Florida by these peoples follows in the next chapter.

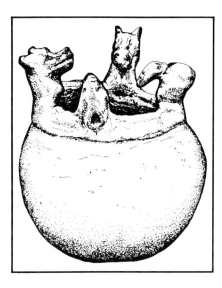

10

Archaeology of the Seminole Peoples

As the last Indian inhabitants of Florida who remain to this day in the state, the Seminole hold a special interest for us. To the anthropologist they have other scientific attractions as they represent a number of special cultural situations. They went through an extreme population "bottleneck" at the end of the Second Seminole War when their number was reduced to a mere 300–400 individuals. Since then they have climbed back to something in excess of 2000, thus affording an example of a group facing extinction which has recovered something like its original population. As migrants from the fall-line area of Georgia and Alabama into a new environment, first in northern Florida, then pushed down into the Everglades and Big Cypress Swamp, they exhibit extreme and rapid accomodation to new environments and the necessity of developing new forms of subsistence (Figure 43). Their extreme isolation until the middle of the twentieth century gives the anthropologist a chance to study the cultural effects of this self-imposed isolation on many aspects of their life. For all of these reasons, the Seminole are of great interest to anthropologists. It is remarkable that so little ethnology and archaeology has been conducted in relation to the Seminole in view of what should have been generated by these factors.

Seminole history in Florida has been described as consisting of five major stages (Fairbanks 1978): (1) Colonization, 1716–1763; (2) Separation, 1763–1790; (3) Resistance and Removal, 1790–1840; (4) Withdrawal, 1840–1880; (5) Modern Crystalization, 1880–present. It is unfortunate

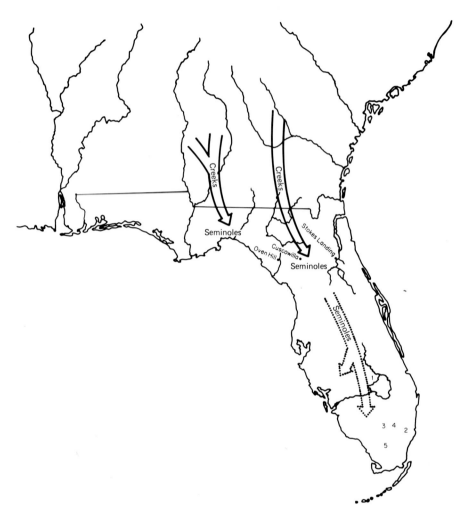

FIGURE 43. *Movement of Creeks into Florida in the eighteenth century and of Seminoles into southern part of state in the nineteenth century. Numbers show modern settlements; (1) Brighton; (2) Dania; (3–4) Big Cypress federal and state reserves; (5) Tamiami Trail.*

that, due to a lack of archaeological research, only the first three stages can be described, and those not in the detail that would be desired.

The earlier Indian occupations of Florida have been discussed in previous chapters and we have seen how the attacks by Creek Indians, led by South Carolina slavers, virtually destroyed the Apalachee, Timucua, and other Indian societies in the whole area that is now northern Florida. Into this population vacuum came small bands of Creek Indians from the central and western parts of Georgia. While vacant lands, especially those as lush as these, are always a magnet for populations, these Creeks were given incentives to become colonists aside from the mere attraction of new territories. Perhaps the strongest was that many of them felt a need to get away from the increasing presence of Anglo-American colonial traders. The disruption of traditional ways of life caused by learning to accomodate to the deerskin trade with its attendant changes, fear of retaliation for the Yamassee War of 1715, and the disorderliness of the frontiersmen, all contributed to the pressures on the Creeks. These influences were strongest on those towns in central Georgia on the Oconee and Ocmulgee rivers at the fall lines. Somewhat less pressure was felt by the towns along the lower Chattahoochee and Flint rivers in what is now the southwestern corner of Georgia.

Additional support for the move came from efforts by the Spaniards to encourage these migrations. The Spanish colonial authorities well recognized that the colony of Florida urgently needed a supporting population in the country back of St. Augustine and Pensacola. In the immediate aftermath of the Yamassee War, the governor in St. Augustine sent a Lieutenant Peña across the abandoned country of Alachua and Apalachee to lure Creeks from the lower Chattahoochee into the Spanish domain (Boyd 1949). Although the Spaniards were at the same time formulating plans to bring in peasantry from the Old World to replace the missing Indians, those plans never materialized to any extent. Lieutanant Peña's proposals, however, did produce some settlers. This ushers in the first phase of the Seminole occupation of Florida, that of Colonization. These new Creek residents may have been joined by some remnants of the original Timucua and Apalachee towns but they were not organized into towns and were in effect submerged in Creek population. The known sites of this phase of colonization show no evidence of relationship to the earlier St. Johns, Apalachee, or San Marcos complexes previously seen in Florida. The people seem to have spoken dialects of Lower Creek or Hitchiti which has remained a basic language of the modern Seminole. While in a few cases old abandoned towns were reoccupied, in most cases new locations were selected. The material culture shows very clear and close derivation from the early historic Creek complex. As is usual in archaeological descriptions, the pottery of these historic Creek is better known than other traits. From central Georgia westward to central Alabama, the ceramics are composed of Ocmulgee Fields Incised, Walnut Roughened, and its equivalent form on the Chattahoochee, Chattahoochee Brushed (Goggin 1958). These brushed and roughened types seem to have been made by malleating the coils of the pot under construction with a corncob and then finishing the outer surface by brushing or scraping with the same cob (Figure 44). This produced a striated surface quite different, although technically related, from the stippled surfaces of Alachua Cob Marked of the late Timucua peoples in North-Central Florida. While the incised types of Creek and Apalachee mission period were somewhat similar, the common cooking pots were significantly different. The rare red-painted and somewhat more common plain pottery are very nearly the same in both cultures. The mission sites of the Apalachee have a consistent representation of late complicated-stamped pottery that seems virtually absent from historic Creek sites.

What this meant in terms of the Seminole stage of Colonization is that the early sites in Florida are rather easily distinguished from the earlier Apalachee or Timucuan sites. As pottery making was women's work among the southeastern Indians and as women participated less in the trade for deer skins with the Carolinians, ceramics was one of the most conservative elements of southeastern culture. Men's tools and equipment changed much more rapidly, as they were replaced by European trade goods. Small triangular projectile points indicate that the early Seminole still occasionally used the bow and arrow. Most hunting and fighting, however, was with the aid of the flintlock musket that British traders readily supplied. While the Spaniards recognized the need to supply these newly arrived Indians with trade goods, Spanish industry simply was not able to fill the demand. It was only with the cession of Florida to England that British traders could establish stores in northern Florida. Under these conditions, early Seminole sites have fewer trade goods than do contemporary Creek sites in Georgia and Alabama.

Perhaps the major change in the culture of the migrant Creek as they colonized Florida was in subsistence practices as they are reflected in their settlements. The basic Creek town was a quite permanent affair with a large squareground in the center flanked by summer and winter ritual buildings, often on mounds. By 1700 the Creeks had stopped building mounds but still retained the central public square. In Florida it has not been possible to locate any formal, squareground towns, and it seems certain that the Seminole simply were not building them. The causes of this probably lay in a shift, at least in the Alachua area, to a greater dependence on the herds of feral cattle that had made themselves at home there following the collapse of the Spanish ranches. William Bartram (Harper 1958) described this dependence on cattle as a distinctive Seminole way of life. Although his description of the Seminole town of Cuscowilla near the present Micanopy implies a formal settlement, archaeologically we see an increasingly diffuse settlement pattern of somewhat separated farmsteads. The separation of the early Seminole from the organized political confederation in Georgia and Alabama

FIGURE 44. *Seminole artifacts from northern Florida;* **a,** *Chattahochee Brushed bowl;* **b,** *gun flint;* **c – d,** *Chattahochee Brushed sherds. The bowl is approximately 17 cm high at the lip.*

meant that there was less need for the public squares. Adaptation to new climate, soils, and other resources helped produce a new relationship of the Indians to the land. We know from early documents that the Indians still grew corn, beans, and pumpkins. Spanish crops such as potatoes derived from South America, watermelons, and probably other plants were adopted. This borrowing from the Spaniards does not mean that the early Seminole were intimately interacting with their neighbors. Seminole sites show very few items of Spanish origin and the relevant documents make little mention of Seminole in and around St. Augustine or Pensacola. The major centers of Seminole colonization near Alachua and Tallahassee were remote from the steadily weakening Spanish government. It is also probable that these migrants, having left Georgia to weaken contacts with the British, were not overly eager to establish new ties with other Europeans. While the Indians continued to supply deer skins to the traders, it seems likely that a large part of their skins were from feral cattle that had proliferated in the Alachua and Tallahassee regions. Wild honey seems also to have been traded and is described as being eaten by the Indians from hollowed out wild oranges that had spread from Spanish groves. These changes in settlement pattern and subsistence paralleled the common British frontier patterns with some dependence on agriculture and on free-ranging cattle. The Seminole probably cannot be called cattle herders at this time, but rather cattle predators, as they probably did not actually pen or tend the stock. A diffuse settlement pattern clearly suited their new conditions and was part of their adaptation to the new country.

The arrival of the British in Florida in 1763 meant that lax Spanish colonial government was replaced by a well-defined Indian policy conforming to the Proclamation of 1763 for the establishment of British—Indian relationships. Many of the Seminole seem to have resented the British and plotted with the Spaniards in Cuba. The treaty signed at Picolata on the St. Johns River in 1765 set the stage for control of the Seminole. It is clear from the documents concerning this treaty that the Seminole in Florida had already severed much of the formal affiliation with the Creek Confederacy to the north. This policy of separation from their kinfolk was extended to an increasing isolation from Europeans as well. It is as if the Seminole, having fled from advancing British trade and settlement in Georgia, now found themselves in the presence of the same dominating people in their new home. They reacted by becoming more aloof and frequently more hostile. An added factor was the increasing numbers of runaway blacks in Florida where they had traditionally found a haven under the Spaniards. For the most part these "maroons" formed separate hamlets under the protection of their Indian hosts and assuredly helped promote a mistrust of white American settlers.

Besides the treaty, regarrisoning of Fort St. Marks, and the sporadic presence of the Superintendent for Indian Affairs or his deputy, the British encouraged the establishment of trading posts among the Seminole as among other Indian tribes. These offered an outlet for British manufactured goods, a profit to the traders, and a means of control of the Indians. As the natives became dependent on British trade goods they could be coerced into obedience by threats of withdrawal of the trade. Spalding established posts on the St. Johns at Stokes Landing and near Astor. The Lower Store at Stoke's Landing has given us our best picture of Seminole material culture during the period of Separation (Lewis 1969). The Indians reported there in large numbers to trade and inevitably camped in the vicinity for varying periods. The British firm of Panton, Leslie, and Company with headquarters in Pensacola had a store on the Wakulla River near Fort St. Marks which served the Seminole in the Tallahassee—Miccosukee region. These trading posts, especially those of Panton, became so thoroughly entrenched that they secured permission to remain after Florida was ceded back to the Spaniards in 1783. This is the period of what was probably the greatest consumption of European goods by the Seminole although the sites show adherence to the traditional brushed pottery. Few other material traits remained Indian in style, with the possible exception of housing. The burials of the period show such trade objects as an iron pipe-tomahawk, iron knives, muskets, balls and flints (Figure 44b), brass buckles and brass kettles, glass mirrors, and many glass beads (Goggin *et al.* 1949). More perishable items include woven cloth, ostrich feathers, and of course, rum in considerable quantities. Seminole settlements were largely confined to the same three areas that had been occupied earlier: Alachua and an area extending to the lower Suwannee, the Tallahassee—Miccosukee area, and settlements along the Apalachicola. The Seminole took little part in the American Revolution, as Florida was not an active theater of combat. Probably the strength of British trade and their fear of advancing colonists kept them from making active alliances with the Georgian rebels. While it seems to have been a time of economic prosperity, it was also a period in which Indian debts increased as the traders usually extended liberal credit. Eventually these debts were to be a lever by which land grants were extorted from the Indians.

The Second Spanish Dominion was a time of weak colonial government in Florida and increasing settlement pressures in the northern territories. The colonial authorities recognized that the example of British cheap trade goods must be continued and they were forced to leave British firms in possession as Spain could not supply the goods. Thus, sites of the period still show many British goods and few articles of Hispanic origin. Traders from the United States were also active in Georgia and were controlled to some extent by an American Indian agent. Seminole sites became even more dispersed, perhaps in part as a reflection of increasing frontier tensions. Few locations of this period have been investigated as concentrated middens are difficult to locate. Pottery still remained the most conservative element in the material culture, although from the Oven Hill site (Gluckman and Peebles 1974) on the Suwannee we find one brushed Seminole pot with three legs in imitation of iron trade kettles. Probably sherds of glass bottles are the most common artifact from the trade sites, although they cannot indicate the tremendous impact that rum had on the native culture.

As Spanish colonial government weakened, the influence of the United States to the north correspondingly increased bringing tension and eventually conflict. As an aftermath of the Creek War, great numbers of Upper Creeks from central Alabama fled to Florida. The population of Florida Indians just about doubled to around 5000 with these refugees. Some certainly were absorbed into existing towns, but most formed new communities between existing towns, or more commonly leap-frogged through the resident Seminole. Thus, we see, after 1814, an increase in Seminole sites and a sprinkling of them southward of the earlier ones. Between Ocala and Tampa Bay, a few villages of the new Muskogee-speaking refugees began to be established. In a few cases where these sites are known, they exhibit hints of central Alabama artifacts differing in minor ways from the established Seminole patterns.

The First Seminole War of 1818 arose out of this increased Seminole population and the consequent friction with frontiersmen in Georgia. It probably reflects, in another sense, a reinforcement of the traditional Seminole distrust of whites. Its lasting effects were minimal except to demonstrate that the Spaniards were unable to maintain order in their colony. Thus it led directly to the cession of Florida to the United States in 1819, although the transfer took some time to complete. Seminole response to American settlement was to withdraw eastward from the Tallahassee region and gradually expand the number of villages southward into the waste lands south of the Alachua area. Confined by the Treaty of Moultrie Creek in 1823 to an area south of Ocala, they became increasingly restive because of lack of food and more intense friction with the new Anglo-American settlers. The sites of this period have not been investigated to any extent but seem to show a poverty of materials and a quite diffuse settlement pattern. Political and war leaders are depicted in a number of paintings from the period of the Second Seminole War, which continued from the early 1830s until about 1840. No sites of the war years have been excavated although the beginning of study of the military forts of the period may show some occupation by Seminole after the army abandoned the spot. The final result of the war was the removal of most of the Seminole to Indian territory while a very few found refuge in the Everglades. There they had to adapt again to a new environment and new subsistence strategies. There has been no scientific investigation of Seminole sites in the extreme southern part of the state, although there are indications that the pattern of diffuse, small settlements that had begun in the northern area continued in their new home. The lack of the formal squaregrounds in the center of towns has continued, although Seminole religion had retained early traits until very late times. The only excavation in these Everglades sites has been looting by collectors who have found graves placed by the Seminole in earlier sand burial mounds. The burials are accompanied by quantities of glass faceted beads, usually blue or green. Controlled excavation of the Seminole sites dating from the earlier periods in northern Florida is urgently needed to clarify the process of their adaptation to the Florida environment.

Epilogue

We hope that this introduction to archaeology in Florida has provided the reader with some understanding of the aboriginal peoples of Florida and an appreciation for their past. Although Indians have lived in Florida for at least 12,000 years, we have only documentary evidence for the historic period, the last 350 years. All of our information concerning the prehistoric period must come from archaeological investigations of Indian sites.

Today, although we have more archaeologists employed in the state than at any previous time, we also have many fewer archaeological sites. Yearly, hundreds of sites are destroyed or heavily disturbed by construction activities, land clearing, and treasure hunting. The number of sites is not infinite, nor are sites a renewable resource. They cannot be bred or planted like whooping cranes or trees. Once a site is destroyed, it is forever gone from the face of the earth.

Few people, once they realize that each archaeological site, whether large or small, is a unique piece in the puzzle that is the past, would intentionally destroy such an important cultural resource any more than they would shoot a whooping crane. But many people simply do not recognize that archaeological sites are a resource that can provide whole new vistas on the past and the forgotten people who lived in those past times. All of us interested in the Florida Indians—professional and avocational archaeologists, historians, and others—have a responsibility to educate the public concerning the need to preserve and protect our heritage. State and federal laws and regulations are not enough; the demand that we use our cultural resources wisely must come from the public, from ourselves. Statewide organizations like the Florida Anthropological Society and the Florida Historical Society and the many local and regional groups interested in the archaeology and history of Florida provide an excellent means through which we can jointly demand that our resources are cared for and used efficiently. It is our hope that this study will prompt more of us to become active in such organizations that are dedicated to learning about and protecting our past.

References

Allen, Ross
  1948   The big circle mounds. *Florida Anthropologist* 1:17–21.
Andrews, Evangeline Walker, and Charles McLean Andrews (editors)
  1975   Jonathan Dickinson's journal. Stuart, Florida: Valentine Books.
Barrientos, Bartolomé
  1965   *Pedro Menéndez de Avilés*, [translated by Anthony Kerrigan]. Gainesville: University of Florida Press.
Bell, James
  1883   Mounds in Alachua County, Florida. *Annual Report of the Smithsonian Institution, 1881.* pp. 635–637.
Benson, Carl A.
  1959   Some pottery contributions to the early fabric techniques. *Florida Anthropologist* 12:65–70.
Boyd, Mark F.
  1949   Diego Peña's expedition to Apalachee and Apalachicola in 1716. *Florida Historical Quarterly* 28:1–27.
Boyd, Mark F., Hale G. Smith, and John W. Griffin
  1951   *Here they once stood: The tragic end of the Apalachee missions.* Gainesville: University of Florida Press.
Brinton, Daniel G.
  1859   *Florida peninsula, its literary history, Indian tribes, and antiquities.* Philadelphia: J. Sabin.
Bullen, Adelaide K.
  1965   Florida Indians of past and present. In *Florida from Indian trails to space age, a history* (vol. 1), by Charlton W. Tebeau, Ruby Leach Carson *et al.* pp. 317–350. Delray Beach, Florida: Southern Publishing Company.
  1972   Paleoepidemiology and distribution of prehistoric treponemiasis (syphilis) in Florida. *Florida Anthropologist* 25:133–174.

Bullen, Adelaide, and Ripley P. Bullen
  1950   The Johns Island site, Hernando County, Florida. *American Antiquity* 16:23 – 45.
  1953   The Battery Point site, Bayport, Hernando County, Florida. *Florida Anthropologist* 6:85 – 92.
  1963   The Wash Island site, Crystal River, Florida. *Florida Anthropologist* 16:81 – 92.
Bullen, Ripley P.
  1949   The Woodward site. *Florida Anthropologist* 2:49 – 64.
  1951   The Terra Ceia site, Manatee County, Florida. *Florida Anthropological Society Publications* 3.
  1952a De Soto's Ucita and the Terra Ceia site. *Florida Historical Quarterly* 30:317 – 323.
  1952b Eleven archaeological sites in Hillsborough County, Florida. *Florida Geological Survey, Report of Investigations* 8.
  1955a Archeology of the Tampa Bay area. *Florida Historical Quarterly* 34:51 – 63.
  1955b Carved owl totem, Deland, Florida. *Florida Anthropologist* 8:61 – 73.
  1955c Stratigraphic tests at Bluffton, Volusia County, Florida. *Florida Anthropologist* 8:1 – 16.
  1958   Six sites near the Chattahoochee River in the Jim Woodruff Reservoir area, Florida. In *River basin survey papers*, edited by Frank H. H. Roberts, Jr., pp. 315 – 357. *Bureau of American Ethnology, Bulletin* 169. Smithsonian Institution, Washington, D.C.
  1959   The Transitional period of Florida. *Southeastern Archaeological Conference, Newsletter* 6:43 – 53.
  1962   Indian burials at Tick Island. *American Philosophical Society, Yearbook 1961:* 477 – 480.
  1969   Excavations at Sunday Bluff, Florida. *Contributions of the Florida State Museum, Social Sciences* 15.
  1971   The **Sarasota** County mound, Englewood, Florida. *Florida Anthropologist* 24:1 – 30.
  1972   The Orange period of peninsular Florida. In *Fiber-tempered pottery in southeastern United States and northern Colombia: Its origins, context, and significance*, edited by Ripley P. Bullen and James B. Stoltman, pp. 9 – 33. *Florida Anthropological Society Publications* 6.
  1975   *A guide to the identification of Florida projectile points.* Gainesville: Kendall Books.
  1978   Tocobaga Indians and the Safety Harbor culture. In *Tacachale: Essays on the Indians of Florida and southeastern Georgia during the historic period*, edited by J. T. Milanich and Samuel Proctor, pp. 50 – 58. *Ripley P. Bullen Monographs in Anthropology and History* 1. Gainesville: University Presses of Florida.
Bullen, Ripley P., Walter Askew, Lee M. Feder, and Richard McDonnell
  1978   The Canton Street site, St. Petersburg, Florida. *Florida Anthropological Society Publications* 9.
Bullen, Ripley P., and Laurence E. Beilman
  1973   The Nalcrest site, Lake Weohyakapka, Florida. *Florida Anthropologist* 26:1 – 22.
Bullen, Ripley P., and Carl A. Benson
  1964   Dixie Lime caves numbers 1 and 2, a preliminary report. *Florida Anthropologist* 17:153 – 164.
Bullen, Ripley P., and W. J. Bryant
  1965   Three Archaic sites in the Ocala National Forest, Florida. *William L. Bryant Foundation, American Studies Report* 6.
Bullen, Ripley P., Adelaide K. Bullen, and W. J. Bryant
  1967   Archaeological investigations at the Ross Hammock site, Florida. *William L. Bryant Foundation, American Studies Report* 7.

Bullen, Ripley P., and Edward M. Dolan
  1959   The Johnson Lake site, Marion County, Florida. *Florida Anthropologist* 12:77−94.
Bullen, Ripley P., and Frederick W. Sleight
  1959   Archaeological investigations of the Castle Windy midden, Florida. *William L. Bryant Foundation, American Studies Report* 1.
  1960   Archaeological investigations of Green Mound, Florida. *William L. Bryant Foundation, American Studies Report* 2.
Clausen, Carl J.
  1964   The A-356 site and the Florida Archaic. Unpublished M. A. thesis, Department of Anthropology, University of Florida.
Clausen, Carl J., H. K. Brooks, and A. B. Wesolowsky
  1975   Florida spring confirmed as 10,000 year old early man site. *Florida Anthropological Society Publications* 7.
Clausen, Carl J., A. D. Cohen, Cesare Emiliani, J. A. Holman, and J. J. Stipp
  1979   Little Salt Spring, Florida: A unique underwater site. *Science* 203:609−614.
Cockrell, W. A., and Larry Murphy
  1978   Pleistocene man in Florida. *Archaeology of Eastern North America* 6:1−13.
Crawford, James M.
  1975   Southeastern Indian language. In *Studies in southeastern Indian languages*, edited by James M. Crawford, pp. 1−120. Athens: University of Georgia Press.
Cumbaa, Stephen L.
  1972   An intensive harvest economy in north-central Florida. Unpublished M.A. thesis, Department of Anthropology, University of Florida.
  1976   A reconsideration of freshwater shellfish exploitation in the Florida Archaic. *Florida Anthropologist* 29:49−59.
Cushing, Frank H.
  1897   Exploration of ancient key-dweller remains on the Gulf coast of Florida. *Proceedings of the American Philosophical Society* 25(153):329−448.
Davis, Frederick T.
  1935   Juan Ponce de Leon's voyages to Florida. *Florida Historical Quarterly* 14:3−70.
Deagan, Kathleen A.
  1974   Sex, status and role in the mestizaje of Spanish colonial Florida. Unpublished Ph.D. dissertation, Department of Anthropology, University of Florida.
  1978   Cultures in transition: Fusion and assimilation among the eastern Timucua. In *Tacachale: Essays on the Indians of Florida and southeastern Georgia during the historic period,* edited by J. T. Milanich and Samuel Proctor, pp. 89−119. *Ripley P. Bullen Monographs in Anthropology and History* 1. Gainesville: University Presses of Florida.
  n.d.   The Apalachee. In *Handbook of North American Indians, The Southeast* (vol. 13). Washington, D.C.: Smithsonian Institution, in press.
Denevan, W. D.
  1970   Aboriginal drained-field cultivation in the Americas. *Science* 169:647−654.
Division of Archives, History and Records Management
  1970   Key Marco reveals early Florida life. *Archives and History News* 1(1):1, 3−4. Tallahassee: Florida Department of State.
Douglass, Andrew E.
  1885   Some characteristics of the Indian earth and shell mounds on the Atlantic coast of Florida. *American Antiquarian* 7:74−82, 140−184.
Dragoo, Don W.
  1973   Wells Creek, an early man site in Stewart County, Tennessee. *Archaeology of Eastern North America* 1:1−56.

Fairbanks, Charles H.
  1957   Ethnohistorical report of the Florida Indians. Presentation before the Indian Claims Commission, Dockets 73, 151. Washington, D.C. (Reprinted in 1974, New York and London: Garland Publishing, Inc.)
  1959   Additional Elliott's Point complex sites. *Florida Anthropologist* 12:95 – 100.
  1971   The Apalachicola River area of Florida. *Southeastern Archaeological Conference, Newsletter* 10(2):38 – 40.
  1978   The ethno-archeology of the Florida Seminole. In *Tacachale: Essays on the Indians of Florida and southeastern Georgia during the historic period,* edited by J. T. Milanich and Samuel Proctor, pp. 163– 193. *Ripley P. Bullen Monographs in Anthropology and History* 1. Gainesville: University Presses of Florida.
Fairbridge, Rhodes W.
  1960   The changing level of the sea. *Scientific American* 202(5):70.
Fewkes, Jesse W.
  1924   Preliminary archeological investigations at Weeden Island, Florida. *Smithsonian Miscellaneous Collections* 76(13):1 – 26.
Fontaneda, Hernando d'Escalante
  1945   *Memoir of Do. d'Escalante Fontaneda respecting Florida, written in Spain about the year 1575.* [Translated by Buckingham Smith and edited by David O. True.] Coral Gables: Glade House.
Fradkin, Arlene
  1976   The Wightman site: A study of prehistoric culture and environment on Sanibel Island, Lee County, Florida. Unpublished M.A. thesis, Department of Anthropology, University of Florida.
Fryman, Frank B., Jr.
  1971a   Highway salvage archaeology in Florida. *Archives and History News* 2(1):1 – 4. Tallahassee: Florida Department of State.
  1971b   Tallahassee's prehistoric political center. *Archives and History News* 2(3):2 – 4. Tallahassee: Florida Department of State.
Gardner, William F.
  1974   Introduction. In *The Flint Run Paleo-Indian complex: A preliminary report, 1971 – 73 seasons,* edited by W. F. Gardner, pp. 1– 4. *Catholic University of America, Department of Anthropology, Archeology Laboratory, Occasional Publication* 1.
Gilliland, Marion S.
  1975   *The material culture of Key Marco, Florida.* Gainesville: University Presses of Florida.
Gluckman, Stephen J., and Christopher S. Peebles
  1974   Oven Hill (Di-15), a refuge site in the Suwannee River. *Florida Anthropologist* 27: 21 – 30.
Goggin, John M.
  1940   The Tekesta Indians of southern Florida. *Florida Historical Quarterly* 18: 274 – 284.
  1947   A preliminary definition of archaeological areas and periods in Florida. *American Antiquity* 13:114 – 127.
  1949   Cultural traditions in Florida prehistory. In *The Florida Indian and his neighbors,* edited by John W. Griffin, pp. 13 – 44. Winter Park, Florida: Rollins College Inter-American Center.
  1950   The Indians and history of the Matecumbe region. *Tequesta* 10:13 -- 24.
  1952   Space and time perspectives in northern St. Johns archeology, Florida. *Yale Uni-*

versity Publications in Anthropology 47.

1958   Seminole pottery. In *Prehistoric pottery of the eastern United States*, edited by James B. Griffin. Ann Arbor: Museum of Anthropology, University of Michigan.

1960   The Spanish olive jar, an introductory study. *Yale University Publications in Anthropology* 62.

1968   Spanish majolica in the New World, types of the sixteenth to eighteenth centuries. *Yale University Publications in Anthropology* 72.

Goggin, John M., Mary E. Godwin, Early Hester, David Prange, and Robert Spangenberg

1949   An historic Indian burial, Alachua County, Florida. *Florida Anthropologist* 2:10–25.

Goggin, John M., and Frank H. Sommer III

1949   Excavations on Upper Matecumbe Key, Florida. *Yale University Publications in Anthropology* 41.

Goggin, John M., and William C. Sturtevant

1964   The Calusa: A stratified, nonagricultural society (with notes on sibling marriage). In *Explorations in cultural anthropology: Essays in honor of George Peter Murdock*, edited by Ward H. Goodenough, pp. 197–219. New York: McGraw-Hill.

Goldburt, Jules S.

1966   The archeology of Shired Island. Unpublished M.A. thesis, Department of Anthropology, University of Florida.

Goodyear, Albert C., and Lyman O. Warren

1972   Further observations on the submarine oyster shell deposits of Tampa Bay. *Florida Anthropologist* 25:52–66.

Griffin, John W.

1949   Notes on the archaeology of Useppa Island. *Florida Anthropologist* 2:92–93.

1950   Test excavations at the Lake Jackson site. *American Antiquity* 16:99–112.

1974   Archaeology and environment in South Florida. In *Environments of South Florida: Present and past*, edited by Patrick J. Gleason, pp. 342–346. *Miami Geological Survey, Memoir* 2.

Griffin, John W. (editor)

1949   *The Florida Indian and his neighbors*. Winter Park, Florida: Rollins College Inter-American Center.

Griffin, John W., and Ripley P. Bullen

1950   The Safety Harbor site, Pinellas County, Florida. *Florida Anthropological Society Publications* 2.

Harper, Francis (editor)

1958   *The travels of William Bartram* (naturalist's edition). New Haven: Yale University Press.

Hemmings, E. Thomas

1975a   An archaeological survey of the South Prong of the Alafia River, Florida. *Florida Anthropologist* 28:41–51.

1975b   The Silver Springs site, prehistory in the Silver Springs Valley, Florida. *Florida Anthropologist* 28:141–158.

1978   Cades Pond subsistence, settlement, and ceremonialism. *Florida Anthropologist* 31:141–150.

Hemmings, E. Thomas, and Kathleen A. Deagan

1973   Excavations on Amelia Island in northeast Florida. *Contributions of the Florida State Museum, Anthropology and History* 18.

Hemmings, E. Thomas, and Tim A. Kohler

1974   The Lake Kanapaha site in north central Florida. *Bureau of Historic Sites and*

Properties, Division of Archives, History and Records Management, Bulletin 4, pp. 45 – 64. Tallahassee: Florida Department of State.

Hoole, W. Stanley
    1974   East Florida in 1834: Letters of Dr. John Durkee. *Florida Historical Quarterly* 52:294 – 308.

Hudson, Charles
    1976   *The southeastern Indians.* Knoxville: University of Tennessee Press.

Jahn, Otto L., and Ripley P. Bullen
    1978   The Tick Island site, St. Johns River, Florida. *Florida Anthropological Society Publications* 10.

Jones, B. Calvin
    1973   A semi-subterranean structure at mission San Joseph de Ocuya, Jefferson County, Florida. *Bureau of Historic Sites and Properties, Division of Archives, History and Records Management, Bulletin* 3, pp. 1 – 50. Tallahassee: Florida Department of State.

Jones, B. Calvin, and John T. Penman
    1973   Windwood: An inland Ft. Walton site in Tallahassee, Florida. *Bureau of Historic Sites and Properties, Division of Archives, History and Records Management, Bulletin* 3, pp. 65 – 90. Tallahassee: Florida Department of State.

Kelly, Arthur R.
    n.d.   A Weeden Island burial mound in Decatur County, Georgia, and related sites on the lower Flint River. *University of Georgia, Laboratory of Archaeology Series, Report* 1.

Kohler, Tim A.
    1975   The Garden Patch site: A minor Weeden Island ceremonial center on the north peninsular Florida Gulf coast. Unpublished M.A. thesis, Department of Anthropology, University of Florida.
    1978   The social and chronological dimensions of village occupation at a north Florida Weeden Island period site. Unpublished Ph.D. dissertation, Department of Anthropology, University of Florida.

Kraft, Herbert C.
    1973   The Plenge site: A Paleo-Indian occupation site in New Jersey. *Archaeology of Eastern North America* 1:56 – 117.

Lazarus, William C.
    1958   A Poverty Point complex in Florida. *Florida Anthropologist* 11:23 – 32.
    1961   Ten middens on the Navy Live Oak Reservation. *Florida Anthropologist* 14:49 – 64.
    1965   Effects of land subsidence and sea level changes on elevation of archaeological sites on the Florida Gulf coast. *Florida Anthropologist* 18:49 – 58.
    1971   The Fort Walton culture west of the Apalachicola River. *Southeastern Archaeological Conference, Newsletter* 10(2):40 – 48.

Lewis, Clifford M.
    1978   The Calusa. In *Tacachale: Essays on the Indians of Florida and southeastern Georgia during the historic period,* edited by J. T. Milanich and Samuel Proctor, pp. 19 – 49. *Ripley P. Bullen Monographs in Anthropology and History* 1. Gainesville: University Presses of Florida.

Lewis, Kenneth E., Jr.
    1969   History and archeology of Spalding's Lower Store (Pu – 23), Putnam County, Florida. Unpublished M.A. thesis, Department of Anthropology, University of Florida.

Lorant, Stefan
    1946   *The New World, the first pictures of America.* New York: Duell, Sloan, and Pearce.
Loucks, L. Jill
    1976   Early Alachua tradition burial ceremonialism: The Henderson mound, Alachua County, Florida. Unpublished M.A. thesis, Department of Anthropology, University of Florida.
Luer, George M.
    1977a   Excavations at the Old Oak site, Sarasota, Florida: A late Weeden Island-Safety Harbor period site. *Florida Anthropologist* 30:37−55.
    1977b   The Roberts Bay site, Sarasota, Florida. *Florida Anthropologist* 30:121−133.
Luer, George M., and Marion M. Almy
    1979   Three aboriginal shell middens on Longboat Key, Florida: Manasota period sites of barrier island exploitation. *Florida Anthropologist* 32:33−45.
Lyon, Eugene
    1976   *The enterprise of Florida, Pedro Menéndez de Avilés and the Spanish conquest of 1565−1568.* Gainesville: University Presses of Florida.
Martin, Robert A., and S. David Webb
    1974   Late Pleistocene mammals from the Devil's Den Fauna, Levy County. In *Pleistocene mammals of Florida*, edited by S. David Webb, pp. 114−145. Gainesville: University Presses of Florida.
McNicoll, Robert E.
    1941   The Caloosa village Tequesta, a Miami of the sixteenth century. *Tequesta* 1:11−20.
Milanich, Jerald T.
    1971   The Alachua tradition of North-central Florida. *Contributions of the Florida State Museum, Anthropology and History* 17.
    1972   Excavations at the Richardson site, Alachua County, Florida: An early 17th century Potano Indian village (with notes on Potano culture change). *Bureau of Historic Sites and Properties, Division of Archives, History and Records Management, Bulletin* 2, pp. 35−61. Tallahassee: Florida Department of State.
    1973   The southeastern Deptford culture: A preliminary definition. *Bureau of Historic Sites and Properties, Division of Archives, History and Records Management, Bulletin* 3, pp. 51−63. Tallahassee: Florida Department of State.
    1974   Life in a 9th century Indian household, a Weeden Island fall-winter site on the upper Apalachicola River, Florida. *Bureau of Historic Sites and Properties, Division of Archives, History and Records Management, Bulletin* 4, pp. 1−44. Tallahassee: Florida Department of State.
    1978a   Two Cades Pond sites in north-central Florida: The occupational nexus as a model of settlement. *Florida Anthropologist* 31:151−173.
    1978b   The western Timucua: Patterns of acculturation and change. In *Tacachale: Essays on the Indians of Florida and southeastern Georgia during the historic period*, edited by J. T. Milanich and Samuel Proctor, pp. 59−88. *Ripley P. Bullen Monographs in Anthropology and History* 1. Gainesville: University Presses of Florida.
Milanich, Jerald T., Carlos A. Martinez, Karl T. Steinen, and Ronald L. Wallace
    1976   Georgia origins of the Alachua tradition. *Bureau of Historic Sites and Properties, Division of Archives, History and Records Management, Bulletin* 5, pp. 47−56. Tallahassee: Florida Department of State.
Milanich, Jerald T., and William C. Sturtevant
    1972   *Francisco Pareja's 1613 Confessionario: A documentary source for Timucuan ethnography.* Tallahassee: Florida Department of State.

Moore, Clarence B.

1893   Certain shell heaps of the St. John's River, Florida, hitherto unexplored (third paper). *American Naturalist* 27:8 – 13, 113 – 117, 605 – 624, 709 – 733.

1894a   Certain sand mounds of the St. John's River, Florida, part 1. *Journal of the Academy of Natural Sciences of Philadelphia* 10:5 – 128.

1894b   Certain sand mounds of the St. John's River, Florida, part 2. *Journal of the Academy of Natural Sciences of Philadelphia* 10:129 – 246.

1903   Aboriginal mounds of the Apalachicola River. *Journal of the Academy of Natural Sciences of Philadelphia* 12:439 – 494.

Morlot, A. von

1861   General views of anthropology. *Annual Report of the Smithsonian Institution, 1860*, pp. 284 – 343.

Morrell, L. Ross, and B. Calvin Jones

1970   San Juan de Aspalaga (a preliminary architectural study). *Bureau of Historic Sites and Properties, Division of Archives, History and Records Management, Bulletin* 1, pp. 25 – 43. Tallahassee: Florida Department of State.

Neill, Wilfred T.

1958   A stratified early site at Silver Springs, Florida. *Florida Anthropologist* 11:33 – 48.

1964   Trilisa Pond, an early site in Marion County, Florida. *Florida Anthropologist* 17:187 – 200.

1971   A Florida Paleo-Indian implement of ground stone. *Florida Anthropologist* 24:61 – 70.

Neuman, Robert W.

1961   Domesticated corn from a Fort Walton mound site in Houston County, Alabama. *Florida Anthropologist* 14:75 – 80.

Padgett, Thomas J.

1976   Hinderland exploitation in the central Gulf coast – Manatee region during the Safety Harbor period. *Florida Anthropologist* 29:39 – 48.

Parsons, J. J., and W. D. Denevan

1967   Precolumbian ridged fields. *Scientific American* 217:93 – 100.

Peebles, Christopher S. (editor)

1974   Current research: Southeast. *American Antiquity* 39:639 – 642.

Penton, Daniel T.

1970   Excavations in the early Swift Creek component at Bird Hammock (8-Wa-30). Unpublished M.A. thesis, Department of Anthropology, Florida State University.

Percy, George W.

1971a   Current research: Florida. *Southeastern Archaeological Conference, Newsletter* 15(1):7 – 8.

1971b   Preliminary report to the Division of Recreation and Parks, Department of Natural Resources, State of Florida, on archaeological work in the Torreya State Park during the year of 1971 by the Department of Anthropology at Florida State University. Manuscript on file, Florida Department of Natural Resources.

1974   A review of evidence for prehistoric Indian use of animals in Northwest Florida. *Bureau of Historic Sites and Properties, Division of Archives, History and Records Management, Bulletin* 4, pp. 65 – 93. Tallahassee: Florida Department of State.

Percy, George W., and David S. Brose

1974   Weeden Island ecology, subsistence, and village life in northwest Florida. Paper presented at the 39th Annual Meeting of the Society for American Archaeology, Washington, D.C.

Phelps, David S.
  1969   Swift Creek and Santa Rosa in Northwest Florida. *Institute of Archeology and Anthropology, University of South Carolina, Notebook* 1(6−9):14−24.
Purdy, Barbara A.
  1973   The temporal and spatial distribution of bone points in the state of Florida. *Florida Anthropologist* 26:143−152.
  1975   The Senator Edwards chipped stone workshop site (Mr-122), Marion County, Florida: A preliminary report of investigations. *Florida Anthropologist* 28:178−189.
Rouse, Irving
  1951   A survey of Indian River archeology, Florida. *Yale University Publications in Anthropology* 44.
Royal, William, and Eugenie Clark
  1960   Natural preservation of human brain, Warm Mineral Springs, Florida. *American Antiquity* 26:285−287.
Schoolcraft, Henry R.
  1854   Antique pottery from the minor mounds occupied by the Indians in feasts to the dead, on the seacoast of Florida and Georgia (vol. 3). In *Historical and statistical information respecting the history, conditions, and prospects of the Indian tribes of the United States* (6 vols.), pp. 75−82. Philadelphia: Lippincott, Grambo, and Co.
Sears, Elsie, and William Sears
  1976   Preliminary report on prehistoric corn pollen from Fort Center, Florida. *Southeastern Archaeological Conference, Bulletin* 19:53−56.
Sears, William H.
  1956a   Excavations at Kolomoki, final report. *University of Georgia Series in Anthropology* 5.
  1956b   Melton Mound Number 3. *Florida Anthropologist* 9:87−100.
  1962   Hopewellian affiliations of certain sites on the Gulf Coast of Florida. *American Antiquity* 28:5−18.
  1963   The Tucker site on Alligator Harbor, Franklin County, Florida. *Contributions of the Florida State Museum, Social Sciences* 9.
  1967   The Tierra Verde burial mound. *Florida Anthropologist* 20:25−73.
  1971a   Food production and village life in prehistoric southeastern United States. *Archaeology* 24:93−102.
  1971b   The Weeden Island site, St. Petersburg, Florida. *Florida Anthropologist* 24:51−60.
  1973   The sacred and the secular in prehistoric ceramics. In *Variation in anthropology: Essays in honor of John McGregor*, edited by D. Lathrop and J. Douglas, pp. 31−42. Urbana: Illinois Archaeological Survey.
  1974   Archaeological perspectives on prehistoric environment in the Okeechobee Basin savannah. In *Environments in South Florida: Present and past*, edited by Patrick J. Gleason, pp. 347−351. *Miami Geological Society, Memoir* 2.
  1977   Seaborne contacts between early cultures in lower southeastern United States and Middle through South America. In *The sea in the pre-columbian world*, edited by Elizabeth P. Benson, pp. 1−13. Washington, D.C.: Dumbarton Oaks Research Library and Collections.
Siemens, Alfred H., and Dennis E. Puleston
  1972   Ridged fields and associated features in southern Campeche: New perspectives on the lowland Maya. *American Antiquity* 37:228−239.

Smith, Buckingham (translator)
  1871   *Relation of Alvar Nuñez Cabeza de Vaca.* Albany, New York: J. Munsell.
  1968   *Narratives of de Soto in the conquest of Florida.* Gainesville: Palmetto Books.
          (Facsimile of the 1866 Bradford Club edition.)
Smith, Hale G.
  1956   The European and the Indian, European-Indian contacts in Georgia and
          Florida. *Florida Anthropological Society Publications* 4.
Smith, Hale G., and Mark Gottlob
  1978   Spanish-Indian relationships: Synoptic history and archaeological evidence,
          1500–1763. In *Tacachale: Essays on the Indians of Florida of southeastern Georgia
          during the historic period,* edited by J. T. Milanich and Samuel Proctor, pp. 1–18.
          Ripley P. Bullen Monographs in Anthropology and History 1. Gainesville: University
          Presses of Florida.
Smith, Samuel D.
  1971a   A reinterpretation of the Cades Pond archeological period. Unpublished M.A.
          thesis, Department of Anthropology, University of Florida.
  1971b   Excavations at the Hope mound with an addendum to the Safford mound report.
          Florida Anthropologist 24:107–134.
Snow, Frankie
  1978   An archeological survey of the Ocmulgee big bend region. *Occasional Papers from
          South Georgia, Number* 3. South Georgia College.
Solís de Merás, Gonzalo
  1894   Memorial que hizo el Doctor Gonzalo Solís de Merás, de todas las jornadas y
          sucesos del Adelantado Pedro Menéndez de Avilés, su cuñado, y de la conquista
          de la Florida. . . . In *La Florida, su conquista y colonización por Pedro Menéndez
          de Avilés* (vol. 1), by Eugenio Ruidíaz y Caravia, pp. 1– 350. Madrid: Hijos de J. A.
          Garcia.
Steinen, Karl T.
  1971   Analysis of the non-ceramic artifacts from a Hopewellian affiliated site in Glades
          County, Florida. Unpublished M.A. thesis, Department of Anthropology, Florida
          Atlantic University.
Stewart, T. Dale
  1946   A re-examination of the fossil human skeletal remains from Melbourne, Florida,
          with further data on the Vero skull. *Smithsonian Miscellaneous Collections*
          106(10):1–28.
Stirling, Matthew W.
  1936   Florida cultural affiliations in relation to adjacent areas. In *Essays in anthropology
          in honor of Alfred Louis Kroeber,* pp. 351–357. Berkeley: University of California
          Press.
Sturtevant, William C.
  1978   The last of the south Florida aborigines. In *Tacachale: Essays on the Indians of
          Florida and southeastern Georgia during the historic period,* edited by J. T.
          Milanich and Samuel Proctor, pp. 141– 162. *Ripley P. Bullen Monographs in An-
          thropology and History* 1. Gainesville: University Presses of Florida.
Swanton, John R.
  1929   The Tawasa language. *American Anthropologist* 31:435–453.
  1946   The Indians of the southeastern United States. *Bureau of American Ethnology,
          Bulletin 137.* Washington, D.C.: Smithsonian Institution.
Swanton, John R. (editor)
  1939   *Final report of the United States de Soto expedition commission.* Seventy-sixth

Congress, 1st Session, House Document 71. Washington, D.C.: U.S. Government Printing Office.

Symes, M. I., and M. E. Stephens
1965 A—272: The Fox Pond site. *Florida Anthropologist* 18:65—72.

Tesar, Louis D.
1976 Site survey success "super." *Archives and History News* 6(6):1—3. Tallahassee: Florida Department of State.

Thomas, Cyrus
1894 Report on the mound explorations of the Bureau of Ethnology *Twelfth Annual Report of the Bureau of American Ethnology*, pp. 3— 730. Washington, D.C.: Smithsonian Institution.

Varner, John, and Jeannette Varner (translators and editors)
1951 *The Florida of the Inca.* Austin: University of Texas Press.

Walker, S. T.
1880 Report on the shell heaps of Tampa Bay, Florida. *Annual Report of the Smithsonian Institution, 1879*, pp. 413—422.
1883 The aborigines of Florida. *Annual Report of the Smithsonian Institution, 1881*, pp. 677—680.
1885 Mounds and shell heaps on the west coast of Florida. *Annual Report of the Smithsonian Institution, 1883*, pp. 854—868.

Waller, Benjamin I.
1970 Some occurrences of Paleo-Indian projectile points in Florida waters. *Florida Anthropologist* 23:129—134.
1971 Hafted flake knives. *Florida Anthropologist* 24:173—174.
1976 Paleo-associated bone tools, Florida. Paper presented at the 28th Annual Meeting of the Florida Anthropological Society, Fort Lauderdale.

Walthall, John A.
1975 Ceramic figurines, Porter Hopewell, and Middle Woodland interaction. *Florida Anthropologist* 28:125—140.

Warren, Lyman O.
1964 Possible submerged oyster shell middens of upper Tampa Bay. *Florida Anthropologist* 17:227—230.
1968 The Apollo Beach site, Hillsborough County. *Florida Anthropologist* 21:83—88.
1970 The Kellog fill from Boca Ciega Bay, Pinellas County, Florida. *Florida Anthropologist* 23:163—167.

Warren, Lyman O., and Ripley P. Bullen
1965 A Dalton complex from Florida. *Florida Anthropologist* 18:29—32.

Warren, Lyman O., William Thompson, and Ripley P. Bullen
1967 The Culbreath Bayou site, Hillsborough County, Florida. *Florida Anthropologist* 20:146—163.

Watts, W. A.
1969 A pollen diagram from Mud Lake, Marion County, North-central Florida. *Geological Society of America, Bulletin* 80:631—642.
1971 Post glacial and interglacial vegetation history of southern Georgia and central Florida. *Ecology* 52:676—689.

Webb, Clarence H.
1977 The Poverty Point culture. *Geoscience and Man* 17. Baton Rouge: School of Geoscience, Lousiana State University.

Wenhold, Lucy L.
1936 A seventeenth-century letter of Gabriel Díaz Vara Calderón, Bishop of Cuba. *Smithsonian Miscellaneous Collections* 95(16):1—14.

Willey, Gordon R.

   1949a   Archeology of the Florida Gulf coast. *Smithsonian Miscellaneous Collections* 113.

   1949b   Excavations in southeast Florida. *Yale University Publications in Anthropology* 42.

Willey, Gordon R., and Jeremy A. Sabloff

   1974   *A history of American archaeology.* San Francisco: W. H. Freeman and Company.

Willey, Gordon R., and Richard B. Woodbury

   1942   A chronological outline for the northwest Florida coast. *American Antiquity* 7:232–254.

Wing, Elizabeth S.

   1965   Animal bones associated with two Indian sites on Marco Island, Florida. *Florida Anthropologist* 18:21–28.

Wyman, Jeffries

   1868   An account of the fresh-water shell heaps of the St. Johns River, east Florida. *American Naturalist* 2:393–403, 440–463.

   1875   Fresh-water shell mounds of the St. Johns River, Florida. *Peabody Academy of Science, Memoir* 4, pp. 3–94. Salem, Mass.

Zubillaga, Félix (editor)

   1946   Monumenta Antiquae Floridae (1566–1572). *Monumenta Historica Societatis Iesu 69, Monumenta Missionum Societatis Iesu* 3. Rome.

Index

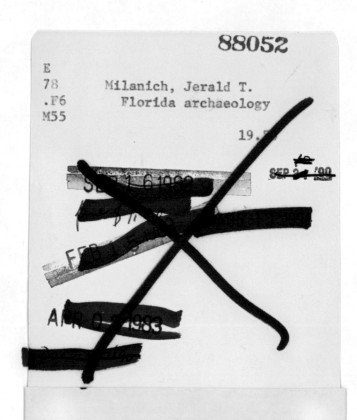